Old Times, Good Times

A rock and roll story

Peter Wonson

 INFINITY
PUBLISHING

"Turn the Page," Written by Bob Seger, Copyright 1973 Gear Publishing Company (ASCAP), reprinted with permission.

ISBN 0-7414-6663-5 Paperback
ISBN 0-7414-6445-4 Hardcover

Printed in the United States of America

Published August 2011

INFINITY PUBLISHING
1094 New DeHaven Street, Suite 100
West Conshohocken, PA 19428-2713
Toll-free (877) BUY BOOK
Local Phone (610) 941-9999
Fax (610) 941-9959
Info@buybooksontheweb.com
www.buybooksontheweb.com

To Wayne Wadhams, Eddie Kistler, Dom "Pooch" Puccio, Dan Morgenroth, and our other friends who left too soon. They helped us make our music, and I wish they were here to enjoy this tale.

The book is also dedicated to the memory of Robert Hill, a former teaching colleague. Robert was a talented singer and songwriter, a "lights out" guitar player, an outstanding science teacher, a loving and devoted family man, and a human being filled with grace and goodness.

Contents

Foreword   ix

1. Nodah   1

2. Nexus   4

3. "Momma, Are They Body Snatchers?"   7

4. Tin Soldiers   11

5. Wayne Wadhams   14

6. Sixties Dartmouth Bands   21

7. The Café Bizarre   33

8. The Acorn and the Tree   38

9. Back Stories and the Road to…Good Intentions   47

10. The Sprites / Nickel Misery   50

11. Whitcomb's Music Center   60

12. The Barn   67

13. Ed Was an Empire   77

14. Anvil   86

15. Kemeny's Lemon   98

16. Can't Get Theah from Heah   104

17. Ragweed   111

18. Gunnison Brook   120

19. Home Is Where the Band House Is   132

20. Rodney Diamond and the Studs   142

21. Then The Muse Tapped Me on the Shoulder   149

22. An Italian Opera Singer   156

23. Hard Times on the Road   161

24. "Hey Leadah…" (Tracks)   167

25. Gar Anderson   182

26. The Rusty Nail   191

27. Davis Brothers Garage Band   202

28. The Wobbly Barn   212

29. "Flash" Gordon and the Jefferson Light Show   220

30. Fox Chase   229

31. Yvonne and Jere Eames   240

32. The Galleon / Jeremiah's   249

33. Gerry's Song   259

34. Fox and Company   268

35. Newell's Casino   278

36. Aerosmith   287

37. Stone Cross   297

38. Joy's Home for Wayward Musicians   306

39. Better Days and Company   317

40. Aha!   327

41. "Huh? What?"   334

42. Where Do We Go from Here   340

43. The Last One Night Stand   347

Acknowledgements   349

Endnotes   353

Photo Credits   357

Players Index   361

Index   368

Foreword

When the surviving members of Tracks released the band's triple album in 1974, Russell Pinkston's liner notes began: "Something significant should probably be said here about what it all means...." Russell's words were prescient, but for almost forty years no one tried to write the story.

This book is not just a Tracks' story. It is a story of a convergence of time, space, and talent that produced a scene extraordinary for its music, bands, and personalities. Forty years later you mention a place or an individual to people who lived that scene, then sit back and watch their faces light up. Their eyes sparkle, and their voices become animated as they reminisce.

It was, simply put, a magical time that will not come this way again. As Joy Moffat, one of "The Waitri" at Eleazar's in White River Junction, Vermont, and the #1 Gunnison Brook fan in the world, says, "The bonds that were forged between people during that time are still very strong, and we keep in touch all these decades later." Don Coulombe of Fox and Company declares, "This was the best time of my life. I made so many friends on the road, and many of them are still in touch."

I could see from the beginning that writing this book would be an impossible task. I could write until the year 2525 and not get it all on paper. But the support and encouragement I received from friends and strangers alike who embraced this project with a passion, who shared their stories and those of long ago mates, convinced me this was a tale worth telling.

Unfortunately, many of the stories have been lost to the intervening years, memories fogged by the passage of time. One of my frequent sources claims to have been "dain bread" throughout much of the book's time period.

Chronology? Forget it! I have come to the conclusion that even if I could magically transport myself back in time to the 1960s and 1970s and get inside the brain of every "eyewitless" (assuming those brains weren't tripping), I still could never get a perfectly accurate story. Thus at times I found myself satisfied with the closest approximation I could manage. So, for readers who may say of a story or an event, "Hey, that's wrong"—you're probably right.

You know the part where the author always says "I take complete responsibility for all the errors in this book" while crediting all the good stuff to sources, collaborators, interviewees? Here it is. I do.

And yet, as I reflect on the triangulation problem I often had in interviews, and the difficulties I encountered with fact checking, this little voice keeps piping up and saying that maybe it isn't just the march of time that has fogged some memories. Truthfully, there was "fogging" going on back in the moment those many years ago. As in, on more than one occasion there were drugs and alcohol on the premises!

Still, the reader looking for "drugs, sex, and rock and roll" is going to be largely disappointed. That tired debauchery angle has been done to death, and I determined early on to write a book which grandchildren could read without grandpa worrying too much about my lifting the lid on certain youthful indiscretions. Not that some of those indiscretions aren't included, but when I write about them I mostly will do so anonymously.

One last thought before you soldier on. Musicians like Pete Merrigan and Mario Casella of Gunnison Brook, Ken Aldrich of Tracks, Norm Coulombe of Fox and Company, Bobby Gagnier of Anvil and Better Days, and Gardner Berry of Stone Cross, all of whom also played in many other bands over the years, have been in the music business continuously for forty-five years or more. The events they have witnessed could fill an airplane hangar. How do you track all those memories and stories? The answer is, you can't.

Dozens of bands, hundreds of stories, fell to the cutting room floor, to my deep regret. But, as Russell Pinkston concluded in his liner notes, while lamenting all the songs Tracks played that had been left off that 1974 album, "We hope, however, that there are more than a few here for everyone."

Peter Wonson
Roanoke, Virginia
May, 2011

Nodah

August 16, 1538. The five men had made camp by the river known to the people of the dawnland as *Wobigentekw*. (1) Two nights earlier, ritual drums and song had echoed through the sacred gorge called Quechee. Tonight, they were just upstream from the point of land where the *Wobigentekw* flowed into the mighty *Kwanitekw*.

Many generations ago, two esteemed warriors arrived at the rivers' confluence during April high water season and pointed their canoe south. Carried along by the swiftly flowing *Kwanitekw*, they had never returned. The people said they eventually reached the endless waters of *Sobakw* and crossed over into heaven to hunt with the manitou.

The hunting party's destination tomorrow was five miles almost due north, then across the *Kwanitekw* to the towering pine forest just back from the river. Tomorrow would be the last day before they turned for home, and the old growth forest, teeming with wildlife, was a favored destination.

It would likely be the last hunt for the oldest, now in his forty-fifth year and noticeably slowed by the years and a savage encounter with wolves during the winter of the starving moons. Still, he knew the trails and the signs, and so was invaluable. The youngest of the party was two months shy of fifteen years, and possessed of a reckless courage the people found at once praiseworthy and unnerving.

Their bonfire on the banks of the *Wobigentekw* leaped and crackled in the summer night. The ancient shale cliffs on either side of the river rose steeply into the darkness beyond the firelight.

1

Earlier, the party had sated their hunger on fresh deer meat cooked over the fire while it was burning lower in the twilight. The men savored blackberries and the delicate cloudberry gathered from the wildflower-filled meadow they traversed before they descended down the path to the clear waters of the *Wobigentekw*. After dinner they threw more driftwood onto the fire until it blazed like a fall wildfire in a pine forest, then rested as the familiar sounds of the night rose outside the flare of the bonfire.

Now, they took out the small drums which they carried with them on any hunt no more than four days distant from their summer camp. They began to chant and sing, their voices melding with the dull sound of the drums. Seated at the core of the people's existence, music was not an accompaniment to life, but the embodiment of life itself. Legend said that from the very moment of the creation of Mother Earth, the Creator had allowed the spirit of the drum to accompany the people's voices. (2)

They sang the old songs, passed down through the generations, asking for good hunting, sufficient rain, a bountiful fall gathering season, and protection in battle from the Mahican, their fierce rivals across the high mountains to the west. As they sang and drummed, they paused to light their reed pipes with the red stone bowls, and smoked the ceremonial *kinnikinnick*, which men traditionally carried with them on the hunt. After a time they turned inward on themselves, and the sound ebbed, for the smoke allowed them to see into the future.

All at once the youngest leapt to his feet, flung his head back and howled at the full moon above the rim of the river valley. As if in answer, far away and above them, came the howl of one wolf, then a more distant second. In response the young brave sang again and again, in a voice both higher and stronger than any of the others could muster, "*Nodah,*

2

Ketsinioueskou" ("Hear me, Great Spirit"). The other party members smiled, both at the youngest and in appreciation of the harmony in which *Ketsinioueskou* allowed them to live with all his creatures, and all his creations. Here, at the crossroads of *Ndakinna*, the place where the great traveling paths had for centuries intersected, the men felt both born anew and as ancient as the earth they rested on. Their visions, their drums, and their singing provided sustenance, comfort, and faith.

Sketch by Rick Hunt

3

Nexus

Exit off Interstate 89 and drive up Interstate 91, through White River Junction, Vermont, headed toward Canada. While crossing the bridge over the White River, look to your left. You will see the site where the Abenaki hunting party camped in 1538, half a mile upstream from where the White empties into the Connecticut River.

Those readers who know the land near the confluence of the two rivers will recognize that I have taken literary license with the topography of the White River valley along this stretch of the river. The steep, shale cliffs stand farther upstream. But I have no doubt that the Abenaki, the primary native tribe of "pre-contact" Vermont, made many a campsite along the banks of the White River. I am also certain that a thousand years ago the Abenaki gazed with awe on the canyon of Quechee Gorge, just as we in rock bands did when we drove over the bridge spanning the gorge on our way along Vermont Route 4 to gigs in Killington or Rutland, Vermont, or at New York's Hampton Manor.

Five miles north of the hunting party's camp site, the old growth pine forest, which Eleazar Wheelock encountered when he arrived in Hanover, New Hampshire, in 1768, is today the location of Dartmouth College. I can say with assurance that the wildlife the Abenaki hunted in 1538 were not the same "wildlife" one found on the Hanover plain in the late 1960s and early 1970s.

As you continue traveling I-91 north of Hanover and Norwich, VT, where the interstate cuts through empty fields and forests and the deer kill on the highway is still excessive forty years after the road first opened, look out the car window. Suspend disbelief in terms of your mode of transportation, ignore the speed and glass windows of the vehicle and the concrete of the interstate. You are seeing *Ndakinna*, the homeland, as the Abenaki saw it five centuries ago. This land that many of us call God's country is jaw-dropping in its beauty. If you have never seen New England in the fall, during leaf peeping season, you have missed one of nature's most spectacular shows, an awe-inspiring, even divinely inspired canvas of flaming, flashing color.

The I-89/I-91 interchange south of White River Junction is the geographic center of this story. At one time or another every band in this tale traveled both of those roads to and from performances at ski resorts, now-defunct clubs, and small, local high schools that are long since gone.

The Upper Valley of New Hampshire and Vermont, as the area is known, was also the epicenter of a ten-year crucible of creativity. Rick Saltman, the original drummer for Dream Engine, several of whose members later joined other bands that populate this book, notes incisively that a multi-faceted cultural explosion took place in the Upper Valley from the mid-1960s to the mid-1970s. The *Gestalt* of the times gave birth to figures who are internationally known in their fields. For example, Wayne Wadhams, who honed his cinema genius as well as his musical talents; double Tony Award-winning director Jerry Zaks; Chris Miller, co-author of *Animal House*; and the Pilobolus dance company, which began in 1971 at Dartmouth.

In this nexus, an area with a radius extending out fifty miles from the Upper Valley, talented rock bands rooted and grew during the same decade. Maybe there was something in the water? Maybe it was a Commie plot! A primary ingredient of this creative gumbo likely was a great liberal arts college. Ford Daley, a Norwich retiree who taught at Hanover High School from 1964 to 1984, describes Dartmouth's Hopkins Center as a cultural lodestone for the entire Upper Valley.

Whatever the reason, rock music moved front and center in the nexus during that decade.

This book celebrates a remarkable era in a particular location, a place in time unique in that so many truly talented bands formed. Yet I am mindful that in another very important way this place and time was not unique. All around the country, the same vibrant music scene was unfolding. Steve Calvert, the keyboard and rhythm guitar player for The Night Watchmen, recalls the milieu in his home state of New Jersey during the 1960s, which featured such luminaries as Joey Dee and the Starlighters at the Peppermint Lounge, and a neophyte later known simply as "The Boss."

For those of us in bands, it was an amazing time to be young, and making a joyful noise. So, to our musical brothers and sisters in arms, most of whom we will never know but with whom we shared a transcendent love for music and so many memorable times: our story speaks to yours, across the miles and across the years.

"Momma, Are They Body Snatchers?"

In the valley of the Connecticut River, between the presidential White Mountains of New Hampshire and the Green Mountains of Vermont, lay a sprinkling of townships sharing a peaceful life far removed from the big cities of New England. The warm summers and cold winters, the mills and the family farms, defined the conservative lives of the families who resided here. Working to assure their survival through the long winters, these upstanding citizens spent summers farming, selectively harvesting trees for fuel, waking with the birds before the sun, tending the animals and letting them out to pasture. That was about to change.

The peace and harmony of their simple life was about to be forever altered by an invasive, non-indigenous species—the rock musician. (1) They came from Tennessee, they came from New Jersey, Washington, D.C., New York, Ohio, California, Oregon. They came from everywhere, and soon would be everywhere!

The natives were horrified. But life was not easy for the invaders, either. Listen to "Scapegoat," a song written by Tracks' guitarist Russell Pinkston.

I'm your old man's scapegoat,
a dyed in the wool coyote,
and I keep my company with cutthroats and thieves
of every ilk.

I'm a common foot soldier,
kept fighting though the war was over,
and I'll take your sister and your mama, for a thrill.
If you start trouble, I'm the one they get the law on....

7

If you start seeing double I'm the one who gets the blame.

I'm the nightmare of the high class,
I'm an outlaw, and an outcast,
I started out dead last, I got nothing to lose.

I'm a communist sympathizer, revolutionary organizer,
the man money can't buy, I don't play by your rules.

If you start trouble, I'm the one they get the law on....
If you start seeing double I'm the one that gets the blame.
Ain't it a shame.

I can fast talk, I can get your goat,
I'm the man on the corner with the leather coat.
I'm the footsteps just behind you, don't turn around.

I'm the hoodlum your daddy told you about,
I'm a no good, and a drop out.
I'm a drugged crazed hippie, you better look out,
I'll sneak up behind you before you can shout,
and whip out my needle, and give you a shot,
and hook you on some of that LSD pot.

If you start trouble, I'm the one they get the law on....
If you start seeing double, I'm the one that gets the blame.
Ain't it a shame. (2)

As a "charter member" of the invaders, I'm speaking to all of you whose hair was a bit too long, whose clothes were a bit too out of the ordinary. Remember standing on the corner of Small Town, USA, anywhere in the Lower Forty-Eight? Citizens are walking by, giving you the widest possible berth, looking askance as if you had three eyes or two heads. Mothers are steering their children away from you, shielding them from even fleeting, incidental contact. If you are now fifty to sixty-five and you say it never happened—I'll say you weren't there. Or, maybe, you were still channeling Richie Cunningham.

The reaction of "civilians" was pretty consistent and pretty ubiquitous: at 2:00 p.m. on a sunny afternoon outside Whitcomb's Music Center in Claremont, NH; at 3:00 in the morning at the Talley House, an "Open 24 Hours" restaurant in White River; after a gig at the Dunkin' Donuts in Burlington, VT. Sometimes we were (pleasantly) fooled when a regular Joe or Jolene reacted to us as if we were not contagious. More often than not, you would have thought our foreheads carried the mark of Satan. I suspect New England was not the only part of the country in which rockers were doing the Devil's work.

Take note of the fact that we "rock stars" were mostly in our teens and twenties, quite taken with ourselves, and not as mature as we might have been. Add in the intoxicating notion that the average citizen seemed to think we humble musicians possessed some sort of power that might threaten the very foundations of society. You are now armed with the knowledge that we didn't always handle the attention well. However, there were times when we overcame our own shortcomings and rose to the occasion.

One night in 1969, on a road trip to play a gig south of Boston, Tracks stopped for dinner at a family restaurant in Brockton, MA. We walked in, found ourselves a long, rectangular table in the center of the dining room, and waited. And waited…. We must have looked unusually disagreeable that evening. Two or three times we shot pointed glances at the klatch of three waitresses standing about thirty feet across the room, encumbered with nothing but avoiding us. Eventually, the waitress who apparently drew the short straw came to our table.

Once we broke the ice with our server we had a pleasant dinner, scowling glances from other patrons excepted. We were exquisitely polite to the young lady. At some point over dinner, someone, perhaps southern gentleman Ned Berndt, had a stroke of genius. "Hey, let's leave her the biggest tip we can." When the waitress brought our bill (about $25 for seven dinners), we cobbled together a tip that approached $100, a princely sum in 1969.

We were in the parking lot when the waitress came flying out the door after us. Somewhere down the road, she would pay forward the lesson she had learned.

We all did what we could. But all of us in bands shared this common experience: people see you and immediately, without reservation or hesitation, distrust and despise you, simply because of how you look. It is an extraordinarily powerful experience, to feel directly the sting of prejudice, and it leaves a profound impression.

I believe that today, forty years later, rockers from the 1960s and 1970s are among the most tolerant people on earth. You learn and forever appreciate the hard lesson of fear and hatred once you've been on the receiving end.

Tin Soldiers

When I think of The Sixties, I reflexively call up a scene from the movie, *Field of Dreams*. Kevin Costner's character, Ray Kinsella, has wormed his way into the apartment of Terence Mann, a character played by James Earl Jones. While fending off Kinsella with an insecticide sprayer, Mann remarks sardonically that his uninvited guest must be from The Sixties.

For many of us, "The Sixties" were not a neat, numerical decade from January 1, 1960, to December 31, 1969. In the early part of that numerical decade life was more like the Eisenhower years, as celebrated in the television series *Happy Days*. You know: buzz cuts, stay-at-home Harriet Nelsons, authority going mostly unchallenged. "Okay, coach, how high?" But somewhere in the middle of that decade, control started slipping away from "The Man."

For me, "The Sixties" span the decade from 1966 to 1975, a time of extraordinary and lasting change, of tumultuous events, culturally, politically, musically. When I think of "The Sixties," I think of the Summer of Love, Martin, Bobby, and the first man on the moon. But I also think of Watergate, a helicopter toppling off a Saigon rooftop, and Richard Nixon in August of 1974: "Therefore, I shall resign the office of the presidency." And, I think of May 4, 1970.

Richard F. Nixon. (1) I suppose it's just me, but I don't believe any other person dominated those years like "Tricky Dick." Hero, or arch enemy? There was virtually no middle ground. For the vast majority of us in the music scene, he represented evil incarnate, all that was wrong with the world.

Change came like a sledgehammer in the mid- to late (numerical) Sixties, and often arrived at the speed of light.

Bob Reich, noted economist and Bill Clinton's Secretary of Labor, was a classmate at Dartmouth and president of the Class of 1968. He remembers an incident in Hanover when *Happy Days* was morphing into "The Sixties."

"In 1967...George Wallace tried to get out of town after having delivered a speech at which several members of the class charged the podium. His car was surrounded by so many Dartmouth students, his driver couldn't move it, and students began rocking the car and climbing on top of it. Thad Seymour [the Dean of The College] ran up to me, eyes ablaze, asking for my help in dispersing the crowd. He and I moved in, yelling at the top of our lungs. We had no effect whatsoever. Wallace eventually got away, but the next week, the campus was caught up in a heated and important debate about what had happened and who was to be held responsible for what. To me, that marked the beginning of a different kind of Dartmouth than the one I'd entered my freshman year, and a different kind of nation, too, for that matter. Crowds can get ugly...demagogues on the right and left can be uglier still.... Sometimes out of anger and resentment a community can change for the better, and any kind of social change—especially involving race or any other deep scar on a nation—can be painful." (2)

May 4, 1970. Every American who was over the age of ten on that date remembers Kent State, and the deaths of four students at the hands of the Ohio National Guard. Many Americans also remember "Ohio," Crosby, Stills, Nash and Young's response to that terrible event. Neil Young wrote the lyrics after seeing photos of the incident in *Life* magazine. The group recorded the song in Los Angeles on May 21, and it was quickly released in June. The song was banned on many radio stations because of its direct reference to President Nixon. The record's B side was Stephen Stills' "Find the Cost of Freedom." Sung a cappella after an acoustic guitar introduction, with a single verse repeated twice, the song is as poignant and painful in its simplicity as "Ohio" is with its anguished, raging vocals, dominant guitar riff, and bass-driven marching meter.

Tracks debuted "Ohio" in our repertoire on August 15, 1970, and for me it was a memorable night. We were playing a club in Ludlow, VT, and as I introduced the song I noticed a policeman at the back of the room, arms crossed over a barrel chest, glaring at me while I spoke. As Russell Pinkston began playing the opening guitar riff, I glared directly back at the cop, and did so through the whole song.

A difficult truth in our society is that while most people remember "Ohio," they do not remember The Steve Miller Band's "Jackson-Kent Blues," or the violence that prompted it. Ten days after Kent State, at Jackson State College, an historically black school in Mississippi, two young men were shot to death following two days of campus protests. On the evening of May 14, a crowd of students became unruly, and approximately seventy-five Jackson City and Mississippi State Police responded. Shortly after midnight, the officers opened fire, killing one student and wounding more than a dozen others. Also killed by a bullet was a black high school student who had stopped on his way home from work to watch the incident unfold.

While Kent State sparked outrage around the country, Jackson State barely caused a ripple.

In Memoriam

Phillip Lafayette Gibbs
James Earl Green
Allison Beth Krause
Jeffrey Glenn Miller
Sandra Lee Scheuer
William Knox Schroeder

Wayne Wadhams

For many of us whose lives reflect off these pages, the story begins in Hanover, NH, between 1964 and 1969. During those years we lived in the presence of, and were inspired directly or indirectly by, the genius of Wayne Wadhams.

For me, the moment of inspiration came in the late fall of my junior year at Dartmouth. One night I was walking by Webster Hall, across the street from my dorm, and heard some damn fine music coming out of the building. I wandered in, sat down, and listened for a spell to Wayne and his band, The Fifth Estate. I can't tell you how long I sat in Webster Hall, but I can tell you it was a primal experience. I watched, mesmerized, as the band created this powerful sound, this incredible energy. Music had gripped me since 1957, when I had purchased my first 45 rpm record (1), but this was an epiphany. As I exited Webster that night I remember thinking, "I'd really like to do that." About a year later I was doing that, thanks in part to Wayne Wadhams.

Who was this necromancer?

According to our Dartmouth Class of 1968 Freshman "Green Book," Wayne Wadhams attended Rippowam High School in Stamford, CT, participated in such activities as yearbook, glee club, and National Honor Society, and graduated cum laude. Wayne matriculated on the Hanover Plain with us Pea Green '68s in September 1964.

Only a few months earlier, in Stamford, Wayne had helped found a band, The D-Men, with singer Don Askew, guitarists Rick Engler and Ken Evans, bass player Doug Ferrara, drummer Bill Shute, and Wayne on keyboards. The group signed a recording contract in the fall of 1964, and released several singles that received little notice outside of the New York area. But in March of 1965 The D-Men appeared on *Hullabaloo* (2), a hit national television show briefly co-hosted by Brian Epstein. (Epstein, The Beatles' manager, filmed his segments on the show from the UK.) In 1966, the band changed its name to The Fifth Estate and hoped to sign with Epstein. But in March of that year John Lennon had caused a furor in America by popping off about his band being more popular than Jesus Christ, and by August of 1967 Epstein was dead of an accidental drug overdose.

On December 31, 1966, Wayne attended a New Year's Eve party and someone bet him that the Fifth Estate couldn't make a rock hit out of a song from *The Wizard of Oz.* Wayne and his band mates rose to the challenge, and in April of 1967 released "Ding Dong! The Witch Is Dead." In June the song reached #11 on the *Billboard* Hot 100 charts, and finished 1967 among the top 100 record releases of the year. (3) The band toured incessantly behind the record, playing with such rock icons as Gene Pitney, The Lovin' Spoonful, and The Byrds. Touring forced Wayne to drop out of Dartmouth prior to his senior year, but he returned to graduate in June of 1969 with a major in English.

"Ding Dong! The Witch Is Dead" illustrates clearly the genius of Wayne Wadhams. In addition to containing all the elements of a successful bubblegum song, The Fifth Estate's version features an anomalous classical music influence that was not in the original song. Wayne had played classical piano since his early teens, and wrote an interlude derived from a piece called "Terpsichore," written by the German composer Michael Praetorius in 1612. The band collaborated on the unusual arrangement, including extensive use of a piccolo, hardly your garden variety rock instrument. But the band's members gave sole credit to Wayne for the inspiration. Who'd have thought you could get away with such a thing in 1966? But that was Wayne, always thinking outside the box.

A top ten hit earns a band instant stardom, but fame came with a significant downside. The group had hoped that its big hit would allow them to write and record more serious, sophisticated music. The record label wanted more pop hits like "Ding Dong!" Two follow up efforts, "The Goofin' Song" and "Heigh Ho!" (a take-off on the Disney film, *Snow White*), met with little commercial success.

More than once in my time with Wayne he referred to The Fifth Estate's "sell your soul" recording contract, including in his commentary various colorful, disparaging remarks about five years of indentured servitude. Jubilee Records folded in 1970, preceded by the Fifth Estate in 1969.

Wayne Wadhams was a larger-than-life figure on a campus filled with big personalities and super achievers. In addition to his widely recognized musical talents he was particularly known as the head of the Dartmouth Film Society. His hilarious, playful brilliance lives on in his classmates' and fellow musicians' many memories. Here are a few.

Gene Mackles: "Freshman year, Wayne Wadhams lived a few doors down from me in Topliff Hall. He was very outgoing and creative, and usually a little on the wild side. But he was lots of fun." Wayne and Gene played piano duets at the "Top of the Hop" in the Hopkins Center. They did a lot of Beatles tunes and took requests almost every afternoon. Gene recalls that, in addition to the Beatles, "We did a lot of popular music of the time, either four-handed or duo piano. Wayne had a great ear, and since my training was in classical piano, it was all new and exciting to me.

"One vacation break I went with Wayne and some members of his band, The Fifth Estate, along with their manager, to see a rock show at the Brooklyn Paramount. The show was put together by Murray the K, a well-known DJ of the time, and it was amazing! Mandala, The Lovin' Spoonful, Cream, The Four Tops—I 'm sure there were others.

"Senior year we collaborated on a film entitled 'Garden' which was based on Hieronymous Bosch's 'Garden of Earthly Delights.' Wayne did most of the heavy lifting on the shooting and editing of the piece. I was more involved in it conceptually, in the selection process, music included, and graphics. Shortly after graduation, Wayne somehow managed to sell the rights to the film to a small publisher in New York City. He was nothing if not energetic."

According to Steve Calvert, another dorm hall mate for three years, Wayne was "almost from another planet smart" in several ways. (This from a Dartmouth grad who earned his Ph.D. in English!) "Wayne was a good friend to me, but so smart and so far ahead musically that I was too intimidated to take much advantage of our time together. I remember he bought a harpsichord kit and built the instrument right in his dorm room. He also developed a board game, in his room, which Parker Brothers paid him *not* to market so it wouldn't compete with 'Monopoly.' 'Wads' called his game 'Theopoly,' and all I remember of the board squares is that in 'Monopoly,' where a square said 'Go to Jail' [Do not pass Go, do not collect $100], 'Theopoly' said 'Go to Hell'….

"When Wayne wrote 'The Goofin' Song' as the follow-up to 'Ding Dong! The Witch Is Dead,' he invited a few of us down to New York City for the last day of recording. He had most of the basic tracks and all the vocals done, but he wrote the flute parts on the train from his mother's house in Stamford, CT, as we watched in disbelief. He had recruited us to go with him because he wanted half a dozen of us to be recorded as a chorus of finger snappers and hand clappers. It was a kick to be on that record, even though it didn't go nearly as far as 'Ding Dong!'"

Steve also reminisces: "One afternoon Wads came down the hall, pulled the book out of my lap, and walked me to a concert in Spaulding Auditorium at the Hop. He had two second row seats to a full piano concert by my mother's favorite recording artist for classical piano, Rudolph Serkin. I was surprised and slightly horrified, though it didn't seem to bother Wads in the least, that Serkin hummed other music to himself, loud enough so that we could hear it in the first two rows, as he played his two-hour concert."

David Soren, referencing Wayne's work with The D-Men and The Fifth Estate, says, "Wayne was brilliant in the studio and had a definite idea of how to market his work. Wayne was the prince of cool and we admired him."

Speaking of the Dartmouth Film Society, Ned Berndt, drummer for Tracks, has this memory of Wayne as it entwines with the Film Society. "In the fall of 1969, Tracks was in the cafe at the Hop. I think it was near Halloween. We had realized that the only person any of us knew, or had heard of, who had been in a real recording studio was Wayne Wadhams. At that very moment he walked past us, dressed in a long, black cape, headed towards Spaulding Auditorium. I jumped up and followed him but there was a lot of traffic coming from Spaulding, as a movie had just let out. He turned into the men's room, so I followed him in, stood next to him at the urinal and introduced myself. I gave him the Tracks card, he said he would call but never did. Five or six weeks later we got his Boston number from someone and I called him. He said that he had found our card in his pocket several days later but could not recall how he came to get it, as he was tripping in the men's room right before going into Spaulding to play the organ for some horror movie."

That phone call from Ned Berndt eventually led to Wayne becoming Tracks' engineer and producer. He helmed half a dozen recording sessions that resulted in the band's 1974 triple album and 1991 CD. In the studio Wayne was highly skilled and patient beyond words, especially when called upon to explain to us studio neophytes why certain things had to be the way they had to be. More than once, with a bemused look on his face, Wayne intoned one of his pet phrases, "What it is, is," as he gently explained to us what we didn't know while trying to make it look like we at least knew something. Wayne was more than just our engineer and producer. He was a good friend.

Wayne Wadhams (center) with Tracks, circa 1974. Standing left is Russell Pinkston, standing right is Bob Neale, seated is Ned Berndt.

After his Dartmouth years Wayne moved to Boston. In 1970 he co-founded an award-winning production company called Film Associates with Dartmouth classmate Austin de Besche. In the fall of 1971, Wayne, de Besche, and another

Dartmouth grad, Bob Gitt '63, founded the Orson Welles Film School and Studio B recording studios. In 1982 the renowned Berklee College of Music came calling, and Wayne taught there until 1996, while designing Berklee's Music Production and Engineering Department, which debuted in 1984.

In 1990 Wayne became a record label owner, founding Boston Skyline Music. Along the way he also authored several highly regarded books, including the well-known *Inside the Hits*, which dissected prominent rock and roll songs and what made them work. What did Gene Mackles say about Wayne? "He was nothing if not energetic!"

Wayne died on August 19, 2008, his passing mourned by many in the music and film industries. He was a talented artist in the broadest sense, but he was far more than that. He was a fine human being, the kind of person the world needs many more of. For those of us who spent our college years in Hanover during the mid- and late Sixties, Wayne's multi-faceted genius will always have a place in our hearts, our minds, and our music.

Sixties Dartmouth Bands

The story of Dartmouth's campus bands in the late Sixties has to start with Webster Hall. Webster, completed in 1907 after six years of construction, was a large building that abutted the College Green and flanked Baker Library. Its first floor was a cavernous auditorium that seated 850 on the main level and in a balcony that loomed above three sides of the main level. The auditorium's stage was huge—deep and wide. The basement level had been cut up into narrow rooms, for storage and other uses.

Webster was used irregularly for "real" College events, and Dartmouth allowed rock bands to rehearse there, both on the main stage and in two basement rooms. A check with members of other bands who attended the University of Vermont, the University of New Hampshire, and Plymouth State (NH) College revealed that none of them remember their schools providing rehearsal space. Pamela Brandt of the Moppets, Ariel, and Deadly Nightshade recalls Mount Holyoke letting the Moppets rehearse in a campus cottage. But no one else had a Webster Hall.

Bob Lundquist of The Coming Thing remembers a signup sheet for reserving space, and that was it; no cost, no hassle, and generous hours for rehearsal. Bob remembers hanging out to see other bands before and after his band's time slot, and feeling both the fellowship and motivation that resulted. The "end up in the middle of that rock and roll stew" effect.

A particularly interesting facet of rehearsing on the main stage was that you always had an audience. Dave Cross, who played in three different campus bands, recalls that "the main stage was a great stage. Plenty of room to spread out, and you got the feeling of performing when you were rehearsing.

There seemed to always be at least a couple of people listening. The College left the building open, and people seemed to always be wandering through." Even at 1:00 in the morning a musician could look up and see people scattered around the balcony.

Webster was pretty much ours to inhabit. In retrospect it seems no surprise that there were so many rock bands on campus each year. Webster was a unique opportunity, Dartmouth's gift to its aspiring rock stars.

The Coming Thing formed in 1966, and featured Dan Morgenroth on bass and lead vocal, Bob Lundquist playing a Wurlitzer electric piano, Eldon Hall on guitar and vocals, and Dave Cross on drums. Bob was on the football team, and sometimes the group had to play the first set without him on the night of an away game. The gridders would return to town and Bob would hustle over to the gig.

Dave Cross remembers that "Dan was one really talented guy. The Coming Thing was my first band, and my first gig was at a Dartmouth fraternity house. From my relatively safe spot behind the drums, I was witness to what, at the time, impressed me as a highly entertaining and somewhat bizarre freak show. But playing was a blast and when it was over I got cash. That's all it took! Over the next year I became a credible drummer, thanks mainly to the patience and persistence of Eldon, Dan, and Bob. Thanks, guys.

"I also remember, very early on, pushing a wheelbarrow full of drums from the storage room in New Hampshire Hall to fraternity row for a gig." What, Dave, no roadies?

The Crowd was composed of three members of the Class of 1968: David Soren, Calvin Jones, and Chuck Berry (the other one). David says, "I had to play rhythm and lead guitar at the same time, Cal played drums, Chuck played bass and we all sang. It was a lot of work making three guys sound like four, but the paychecks were split three ways even if I had to fake the leads. Our motto was 'Two's company but three's The Crowd!'"

In the fall of 1964, freshmen Rich Olin, Don Russell, and Eric Ebbeson shared a suite in Cohen Hall, and discovered that Rich and Eric played guitar and Don played drums. They were also members of the Dartmouth Corinthian Yacht Club, hence the name they gave their band, The Corinthians. At the end of their freshman year they added Steve Giddings on bass, and after a summer upgrade of equipment the band played on fraternity row just about every weekend.

Eric says, "We were strictly a cover band, never wrote anything of our own. Our signature songs were 'Sea of Love,' with which we ended every gig, and 'Long Tall Texan,' with a verse about a long, tall Emmet—me. We clowned around a lot and played good time music. For a while in the Corinthians we had a keyboardist, Mike Crabtree, playing with us. We didn't want one at first because that would mean splitting the money with one other person. He had this Hammond organ that was enormously heavy and really not portable, but we schlepped it around anyway." Seems The Corinthians had the same love/hate relationship with their Hammond that a lot of bands did.

Uncle Tom's Cabinet was another band with a politically incorrect name. The group included band leader Tom Parker on bass; original lead singer Ocie Sydnor; Nelson Armstrong, who took over the vocals when Ocie graduated in 1968; Jim Shafer on keyboard; Phil Lucas on tenor sax; Anthony "Fa Fa" Harley on trumpet; multi-instrumentalist Rich Johnson on bass, guitar, piano, and trumpet; and Dave Cross on drums. Yeah, Tom Parker was black.

As Jim Shafer remembers it, "Phil Lucas was the heart of the band. Phil had studied for several years in his home town of

Indianapolis with a professor from the University of Indiana. Indiana was, and is, a major jazz school." The band played soul hits like "Midnight Hour" and "Mustang Sally" by Wilson Pickett, "Knock on Wood" by Eddie Floyd, The Temptations' "My Girl," "Hold On, I'm Comin'" by Sam and Dave, Otis Redding's "Dock of the Bay," and "Tighten Up" by "Archie Bell and the Drells from Houston, Texas." Uncle Tom's Cabinet performed a Jimi Hendrix set, as well as several original songs written by Tom Parker. Nels Armstrong recalls recording those originals one day in Spaulding Auditorium.

Upon the demise of The Corinthians and The Crowd, Eric Ebbeson, Steve Giddings, and David Soren formed Sphinx. Eric recalls that "The early days of Sphinx started with Steve Giddings and me trying to form a blues band. I had been to the Newport Folk Festival back in the summer of 1965 and saw Mimi and Richard Farina perform electrified with Paul Butterfield backing them up. I also saw the Chambers Brothers, the Blues Project, and others. Steve and I, the last of The Corinthians, tried to get something going. Steve found Howie [David] Soren and I think I asked Gene Mackles, because we were both art majors and I knew he played a killer keyboard." The band was Soren on lead vocal and rhythm guitar, Ebbeson on lead guitar, Giddings on bass, Mackles on keyboard, and Dave Seidman on drums.

David Soren had wanted to front a group and Sphinx proved the right vehicle. Eric says that "Howie was really into psychedelic music and was writing some originals, so the complexion of the group shifted away from blues and we became a psychedelic band. That was okay with me 'cause I just wanted to play."

Gene Mackles relates that "After agreeing to join the band, I went down to Boston to Jack's Drum Shop and picked up an Acetone organ and an Ampeg amp. We rehearsed in Webster Hall. We did mostly covers of popular songs, but also a few of our own. Our first gig was at Hanover High School. I don't think we were very good and my memory was that the crowd agreed. We did, however, gel after time and played lots of frat parties. My most vivid memory involves playing in the basement of a frat house, wading in a few inches of beer slosh. And then there was the smell...."

1968 Sphinx rehearsal at one of Dartmouth's Choate Road dorms, L – R: Gene Mackles, Steve Giddings, Dave Seidman, David Soren, Eric Ebbeson

Sphinx began doing very well, helped by the addition of David's wife, Noelle Soren, a female singer who people compared to Michelle Phillips of The Mamas and The Papas. The band also had drummer Seidman, who could really cook on songs like "Midnight Hour," which featured David Soren rolling around on the floor and screaming. But Seidman decided to leave the band to pursue his first love, and the band struggled to find a drummer to replace him.

Dave Seidman was not only a strong, instinctive drummer, but a world-class mountaineer as well. In April 1969 he was part of an eleven-member American team attempting a never before tried route up Dhaulagiri in Nepal. Dhaulagiri is the seventh highest mountain in the world at 26,795 feet. It had first been "summited" in 1960 by a Swiss/Austrian team. On April 29, an advance party of seven Americans and one Sherpa guide was caught in an avalanche while building a log bridge over a crevasse. David, team leader Boyd Everett, and five others were killed, their bodies never found. American Lou Reichardt was the lone survivor.

The Night Watchmen was mostly a Dartmouth Class of 1970 group. Russell Pinkston posted an open audition notice on the Hopkins Center's Hinman Post Office bulletin board during his Freshman Week in September of 1966. As Russell puts it, "Believe it, or not, that one sign brought in Jeff Wilkes, Pete Logan, a rhythm guitarist named Al Kaplan, and eventually Steve Calvert. Steve could sing, knew a bunch of tunes, had some microphones, a guitar, some kind of keyboard, two Fender twin amps, and was already a very old man—a junior—who had connections. It was really Steve's band, obviously, even though I did put up the sign that started everything. We called ourselves The Embryos, and we played a few gigs together that first year. Al left at some point, because he was superfluous since Steve also played rhythm guitar."

The next year the band renamed itself The Night Watchmen, played a lot of campus gigs, and spent many hours in Webster Hall. In fact it was in Webster Hall that the band came up with the new name. Steve Calvert recalls that "When Hanover High didn't want a band named The Embryos playing one of their dances, we looked around a darkened Webster Hall one night during rehearsal, spotted the night watchman wandering around with his flashlight, and had our new name."

By the end of that year, says Russell, "We were pretty good, or thought we were." The band auditioned for a summer gig at a club in Saratoga Springs, NY, passed the audition, but then was fired after being outed by the clearly superior house band, the Lime Cirrus from Burlington, VT. The boys retreated to the Pocono Mountains vacation home of Russell's parents for a couple of weeks to sharpen their game. Then they went to New York City, where they lived at

Russell's house in Brooklyn for the summer and found work by playing in Greenwich Village at the Café Bizarre, where the Lovin' Spoonful got its start and the owner, Solange, befriended the band.

Speaking of auditions, Peter Logan remembers that in March 1968 "we were auditioning at the Hampton Manor and while we were there President Lyndon Johnson announced he would not run for re-election. We thought this surely meant the Vietnam War was about to end, and maybe even that Steve wouldn't have to go into the Navy when he graduated in June."

The Night Watchmen's play list included many of the great bands of the mid- to late Sixties: Beatles, Stones, Doors, The Who, Jefferson Airplane, The Lovin' Spoonful, Spencer Davis, The Young Rascals. The group also played a lot of Cream and Hendrix, to take advantage of Russell's increasing skill as a lead guitarist. Among the band's enduring memories: the drive in Jeff Wilkes' 1956 Cadillac hearse to Boston to buy its first real guitar amplifiers. The hearse lost its brakes at sixty miles an hour, but the boys survived. Whoa, three-fifths of a mile in ten seconds!

Dream Engine was a seven-piece band with a lot of flexibility, serious chops, a broad play list, and a great name. The band got the name when guitarist Tom Maddron told the other band members that he had a dream about a train engine and a tunnel, thus the group became the Dream Engine. There was Maddron on guitar and vocals; Oliver Hess on guitar; Andy Raymond on bass and vocals; John Maxfield on keyboard, trumpet, and vocals; Peter Christenson on trumpet and lead vocals; Dave Gilliatt on harmonica and vocals; and Rick Saltman on drums, later to be replaced by Dave Cross.

Cross remembers that "Dream Engine was the first band I was in that played original material. Tom Maddron was the principal songwriter, and at that time I didn't even care if a

27

tune was marketable or not. I considered myself a budding 'artiste' and I think most of the musicians around had this disdain for anything 'commercial'…almost a pejorative term. But I don't think we always thought through very well things like, 'Is this danceable, will this help us get gigs?' It was more like how artistic we could be, how creative, and then if we couldn't sell it, it wasn't our fault, it was the people who didn't recognize quality music."

Despite Cross' description of a group that disdained the commercial, the band did play a mix of well-known covers, including "Midnight Hour," "Try a Little Tenderness" by Otis Redding, and "Born in Chicago" by The Paul Butterfield Blues Band. Peter Christenson remarks that "Having two trumpeters moved us toward soul and blues a bit, though not as far as I would have liked. We also played some Beatles and Stones, but in addition we did a bunch of other stuff that didn't fit anywhere, including jazz fusion. Try that at a frat party!"

Dream Engine would re-emerge in a future life as the band Ragweed. In August 2009 I sent a Ragweed CD to Gerry Bell, a Dartmouth classmate, and asked him what he remembered about Dream Engine. His memory, more than 40 years later: "More than the type of music Dream Engine played when I listened to them one night in Webster Hall, I remember what good musicians they were. I recall some rock, not driving hard rock so much as fluid stuff, maybe a touch of soul. But mostly I stayed in Webster and listened because they played so well. There were no vocals that I recall now, but I was really impressed by how professional the music was—so much better than the hack bands that frequented Alpha Theta."

The Ham Sandwich was not really a Dartmouth band, although when the Sandwich broke up in June 1968 three of its five members were Dartmouth students. In any event, with apologies to Skip Truman and Ken Aldrich, I am including Ham Sandwich in this chapter.

The roots of the Ham Sandwich lead back to a Hanover High School band. The Stingrays formed in 1962 when Ken Aldrich was a sophomore, and broke up when he graduated in June 1965. "It started before I had a driver's license, and our parents drove us around for the first few gigs. Skip Truman was the drummer, and in the fall of 1962 he was a seventh grader. We had to go get permission from his folks for him to play in the band." In 1966 Ken and Skip played in a band called The Night Crawlers with two Dartmouth students, Steve MacIntosh and Hare Naylor. Ken was in engineering school in Concord and drove an hour to Hanover on weekends.

Some time early in 1967 Ken and Skip joined forces with guitarist Dan Morgenroth to form the Ham Sandwich. Ken played organ and keyboard bass with his left hand, Skip manned the drums, and all three sang. Early in 1968, when I joined the group, fellow Minnesotan Eldon Hall had replaced Dan on lead guitar.

Even back in 1968 I thought my being asked to join Ham Sandwich was ridiculous, and I certainly think so with forty-three years of hindsight. I'd always loved rock and roll, always loved singing along, but I came to music absolutely unwashed. I was no musician, I was a "jock" for chrissake!

One night in late 1967, in the basement of Sigma Nu, we had some cheap, junky band playing. They took a break, three of the brothers grabbed the guitar, bass and drums, and I sang two staples of that era, The Kingsmen's "Louie, Louie," and "G-L-O-R-I-A" by the Shadows of Knight. Naturally, the inebriated frat bros loved it. More importantly, Scott McQueen, a 1968 classmate who happened to be there and who was Ham Sandwich's agent, also thought it was pretty good. The next week he offered me a tryout as lead singer for the Sandwich. I thought, "Hey, that would be cool, singing rock and roll," so I auditioned and got the job.

What was such a joke was that I knew nothing about being in a rock band or being on stage. I didn't play an instrument, and I had no equipment. On top of all that, both Ken and Skip were clearly better singers than I was for the entire time I was in the band. But Scott wanted to go with the hot concept of the time, the front man. Again, my apologies to Skip and Ken, two dear friends who would probably never tell me, even today, what they really thought when I joined them in January of 1968.

But I wasn't gonna give it back! I was livin' the dream, man, fronting a rock band, groupies, wearing those funky boots and clothes. Shortly after I joined up Dan returned on guitar, Eldon moved on, and we found a Dartmouth freshman from Lawnguyland, Dom "Pooch" Puccio, to play bass. Kenny ditched the keyboard bass, and Pooch gave us a fifth vocalist. It was a blast for six months, driving around Vermont and New Hampshire in the band's hearse, playing great tunes with some fine musicians.

The band's play list included "Light My Fire," the Vanilla Fudge version of "You Keep Me Hangin' On," "Shotgun" by Junior Walker, "My Girl," "Fire" by both Jimi Hendrix and Arthur Brown, several Rascals tunes, "Sweet Lorraine" by Country Joe and the Fish, The Beatles' "Lady Madonna," and that one hit wonder, "Expressway to Your Heart," by The Soul Survivors. The only original song we did was Dan's, a ballad called "Caroline" that Skip sang beautifully.

June of 1968 arrived, and with it graduation for Dan and me. The group played out a string of gigs that month at Dartmouth class reunions and in various backwater clubs and dance halls.

Our final gig was at New York's notorious Hampton Manor. After playing all night and then loading the equipment back into the hearse we were dead tired. But we still had to drive almost two hours back to Hanover over a winding, hilly Vermont road that in the first week of my freshman year at Dartmouth had claimed the lives of four students.

We were complaining to each other about how tired we were, and somebody associated with the Manor said, "Here, try these pills. They're kinda like 'No-Doz,' and they'll keep you awake." Yeah, they did that. The other guys took a different vehicle back home, and Pooch rode shotgun as I drove the hearse. We made it back to Hanover with nary a drooping eyelid. I remember sitting with Pooch on the curb outside Topliff Hall after we had returned, the sun coming up. I looked at him and suggested we go get something to eat, because neither of us was going to sleep any time soon. I don't know what variation of speed was in those little "No-Doz" pills, but neither of us slept for about thirty-six hours.

Ham Sandwich, Hanover, June of 1968, L – R: Peter Wonson, Ken Aldrich, Dan Morgenroth, Dom "Pooch" Puccio, Skip Truman

The Ham Sandwich broke up late in June after that gig at the Hampton Manor. In July, with great trepidation, I returned to Minneapolis to see my Uncle Sam about one little item—my draft physical. At that point I wasn't planning on seeing my friends from the Sandwich ever again.

The Café Bizarre

August 21, 1968
By Steve Calvert
Reprinted with permission

At 8:50 p.m. on a Saturday night in The Village, Solange, the *Café Bizarre*'s owner, displays the patient good humor for which she is known in the pop music world. Her narrow storefront club was once home to The Lovin' Spoonful. Literally. They slept in the loft and Solange fed them hamburgers until they signed with Kama Sutra. Tonight, Solange's headliners aren't John, Zallie, Steve, and Joe.

Tonight, Solange features The Night Watchmen, a two-year-old cover band of Dartmouth College students. The group finds it cosmic, our name on a marquee under the café's name. It is bizarre, landing a two-month gig in a New York City hot spot, after getting fired in Saratoga Springs. It wasn't entirely our fault. We can't have been the only band the Lime Cirrus played off the stage. They were tight, soulful, forcing our retreat to Russ' family camp in the Poconos to rethink arrangements, stage presence, what we wanted from the music.

Greenwich Village. Russell Pinkston grew up near here, in Brooklyn, got the audition with Solange; got us tonight's CBS audition. Peter and Jeff stay with Russ at his parents'. I commute, packing brown sugar 8:00 to 4:30 out in Jersey.

Ole, our chief engineer, has jury-rigged a Rube Goldberg contraption to seal brown sugar in plastic bags. When he hears I've been to college, I become his assistant. All day we tinker with screws and bolts, pulleys and belts. The regular workers forgive me for it, invite me to Friday beers, and to play industrial league softball. One fictional world to another, and back: pack sugar, rock music, pack sugar.

Our new act is good enough that Solange hasn't fired us. There's more at stake tonight, though, so we keep wary eyes on the door. That's easy. The house is empty.

Our folksinger arrives with wife and baby Rose. After three weekends, we're family. Sonya told us one night, over Solange's hamburgers, how beautifully Rose travels in the VW Bus if they blow sweet smoke in her face. Danny plays during our band breaks. We cheer, chip in when he passes the hat, request his song about broken glass.

At 8:51 p.m., Russ comes bolt upright. CBS is here, two execs in wool slacks and golf shirts. Couldn't figure out how to dress. They're just kids, our age, but they don't see us. They're checking in with Solange. It will occur to me, forty-three years later, this audition goes on her say-so.

Solange's say-so, and what we bring the next fifty minutes to the worn oak floor and six spotlights that define Solange's stage. We walk to instruments in dead air slumped over us like a Bowery bum.

No generation before us shared music this way: danced to a weekly hit parade; picked up guitars, portable keyboards, horns, and mics to cover the world's music in the basement and the garage. But then, we were Boomers, we had our way, changed the world to fit our image. For generations after, we would sit in concerts where children swooned over our hits, our stars. Did Homer have this power? Beethoven? Puccini? Sinatra or Brubeck?

We know the music cold. In the middle of The Young Rascals' "Love Is a Beautiful Thing," I'm grateful Russ was born with strings in his genes: his mother played violin with

the Brooklyn Philharmonic. In the rhythm section, Jeff
Wilkes is the first true bass player I know, having studied
McCartney's runs on *Meet the Beatles*. And Peter Logan
earned his way out of Russ' doghouse back in the Poconos;
he hits hard now and we trust the beat.

THE NIGHT WATCHMEN

L – R: Jeff Wilkes, Steve Calvert, Peter Logan, Russell Pinkston

The set features our own greatest hits: Beatles in three-part harmony, Stones, Lovin' Spoonful, The Left Banke, Junior Walker, Young Rascals, Steve Winwood's "Gimme Some Lovin'," which Russ has slowed from its original 140 beats per minute to 110, so it passes for soul music. We can't see anything in front of us. Not because of Solange's spotlights. The place has filled with smoke, swirling like a Lava Lamp. We're looking, but we aren't seeing. Or feeling. We can't taste our tongues, can't smell the mics. The world has lost all its senses, except sound, our sound. For all I know, we might be really good right now. I'm not blowing anything.

Funny: I blow it, make mistakes, all the time, in music, on baseball's field of dreams, except when it's for all the marbles. Then I play like I mean it. Funny, and frustrating. I know people who seem to be on all the time.

Peter's throwing off the strong vibes of a future lawyer; Jeff, not much longer than his Precision Bass and shorter than his Kustom amplifier, would cramp if his body moved like that after the music stopped. Russ' guitar licks on "Crossroads" channel Clapton. I switch from keyboard to guitar and back.

In fall 1963, "I Want to Hold Your Hand" awakened me on late-night radio. A month with my best friend's mother's western acoustic and I was hooked. But my parents made me paint the garage for permission to spend $30 I already had on a guitar. Seven years earlier they had sent me to bed before Elvis appeared on "The Ed Sullivan Show." Were they still freaked, not only by the swiveling hips, but by his guitar, not cradled demurely on his knee but slung around his neck? I can't be the only kid who snuck downstairs to peek around the corner and catch "Hound Dog" on TV. Would my parents have stopped paying for piano lessons had they foreseen I could turn Liszt into "Light My Fire?"

For once, it doesn't matter how much I can't sing like Hendrix. The set's almost over. Finale time. "I Can Tell" is early Billy Joel, who was the heart of The Hassles when only New Yorkers like Russ had heard of him. Russ brought the song to us in New Hampshire and we fell in love. Peter tick-tick-tick-ticks and I riff down the Farfisa; Russ makes it a duet on the Gibson double-cutaway; when Peter and Jeff come in, the room fills instantly with us.

When it's over, we're happy, relieved…and awed. The set began in an empty room. As Solange's world comes back into focus, we realize every table is filled, dancers crowd our mics for an encore we don't have. The place is SRO down the walls, across the back, into the street. We hear the line runs down the sidewalk, beyond the marquee.

*   *   *   *   *

The point isn't that magic ends. The point is that it happens. How did Willie Mays catch Vic Wertz' fly ball in the Polo Grounds during the '54 Series? What flew through Lindy's foggy mind as he made the coast of France after an endless moonlit night? I had an inkling, finishing that set in the summer of '68, thanks to three friends, a woman with one name, and our music.

The Acorn and the Tree

"It is my belief, after teaching all age groups from young children to the elderly for fifteen years, that there is no question that anyone who is hugely talented in music, if you trace back through their family tree, almost 100% of the time there are major musical talents in earlier generations."

— Brad French, guitarist for Anvil

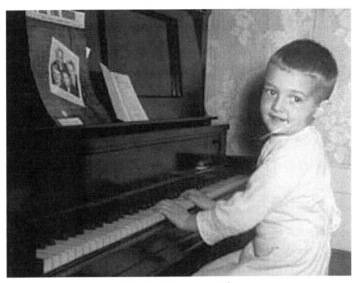

Gardner Berry at age 3

Margaret Fountain was born in Macon, Georgia, where she became known as a child prodigy on the violin. In 1934, when she was fifteen, her parents put her on a train bound for New York City to live with an aunt and attend Juilliard. Margaret studied there for ten years, earning her diploma and then doing post-graduate work. She was the concertmistress of the Juilliard Symphony, and twice runner-up in the Naumburg Competition, a prestigious international competition for pianists and violinists.

After Juilliard, Margaret joined the USO and went to Germany to entertain the troops at the end of World War II. She married James Pinkston in 1946, and moved to Beirut, Lebanon, where James was dean at the American University medical school. Their first two children were born in Beirut: Betsy in August 1947, and Russell on January 1, 1949. The Pinkstons returned to America when Russell was two years old, and settled in Brooklyn, New York.

Margaret, who had interrupted her musical career to start a family, began playing with the Brooklyn Philharmonic. When Russell was still young "We would go to her concerts, and my biggest memory of that besides the plush, red seats and running up and down the stairs—which I surely was not supposed to do—was eating those big lemon drops. I don't remember what music was played, but it went in and some of it must have stuck."

Indeed, from an early age Russell was exposed to classical music in various ways. His mother gave violin lessons and played in a string quartet, she practiced in the house, and she would play classical music on the record player. Russell grew up listening to her play violin and hearing chamber music, and "when she wasn't playing records she was constantly whistling...like, a violin solo when she was washing dishes."

Russell started, like many of us, on piano, but he didn't want to practice and it didn't take. The first instrument on which he persevered was the cello, which he played for three years. "That was not an entirely joyful experience for me, because like other kids I was much more interested in playing soccer or baseball...anything but school work or practicing. So I quit after a while, I was probably about thirteen, and it was a great disappointment to my mother. I remember her telling me when I quit, 'Some day you are going to want to play music again, and you can play anything you want except drums, trumpet, or electric guitar.'"

It is hardly revelatory that so many children display the same talents and tendencies as their parents, and follow the same career path. It happens with disproportionate frequency, though not as often today as in the middle of the last century. Sons of professional baseball players often become more famous on the diamond than their dads. Sons and daughters of plumbers take over the family business when dad retires. Educators breed little educators. Nature, or nurture? Likely some of both. Regardless of the reason, I would posit there is nothing random about the fact that the players who populate these pages pursued music.

Russell Pinkston is not the only rocker with a Juilliard parent. In June 2010 I had the privilege of interviewing Mr. Victor Tallarico. Victor was 94 years young the morning I sat down with him, and we had a truly enjoyable conversation; I owe a sincere thank you to Lynda, his daughter, for arranging that conversation.

In Steven Tyler's case, as with many other rockers, the musical gifts flowed down through generations. Victor's father, Giovanni, came to the United States from Italy in the early 1900s with his brothers Pasquale, Francesco (Frank), and Michele (Michael). Giovanni was a fine cellist, an excellent saxophone player, and an orchestra leader at many of the grand hotels up and down the East Coast, including the Granliden Hotel in Sunapee, NH.

Giovanni met his wife, Constance, a pianist who had a beautiful voice, at The Virgil Music School in New York. They lived in Manhattan, and "Mrs. T." gave piano lessons. One of her promising pupils was Seymour Kaufman. Giovanni had gone to tune a piano at the Kaufman's house when Seymour was four or five, and the family piano was truly substandard. Constance started giving the little boy lessons, and even went so far as to provide his family with a good piano. Seymour played piano recitals at Carnegie Hall before he was nine, changed his name to Cy Coleman, and won five Tony, three Emmy, and two Grammy Awards.

Giovanni and Constance also opened their home to a pair of Juilliard students, who would use the Tallaricos' pianos to practice. Arthur Ferrante and Louis Teicher later scored such hits as "Exodus," "Midnight Cowboy," and "Tonight."

The Tallarico Brothers formed a quartet, with Giovanni, Pasquale on piano ("He was a child prodigy piano player," says Victor), Frank on violin, and Michael on guitar. The brothers "practiced quite a bit and played enough so they could give concerts. That's how they raised ten dollars or whatever back then," laughs Victor.

Victor Tallarico trained as a pianist at Juilliard, and played professionally for many years. "There was something called society bands and society music, and we would entertain at weddings and bar mitzvahs, at country clubs and at the wealthiest parties." During World War II he was a member of the U.S. Army band at Fort Dix, NJ, where he met his wife, Susan. After the war Susan and Victor moved into a top floor apartment in a new building in the Riverdale section of the Bronx. Victor purchased a grand piano and, as Lynda remembers it, "The piano took up the entire living room. We were on the sixth floor, and they had to take the window out to lift the piano into the apartment."

"Steven used to love to listen to me play" recalls Victor, "Beethoven, Brahms, Schubert, whatever I was playing. He would sit under the piano when I was playing, even when he was two or three, and sometimes I would play for hours. I also gave him piano lessons for three years, and he learned what good music was."

Lynda Tallarico remembers that as a young boy, "Steven had incredible rhythm. My mother used to read him "Over in the Meadow," and they would sing the rhymes and tap out the rhythm as she read. She'd read that over and over, and he loved it; you could see Steven taking off on that one."

Olive A. Wadsworth wrote "Over in the Meadow" in 1870. The first and most well-known verse reads:

Over in the meadow,
In the sand in the sun
Lived an old mother turtle
And her little turtle one.
"Dig!" said the mother,
"I dig!" said the one,
So they dug all day
In the sand in the sun.

Ken Aldrich tells a "third generation" tale. "My maternal grandfather played music for many years, especially clarinet and violin. He also directed an orchestra for silent movies in Keene, NH, until silent movies went out. He played for both of the old movie theaters in town. Being little old movie theaters they couldn't always afford the talkies, so that orchestra gig lasted longer than in bigger cities."

Skip Truman, whom I first met in 1967 when he was the drummer for Ham Sandwich, points out that "My father and grandfather were both musicians. My grandfather was in vaudeville and toured the country. My dad, Ralph, just sort of carried on what my grandfather had done, but his interest was in jazz and country. He was just music, music, music. He was on television, toured with Arthur Godfrey, and was asked to tour with Duke Ellington but refused, because my older sister was born and he wanted to stay home. Then I came along and got the bug. My mother told me I used to pound on the kitchen table all the time."

Ford Daley, Dartmouth Class of 1961, recalls that Ralph Truman used to play stand up bass with his trio at Phi Tau fraternity on Sunday afternoons. Ford remembers, "He was so smooth, a fine musician, with a big smile on his face all the time, and putting out the great tunes."

Mario Casella of Gunnison Brook, who had an amazing tenor voice at age seventeen and still does at age fifty-eight, told me, "I never knew my father, but the story goes that his brother Rosario sang with the New York City Opera. And my grandmother, she never sang professionally but she would constantly sing gospel in the kitchen while she was washing dishes. She was a Baptist and sang all the time; the music was with her and she sang very well."

Carol Mulroy Morton, older sister of Stone Cross and Missing Links drummer Mike Mulroy, remembers "a musical family. Our father, Joe Mulroy, was in a group in the late 1920s and early 1930s in the Manchester, NH, area called 'The Magnolia Trio.' And our mother was a drummer in an all-ladies band called the 'Kitchen Kats' in the mobile home park in Florida where she retired. She played until she was eighty-three!

"While we were growing up mom took piano lessons so she could play, and we always had a record player. Mom and dad would roll up the dining room rug and have friends in on Saturday night, play cards for a while and then dance, just have a wonderful time. We kids would be sitting on the stairs, they'd send us up to bed, and then we'd sneak back down. Mike was really little, and those Saturday nights must have made a big impression on him."

In some instances it was not preceding generations but rather older siblings who inspired rockers. Several of them claim that being the youngest was especially congenial for the development of musical skills.

Says Pete Shackett of Gunnison Brook and Better Days, "By the time I was aware of nearly anything—like my name really wasn't 'Shut up' or 'Go to your room'—my older brother Bill already knew how to play drums and guitar very skillfully. One of the advantages of being the youngest of six siblings is reaping the benefits of all the hard work of those before you. I was somewhere around five when Bill started showing me how to use the bass drum pedal and the sticks on the drums and cymbals. A few years later, he showed me chords on the guitar and I was off to the races."

Bob Neale of Tracks notes that, "My brother is ten years older than I am. When I was around six he was always listening to Elvis, Bill Haley, Jerry Lee Lewis, and the Big Bopper. He was a fanatic about it. I guess some of that early rock and roll rubbed off."

The parental artistic gene can skip to a parallel path. Pamela Brandt of Ariel and Deadly Nightshade says that "My family was not so much a musical family as they were a professional entertainment family. My father and mother both were professional actors. My mother was successful enough in New York, for example *Kraft Music Hall*, that she was offered a Hollywood contract, but she chose husband and family over career. My father was an announcer for NBC in New York. Remember the old peacock thing on television, where the peacock would spread its tail and then a voice would say, 'This program is brought to you in living color on NBC.' That was my dad. And in every house we lived in while I was a kid the doorbell rang with the three note NBC tone."

Brad French is proud that his father, Charles French, was a scientist, engineer, and inventor who graduated with top honors from Harvard Engineering School in 1936. But "Charlie" was also a terrific piano player who earned enough money playing fancy restaurants in Harvard Square to pay his way through Harvard. In the early 1950s he opened the first professional recording studio in Boston that used magnetic tapes. His skills ideally suited him to open the studio. He recorded up and down the East Coast, including the *Amos 'n' Andy Show* in New York and performances by the Boston Symphony and Nat "King" Cole.

And when the sapling matures? In March 1999, I called Russell Pinkston in Austin, Texas. I don't recall what the occasion was, but I sure remember the phone call. In the midst of our conversation, I heard this fantastic blues riff in the background. I instantly wanted the CD Russell was listening to, but when I asked him who the artist was he replied, "Oh, that's just Malcolm messing around on his guitar." At the time Russell's son was fifteen.

Carey Rush, age 2

When Stone Cross was in its prime, Carol Morton was married with two young children, living in Claremont, NH. Stone Cross was on the road a lot, but whenever the band was in the Claremont area they would stay the night at Carol's house, spreading out sleeping bags in the living and dining rooms. Her two sons adored their Uncle Mike, and when the band played where kids were allowed, she would take her sons. Carol says, "The boys were known to sleep in the drum cases, in the middle of all that noise, right next to the sound board." Both those boys grew up to be drummers, as did two of Carol's grandsons.

On September 4, 2010, at Mohegan Sun in Connecticut, Steven Tyler was on stage with Aerosmith. His sister, Lynda Tallarico, to whom Steven sang and dedicated "I Don't Want to Miss a Thing" that evening, describes the scene. "Dad was there, seated on the side of the stage. Cameras were on him when Steven sat next to him to sing and to play his harmonica. It was wonderful to see their images projected onto the huge screens above the stage. Dad was smiling harder than he ever had in his whole life!"

At some level, by sharing his music and the spotlight with his father, Steven was returning the favor for all those hours spent under the grand piano in the living room. Nature, or nurture? No matter, the acorn rarely falls far from the tree.

Back Stories and the
Road to...Good Intentions

Of all the fascinating back stories that band members brought with them to the Sixties and Seventies, perhaps Pete Shackett, red-headed drummer of Gunnison Brook and Better Days, lays claim to the most compelling.

Pete's paternal family, originally the Chaquettes, issued from Québec, Canada. When a great-great-something grandfather moved south to New Hampshah to find work in the mills, he bumped head first into prejudice and could not secure employment until he Anglicized his name. Such experiences are a broadly unfortunate part of American history. On his mother's side, Pete says a great-great-something grandmother was a member of the Algonquian Confederation tribe named the Fakawi.

In telling this tale, I have to fess up. I was one of those academic pinheads at Dartmouth, a double major...in Geography and Runology. I first stumbled across the word fakawi while doing a semester abroad in Oslo in the mid-1960s. I was studying some very old stone tablets in a museum basement, and on one of them was an account of the voyage on which Leif Ericson was blown off course and skirted the coast of Newfoundland. As a dense coniferous forest unexpectedly rose out of the mist, he turned to his navigator and said, "Fakawi?" To which the navigator replied, "Hel uff eino da."

This incident is linguistically as well as historically tantalizing, in that the navigator's answer appears to be the medieval precursor to the modern day, multi-use Norwegian expression, "Uff da!" This descriptive phrase is often heard in my native state of Minnesota. For example, on the one hand it might be used by MCPs sitting in a bar to assess a particularly attractive woman who enters the room. Or, on the other hand, depending on the tone of voice and accompanying facial expression, to disparage a particularly unattractive woman who walks in.

There is, of course, solid archaeological evidence that Leif and his men settled in "Vinland" for some years and intermarried with certain native tribes. They were roundly derided by the other native tribes as "Fakawi," and many of their offspring had red hair. So, having heard of Pete's Québécois forebears coming down to New England from Canada, I believe it just might be possible that we have an extended lineage for Pete directly back through Leif to Erik the Red. All those years we may have had a genealogical celebrity in our midst and we didn't even know it.

In researching the book I wasn't surprised by the dearth of hard evidence regarding the Fakawi, either in print form or on the internet, even on a highly respected site like Wikipedia. I had to dig. Still, it is well documented that the Fakawi originated in the Atlantic coastal region of Canada, so I was also not surprised that there exists a great deal of anecdotal evidence of Fakawi presence in northern New England. In fact, I have seen the rare, vintage photograph, of an ilk similar to the famous 1970s Bigfoot photo from the West Coast, which shows a small group of Fakawi riding their choppers north of Smugglers' Notch on Vermont Route 100 near Morrisville. There are only four of them, and it is a blurry photo, but they are clearly perched on 1928 Harleys.

In the second half of the twentieth century, the Fakawi came to national prominence during the Viet Nam era, when a great many of them worked at the Pentagon. In fact, there were so many tribe members working in the building during the Nixon administration that the password combination for the entire building, written and spoken, went like this: challenge—"Fakawi"; response—"Ella five aclu." Isn't it ironic that pop culturists ascribe to that DOD password response the origin of the acronym for the famous civil liberties organization? (1)

Today, Pete "Motorhead Red" Shackett resides on Florida's Gulf Coast, where he has lived for more than three decades. His 1988 album, *Grouper Republic,* is filled with the language, lifestyle, and lore of the region's beaches, fishermen, and waters. If you ask Pete what his favorite fresh catch is, he will reply with a smile, "Red herring."

Wilfard and Bertha Shackett on Wilfard's 1928 Harley

The Sprites / Nickel Misery

One band, two distinctly different names. The name change came halfway through the band's history, prompted by a dramatic shift in the tenor of American culture. The constants through the band's five years were musical talent and showmanship that knocked people over.

In the early 1960s a young man born in 1951 in Rochester, NY, moved with his parents and five sisters to Brattleboro, VT. Eddie Kistler's father came to practice anesthesiology at Brattleboro Memorial Hospital.

The Sprites formed late in 1964 when Eddie was only thirteen. Over the next decade, in three different bands, his legend grew in northern New England until his untimely death at age twenty-two. While Eddie was the youngest, the entire band was young. Pete Bover was fourteen, as was Jimi Slate, the band's first manager. The lineup was: Eddie on keyboard and lead vocals, Jerry "Bear" Johnson on lead guitar, Dave Trombley on rhythm guitar, Pete on bass, and Chuck Holden on the drums. In 1966, Jimi replaced Chuck as the group's drummer.

I asked Jimi how he came to be The Sprites' manager in 1965. "I was friends with Bear, who used to live right down the hill from me. So from being friends with Bear that's how I met all the guys in the band. That was about the time that everything was getting going with The Beatles, and they had that manager, Brian Epstein. Back then I thought, 'Hey, I could be another Brian Epstein.' That's how I got into doing it, then the next year Chuck left and I took over drumming."

At first Eddie's mother drove the group to performances. From its inception, regardless of where they played, the band attracted a large and loyal fan base. They also hooked up early with a man who would prove to be very successful in promoting the group, Ed Malhoit.

Ed tells the story about the first time he heard The Sprites. "We saw an ad for a Battle of the Bands thing going on in Brattleboro, and The Sprites were on it, as well as a group called the Zip Codes and a group called the Trophies. The Trophies did 'Walking the Dog,' a big song for Rufus Thomas, and they did a good version. All these bands were from Brattleboro, which was beyond me...so many good bands from this one town. We went down to Brattleboro so we could listen to the bands. There were six or seven bands. The Sprites were excellent, but they were so young. I said to myself, 'Jeez, I could make them even better.' Even though I wasn't in the business I could see there were a lot of things they were doing wrong."

Ed really wanted to be in the music business, so after the show he talked with the band and their parents. They reached an agreement, and The Sprites became the first band Ed ever managed. From that point, "We got The Sprites going so well I couldn't keep up with the demand. We were even turning down jobs! It was interesting. I was their chaperone for a time, driving the van, and running their light show which consisted of Christmas tree lights."

Pete Bover remembers being skeptical at first. "We were the very first band Ed booked. He started his career as an agent with The Sprites. One night he showed up in a suit and tie and had a whole line of ideas to sell us."

Jimi Slate liked Ed's approach. "Ed had a Brian Epstein mentality just like I did. He really was professional and insisted we be professional. We had tuxedos we wore, and if you were missing any part of your tux he used to fine you $5. The rule was if you forgot a tie, or any part of the tux, he would deduct $5 from your pay. He took us to Boston for shopping sprees at the best places to buy hip stuff. I had the first Beatle boots in Brattleboro, reproductions of what the Beatles were wearing. I got them in Boston one time when Ed drove us down. We went there several times, got our tuxes, boots, leather vests, things like that."

The Sprites, 1967, L – R: Eddie Kistler, Jimi Slate, Dave Trombley, Jerry "Bear" Johnson, Pete Bover

Maybe it's because they were so young, but Doug Morton from Brattleboro remembers that in addition to their special musical talent the guys in The Sprites were very cordial to, and friendly with, some of their even younger fans, the aspiring musicians like himself who hung around the band.

"Eddie Kistler—oh man, you know, for us kids growing up, we were already hooked on the rock and roll thing, playing in our horrible little rock band, thank God we got better! In that era the local scene was so vibrant we could reach up and touch it. Our heroes were the local guys. They were right there, they were playing in the local schools. The Beatles, the British Invasion, Grass Roots, etc., they were kind of exotic to us, they were untouchable. But Eddie was like a Robert Plant with that stage presence and that amazing voice. For me as a bass player who was starting to sing quite a bit, his stage presence was just unbelievable. Out front he was very charismatic. He had that long, curly blonde hair and I had blonde hair too, so I decided to grow it out. People would say, 'Oh, you're trying to look like Roger Daltry,' and I would say, 'No, I'm trying to look like Eddie Kistler.'

"And those guys, especially Eddie, were so gracious with their time, they didn't mind us bugging them. Whether they were rehearsing down on Williams Street or playing on Flat Street they were so gracious, the epitome of cool. Kistler first, and Bover second, as far as cool. I think Eddie just thought it was part of the deal. 'I want to be a rock star, so I'll act like a rock star, so when people wanna talk to me it's okay.' He wasn't, like, 'Go away kid, you bother me,' he was just really friendly in addition to having that rock star vibe. Kistler stuck out to me in the sense of 'That guy's going places.'

"Also, being a bass player, I followed Pete Bover around like a puppy dog, and I watched everything he did like a hawk. He was giving me bass lessons from the stage and he didn't even know it! At the 'Over 21' clubs the owners used to let us in even though we were under age, because we knew Pete and Eddie and Bear and were sort of protégés of theirs. We weren't even supposed to be in there, but they'd even let us in the front entrance and we could get a table."

The Sprites play list included Beatles, Stones, The Kinks, Paul Revere and the Raiders, and a lot of Young Rascals, for which the band was especially well-known—tunes like "Come On Up," "Good Lovin'," "Love Is A Beautiful Thing," "Baby Let's Wait," and "Groovin'."

Other rockers from the nexus give The Sprites and Nickel Misery uniformly laudatory reviews. Lane Gibson of Davis Brothers Garage recalls that "The first time I saw The Sprites, either in 1965 or 1966, I thought, 'Oh, my God, this is the bomb!' They were just head and shoulders above the other bands I heard."

For Carey Rush, "Nobody was doing anything like they were at the time. They had great vocals. Instead of the usual rock and roll vocals they had studied vocals, and had close harmonies. That was sort of foreign to many people's ears at the time, but it was very exciting, very pleasant, and you were drawn to the good harmonies."

Don Coulombe of Fox and Company says, "The first time I saw them the most impressive thing was they were doing a lot of Rascals, they had the harmonies and that B-3 and it just blew me away. It was at Notre Dame Arena in Berlin, NH, and people who went there had never heard of them before. Ed Malhoit had booked them in there, and they just blew everybody away. To me the key thing was when I heard them doing The Rascals, and also 'Time of the Season' by The Zombies. I heard Eddie sing that and went, 'Oh my God.' The guy just had this magic about him, a great voice, great stage presence, people wanted to see him. That was probably 1966."

One thing that helped to cement The Sprites' reputation and expand their fan base was participation in a large number of Battles of the Bands. According to Jimi Slate, The Sprites won eight of the ten Battles of the Bands in which they competed, an incredible success rate.

An offer to participate in a Battle of the Bands was an interesting proposition. A "BOB" was a great opportunity for a band to showcase itself, but the risk was daunting. Allow me to explain.

In those days a Battle of the Bands was typically scheduled on a Friday or Saturday night, to attract the largest possible crowd of paying customers. (Keep in mind that Friday and Saturday nights were when bands secured their best paying gigs.) Six to eight bands were invited to compete for a grand prize ranging anywhere from $500 to as much as $1,000; therein lay the temptation. On the other hand, each band willing to take a shot at that "big money" was guaranteed only a nominal sum, generally $50.

A Battle of the Bands was usually held in a high school gymnasium or similar space. The bands set up around the edges of the room while the audience listened from the center. As a rule each band played a thirty minute set, with only two or three minutes between sets. The promoter hoped a crowd of hundreds would pay three or four bucks apiece to hear up to four hours of continuous, "outstanding" rock and roll by many "talented, up and coming" bands. In truth, a Battle of the Bands was a terrific entertainment bargain, and most of the time there were at least a couple of good bands.

Now let's analyze this whole proposition from the band's point of view. Let's say there are eight bands competing. That means the mathematical odds of winning round to a superstitious 13%. You figure the risk. Give up a paying gig of maybe $400 on a Friday night for the chance to win $750-$800? With a guarantee of only $50? Hmmm….

The only time I remember Tracks playing a Battle of the Bands was on Friday, May 1, 1970, in Greenfield, MA. Ed Malhoit booked us at the Greenfield High School gymnasium. We were one of eight bands vying for a grand prize of $1,000, with a guarantee of $50. Tracks set one condition, which Ed was able to persuade the promoter to honor—we would go on last. Then we went to work honing a seamless half hour of our best and most popular songs. We ended up a happy bunch of Tracksters that evening.

Now reflect on Jimi's recollection that The Sprites won eight of ten competitions. That winning percentage speaks to the band's talent and popularity.

The Sprites played several notable gigs that are fixed in the group's lore. Pete Bover remembers that "When we were still a young teeny bopper band, Ed got us booked into the gym up in Burlington at the University of Vermont opening for Dionne Warwick. There must have been 5,000 people there. Eddie got a standing ovation for his rendition of 'Summertime.' He used to throw himself down on his knees, and do the whole routine, which was pretty daring for a guy who was fourteen. That night was also an unfortunate mis-booking of Dionne before she became really big with Burt Bacharach songs. It was just her and a lounge trio in a big gymnasium, for this UVM college gang. She played a few songs, getting no response, with people talking, and she quit the show after about six songs. They put us back on the stage and I remember her walking out through the crowd in front of us in a big fur coat and just kinda looking up and smiling at us."

A summer 1967 gig in east-central Massachusetts sticks in Pete's mind as a very appealing opportunity to a group of fifteen-and sixteen-year-old gentlemen. "The majority of our bookings were high school dances in Vermont and New Hampshire, with some private parties mixed in. For this gig we got booked into a bar in Ayer, MA, that served mostly servicemen from Fort Devens. It was a rough joint, a five-night gig, and we stayed at a rundown hotel down the street. It was a big adventure for us, and we even snuck in a few drinks on the stage. We played our popular, teeny bopper songs and people danced and got crazy. I remember being in the hotel and we had a little portable record player we had bought. The *Sgt. Pepper's Lonely Hearts Club Band* album had just come out and we listened to it over and over, this outrageous breakthrough album. For us to be playing there in that bar as young kids, that was a great adventure."

In late 1967 or early 1968 the band exchanged their bubbly, pop name for something darker, more late-'60s hip. Rock music was changing, which affected how bands dressed on stage, as reflected in this chapter's two photos, taken only a year apart. Pete says, "We got tired of having the same name for so long. Things were changing then, that was when the whole pot thing was coming in, you know, a 'nickel bag.' We were sitting around talking about a new name, just coming up with things, and we said, we got a cool name here. Then when we did the new promo pictures we wanted to look real 'edgy,' real Marlon Brando and all James Dean."

For a time Gene Struthers joined the band to replace Dave Trombley on rhythm guitar, and the band's play list evolved as well, reflecting broader musical influences and the more psychedelic, complicated songs of the late '60s. Nickel Misery played the full-length version of "You Keep Me Hanging On" by Vanilla Fudge, and the extended version of the Doors' "Light My Fire." They did Cream, and Jimi Hendrix, and they played some blues by such artists as Bobby "Blue" Bland. But they also kept Eddie's dynamic version of their old standby "Summertime," and they even did some Aretha Franklin songs, like "Respect," to showcase Eddie's phenomenal tenor voice.

Don Coulombe recalls seeing Nickel Misery at Newell's Casino in Whitefield, NH. "They were a great band, Nickel Misery. They did songs like 'Time of the Season' by The Zombies, 'While My Guitar Gently Weeps' by The Beatles, 'I'm a Man' by Spencer Davis and Steve Winwood, Hendrix, Cream, and more. And Eddie Kistler, he was amazing. I loved watching him perform."

Nickel Misery opened once for Al Anderson's Wildweeds at Old Orchard Beach Casino on the coast of Maine. Jimi claims it was "one of the best concerts we ever played. Eddie really shined as a budding talent, and people were asking us for our autographs."

THE **NICKEL MISERY**

BRATTLEBORO, VERMONT　　　　　　　　(FORMERLY THE SPRITES)

THE SOUND WHICH HAS TAKEN THE U.S. BY SURPRISE. APPEARING IN NIGHT CLUBS, COLLEGE CAMPUSES, CLUBS, AND RESORTS ACROSS THE COUNTRY...

Nickel Misery, 1968

The group also played with Buddy Miles of the Buddy Miles Express. Jimi says, "We opened for him in the field house at Windham College in Putney, VT. Half way through his set Buddy got off the drums and went up front and there was nobody on the drums. I should have gone up there. We went to a party with him afterwards, and got to hang out with him for hours. He was a very cool dude."

"One night right before the band broke up," remembers Jimi, "we're playing and I look down on the right hand side of the stage, and Steven Tallarico is right there leaning up on the stage with his arms on the stage. A few weeks later, we're playing somewhere else, Steven Tallarico's on the left hand side of the stage leaning right up against the stage. I saw him three or four different times, and I thought it was kinda cool, since he was such a major talent. But I also thought it was kinda odd."

Jimi would soon find out why Steven was such a frequent visitor. According to Pete Bover, "Steven had a three piece band called Chain, and they would come to Brattleboro to play, and they heard Nickel Misery. In the summer of 1969 they approached us one night and said, 'Let's stop screwin' around, we want to have you and Eddie join with Chain and have a five-piece band, get serious, write some tunes, and try to do something other than playing high school dances.' That's how Fox Chase came to be. So about September of 1969 we made the connection, and I guess Malhoit was probably a little ticked off because now instead of having two great bands to book he only had one."

But what a band it was!

Whitcomb's Music Center

"The first thing when you walked in the door, Don looked up and saw you and his eyes just squinted shut. When he smiled, it was all smile, his eyes squinted shut and he was genuinely happy to see you."

— Carey Rush

Don Whitcomb opened Whitcomb's Music Center on lower Main Street in Claremont in 1961. Several years later he moved to a larger, more propitious location on Pleasant Street, where the store remained a fixture for three decades. Every band and musician has to have a place to buy equipment, and the bands in the nexus had Whitcomb's. In addition to being a businessman, Don and his wife Lady Eve were also talented musicians themselves, so they understood the life we led. When we long-haired, freaky types needed a respite from the straight world's (1) buffeting of insults and assaults, there was no better port of refuge than Whitcomb's Music Center.

Ken Aldrich agrees with Carey Rush: "Don was always laughing, always had a smile on his face. He was just one of those people who was really happy with what he was doing." When you walked in the door, Don, Eve, and their staff let you know—by their smiles, by the tone of their voices, by their body language—that you were part of the family and, as far as they were concerned, you were home.

Don Whitcomb was a local boy, born and raised in Windsor, VT, and living there when he met Eve. Lady Eve was, by contrast, a peripatetic soul until she met Don and settled down. Born in South Carolina, she moved to Toronto, where she graduated from high school. Eve was an exceptional jazz vocalist, and after high school she hit the road, performing all over Canada and the United States with such luminaries as Count Basie, Duke Ellington, The Inkspots, Lou Rawls, B.B. King, and others.

Don was a talented multi-instrumentalist who led his own band and is remembered by Ed Malhoit as "quite the ladies' man." One night in the late 1950s that ladies' man caught a show in White River Junction at which Lady Eve was performing. Don was smitten, introduced himself, and the two of them hit it off.

Eve was finishing a long stretch on the road, and Don asked her to stick around. The story goes that she replied, "You fool," but stick around she did, and they soon married. Eve had a contract with a big band orchestra, it was going back out on tour, and she was headed for the big time. Instead, she traded glamour and fame to live with the man she loved in the back of their first store.

Carol Mulroy Morton still thinks of Eve with great fondness. "In the 1950s Don and his first wife lived in Windsor, where he and I are from, and I used to baby-sit for his children when he played. When Eve came down from Canada she first sang with The Don Whitcomb Trio in White River. She stayed here in the States and went to work in the office of Cone-Blanchard Machine Company in Windsor, the first black woman ever to work there. My mother worked at Cone's and had met Eve at Teddy's in White River. The other women in the office wouldn't have anything to do with Eve and would not even sit with her in the cafeteria. My mother set those women straight and she and Eve remained great friends. Eve sang 'Amazing Grace' at my mother's funeral in 1998 and told the congregation about how my mother had stuck up for her all those years ago.

"My husband and I used to go to parties at Don and Eve's house, and her parents often would come down from Toronto so I knew them as well. They were lovely, lovely people. Eve was a darling, and she was also a hair client of mine at my beauty shop. What a great lady!"

Carey Rush grew up in Claremont, and as a junior and senior high student worked at the Music Center in the late '60s and early '70s. Did he notice the racism that Eve experienced at Cone? "I thought there was a lot, especially when they first started the store. Here they were, a mixed race couple in New Hampshire in the 1960s. Back when I first started around the store a Yankee redneck type would come in the store, and Eve would walk over and ask if he needed any help. There she was, dressed to the nines, looking gorgeous and professional every day, and the response would usually be, 'harrumph.' Then if another employee would walk over you'd see a whole different response.

"But Eve handled everything that was ever thrown in her face and handled it like a true professional. She could manage any type of heckler and any type of hassle that occurred at the store. You have to remember that these were townsfolk from New Hampshire who probably had never seen a black person in their lives."

Carey adds that, "Lady Eve was also the consummate den mother. She took care of everybody, and she was chock full of good advice. I remember her saying to me once, 'Rock and roll is great, but listen to the other things. Listen to the trumpet player, listen to the sax player, because you are gonna hear them doing licks you want to do on the guitar.' Those were wise words."

Another store employee who respected Don and Eve was Annie (Cole) Dolan. "Eve impressed me so much, she was actually kind of imposing. She had this presence, she was just so cool, and I remember being in awe of her. Don was just a wicked, wicked nice guy. He was like everybody's father, and he treated everybody like his child. In 1973 when I first got married and really needed money he offered me a job, which I was really grateful for."

While interviewing aging rockers for this book, I frequently and not surprisingly found their memories fuzzy. Interestingly, when I asked musicians from the Sixties and Seventies what they remembered about Whitcomb's, their memories were remarkably clear and exceptionally positive, and had the same bottom line.

Ken Aldrich says, "I used to buy an awful lot of stuff from Don. He did the best he could for me and for other musicians, too, so I was there a lot. I'd go down there and hang out, even though it was twenty-five miles from home. I started going there in high school, in 1962 or 1963, when I was with the Stingrays. Don was a hub for local bands, where we all did a lot of business. It did seem to me that Don was not as well-off as I thought he should be, given that his store did so much business. I really believe part of the reason why is because he was always cutting great deals for band people, almost subsidizing us."

Pete Shackett: "I worked with Don for many years before Gunnison Brook, during Gunnison Brook, and after. He was always kind, trying to get a good deal for me and still stay in business. I bought all my supplies from him, and really enjoyed going over to Claremont to talk to him. Hell of a nice guy."

Don Coulombe maintains that "Don was really fair with all the musicians. When you went there if you wanted to trade something in and he saw you didn't have a lot of money he would give you terms. It seemed like you got a better deal from him than anywhere else. He would say, 'Oh, just give me so much a month.' Nobody else would do that. Music stores just wouldn't do that with musicians."

Jim Goodrum, bassist for The Other Man's Grass and Anvil, recalls that "We always got really good deals from him. He did Kustom amps and I remember we got a Kustom PA from him. Don's place was where you went if you needed gear."

Another bassist, Doug Morton from Brattleboro, remembers Whitcomb's as "The main place for players down here to go and get instruments, amps, rentals, etc., because he was such a good guy and so gracious with payment plans. Lots of guys got their equipment from Don. I got my first Standell bass amp. He had good quality stuff and he was unique in that he would let you buy gear on a payment plan, which other stores generally wouldn't do. I took my younger brother there to get his first real set of drums. He wanted those blue Ludwig Vistalites. Don had a set, and Don gave the kid a helluva deal."

Doug tells one of the very best Don Whitcomb equipment stories, corroborated by Jimi Slate and Pete Bover. "When I was playing with Bear Johnson in High Altitude, he was playing a Les Paul Junior two pickup model, like a 1956 or 1957, a beautiful sounding guitar. He had stripped it down and he told me the story. One night he was playing in Nickel Misery and he did something to his guitar. So he went into Whitcomb's and Don said he would rent him this white, Les Paul-ish looking guitar that had been painted. Bear rented it, never brought it back, just kept paying on it, and finally bought it for $70 because it sounded so good. A few years later he and Pete Bover stripped it down and there was a Gibson Les Paul underneath—a collector's item!"

Ed Malhoit, whose booking agency, Wain Music (later named EMA), handled most of the successful bands in the area, describes the relationship between his agency and

Don's store. "When I first started booking bands I worked out of my house, and of course Don's store was originally on Main Street. As I grew, Don was growing too. We both moved uptown, to Pleasant Street, where the door to my second floor office was located right next to his store with the office itself directly above his store.

"Don knew the Pleasant Street location was much better. It got a lot more traffic, and he had a loading dock at the back of the store. The Music Center was filled with promotional pictures of the bands that I was booking, so the bands used to visit me and then go down there and shop for equipment. When I told him I had outgrown the upstairs offices and was moving he was concerned and said, 'No, no, I'll pay for your rent.' I said, 'No, Don, I'm moving just across the street, just half a block to the city bank building.' The relationship was very good for both of us."

Cher Mitchell Aubin grew up in Claremont in the 1960s, fled to Boston upon graduating from Stevens High School in 1970, and then returned permanently to the area in 1978. Cher has been in love with music since she started taking piano lessons at age five, and she has been in bands since she was eleven. Today she is still playing out as a member of a band called Club Soda. Cher remembers another way in which the Whitcombs influenced the music scene in Claremont. "My parents hung around with Don and Eve, and there was another musical couple named Paavo and Frances Kangas. Their son, Jeff Kangas, was a very well-known, very good drummer in this area.

"Paavo and his wife Frances owned a cottage on Sunapee. Every weekend they had full-blown jam sessions over there—Friday night, Saturday night, and Sunday. Don and Eve were always there. At any given time there would be forty or fifty people, all musicians. This was during the '60s and '70s. They were doing the jazz/pop scene, while the kids were doing the rock and roll. The adults would do a jazz set, then take a break and go have a drink and say, 'Okay let the kids take over.' So then it would be Jeff and me, whoever was there. The younger musicians would take over the equipment and play some songs. It was pretty well known, their cottage jam sessions, and all the area musicians, all of whom knew the Kangases and Don and Eve, would attend."

Don Whitcomb passed away on May 31, 1991. Eve tried to run the store at 10 Pleasant Street for a while, but it got to be too much. Then their son, Aaron, opened the store again for a couple of years. He couldn't make a go of it, either. Lady Eve passed away on February 19, 2003.

Perhaps the difficulties Eve and Aaron experienced in trying to run the Music Center in the 1990s are best explained by Carey Rush. "The way Don ran the store, no way you could make it work today. Their approach was a family thing, just treating people well all the time. They made it for so long despite the fact they ran the store like musicians, rather than like business people."

Bands always need some place to buy gear, whether at Whitcomb's in 1970 or in 2011 at Dan Salomon's Northern Lights Music in Littleton, NH. Stuff breaks, or you get the itch to upgrade what a couple of years earlier was state of the art. Yeah, we shopped other stores from time to time—Sam Ash in Brooklyn, E.U. Wurlitzer Music and Sound on the corner of Newbury Street and Mass. Ave. in Boston, Ted Herbert's Music Mart in Manchester, or Louie Catello's in Berlin, NH. But Don Whitcomb was always there, especially when we needed him. For us, Whitcomb's Music Center was an oasis where, in addition to getting great buys on equipment, we could cool our heels, get away from the craziness for a while, and know that we were always welcome. Bands in the nexus couldn't have had a better friend, and we couldn't have been more fortunate.

The Barn

"If you were a teenager in the '60s in this area and you were following the live music scene, one of the hot spots was The Barn in Georges Mills. For me, and my buddies, it was because of this guy Steve Tallarico. He would come up from Yonkers, NY, and spend the summers, and he had two bands, Thee Strangeurs and Chain Reaction. If you walked into The Barn and saw Steve singing Zombies songs, I mean, he was absolutely as good as or better than the original. And he also played half the night on drums, and really, it was like the city coming to us country bumpkins. Thee Strangeurs and Chain Reaction set the bar, make no mistake about it."

— Rick Davis, Davis Brothers Garage

The Sunapee Lake region has long been a summer vacation spot for urbanites from across the northeastern United States. As a consequence, there have always been entrepreneurs in the area determined to seize upon the opportunities provided by the summer folk. One of those entrepreneurs was an impresario named John Conrad, a flamboyant character who in the 1950s decided he wanted Conrad Manor, his inn on Prospect Hill Road, "to be an important stop on the live music circuit. He gussied up his barn, called it a venue, and brought some high-quality blues and jazz acts in from Boston and New York. The Barn became something of a music hot spot. A 1958 issue of *Sports Illustrated* directs skiers from Boston, Worcester, MA, and Providence, RI, to Conrad Manor for dancing." (1)

From 1900 through the late 1950s, the Georges Mills area was rife with Hollywood types, and very nearly became a Hollywood-type town. In the early 1900s Billy B. Van imported theater people and summer stock did very well. Years later John Conrad had many friends in the theater, including Lee Collins. Lee lived nearby and was often found at The Barn and the Conrad Manor.

It was this theatrical influence that set The Barn apart from other venues in the area, according to Pete Merrigan of Gunnison Brook. "The Barn had a certain dramatic appeal and authenticity, an aura, if you will, of show biz. I can clearly remember a mural on the wall in The Barn done by an artist of some renown. The mural depicted John behind the cash register madly ringing up sales while the scene around him was reminiscent of a Dean Martin/Frank Sinatra party movie, all done up in that '50s cartoon style you might see in *Playboy* magazine. Onstage was Lionel Hampton playing vibes. Hampton did play at The Barn in the flesh, though well before my time."

In the 1960s Conrad shifted The Barn's musical offerings from jazz and blues to rock bands, attracting a younger, more local crowd. Soon Conrad's venue was one of the hottest spots in the area.

Lane Gibson of Davis Brothers Garage, who grew up in Metuchen, NJ, but who visited his cousins Jeff and Rick Davis in Brownsville, VT, each summer, reflects fondly on the area's music scene, The Barn in particular. "I went with Jeff and Rick, and we just couldn't wait to get there. Besides Steven Tyler's band, Thee Strangeurs, I couldn't tell you who I saw there, but I remember it was always packed, and that The Barn was *the* place to go. I probably remember The Barn partly because my experience in Vermont was so different than what I knew in New Jersey. There was so much going on in the music scene up here. It was thrilling to go to the Com Tu Club in Springfield, VT, or The Barn, or to go see Eddie Kistler and The Sprites in Claremont...the music was just fabulous." Rick Davis chimes in: "It was a forty-five minute drive over from Brownsville, but

Sunapee Lake was a hot spot. Sunapee Harbor, I mean, it was just 'happening'—a lot of chicks, a lot of great music."

Here's another thing about the scene at The Barn, according to Nick Kanakis, who grew up in the Sunapee area and went to Newport High School. "Like every school, Newport had a group of kids that were a little 'wilder.' Claremont and Newport is a big high school rivalry; but in the '60s kids from Sunapee, Claremont, New London, Springfield, all over really, came to The Barn. It was the place to go if you liked music and you liked to party it up and there was just a huge group of us. But it was also odd that so many kids from so many different schools hung out, and there were never any school problems. It would never break down to 'my school,' but would break down to 'John's a jerk' and that sort of thing. In fact, I'm not that big a guy, but I was defended a couple of times by guys from Claremont and Springfield who knew me from there."

While a number of talented bands played The Barn, there is absolute consensus that the best bands featured Steven Tallarico. Nick Kanakis says, "All of Steve's bands were *the* most popular band at The Barn. It didn't matter what group of guys he brought up from New York that summer. He was kind of legendary, even in his own time, and was very well-respected as a musician by everyone in the area."

Jim Goodrum, bass player for Anvil and The Other Man's Grass, concurs. "My memories are basically Thee Strangeurs. When we were fourteen years old we would hitch rides with older kids from Springfield to The Barn and that's where we first saw Tallarico. I was pretty impressed with the way he played drums, and it was also the first place I ever saw a fuzz tone and the foot pedal."

When she was a student at Hanover High School, Annie Dolan heard Thee Strangeurs at The Barn "all the time.

Anything Steven was playing in was the reason why we headed down there. I especially remember about Steven's performances at the Barn that he was always compared to Mick Jagger."

Nick Kanakis, however, remembers one guest of his who wasn't that impressed with Steven and his troops. "I remember seeing Thee Strangeurs there, I saw all Steven's bands from the time I was a sophomore in high school. And I had a cousin from New York, and she used to come up summers. I said to her one time, 'I ought to take you over to The Barn, there's a great band playing there tonight. I'm talking up the band on the way over, and we get over there and she says, 'Eh, I go to high school with those guys!'"

Advertisement for the Barn, Summer 1969

Some people went to even greater lengths to see Steven Tallarico's bands. Lonna LaLonde was a student at Lebanon (NH) High School. "We went there every weekend during the summer. We went to see Steven's bands only. One time I stayed there for a whole week just to meet the band. The Conrad Manor was a hotel-like place with rooms, etc. I rented a room for six days, and I was only sixteen. It was pretty lonely during the day, but at night...I met Tallarico and the band the last night they were there, the last night of the summer."

The Barn was indeed an old barn, a wooden structure with wooden pillars and beams, a dance floor, and two levels of balconies overlooking a very small stage. The building was attached by an ell to the Conrad Manor, and its interior is described consistently by former patrons as "rustic."

The space was carved up into alcoves, small backrooms, and several staircases, which gave the place an intimate feel. The two things former patrons all remember are that The Barn was always hot and always packed. "It was literally sardines in there." "It was one of my favorite places because it was jam packed, totally insane...one of those 'you can't turn around' feelings."

Even with the back door open, as it usually was, air didn't circulate well enough to mitigate the heat. That open door was, however, a boon to those who were under age or impoverished. One regular recalls that "Everyone would always sneak in there. The locals knew that was the way to get in." Annie Dolan says, "We were sixteen, seventeen, Lonna was absolutely gorgeous...big brown eyes, petite, hair down to her butt. She could talk her way into anywhere. But if that didn't work, we'd sneak in the back."

Then there was the parking, or lack thereof. On nights The Barn was open, neighbors must have wished they lived anywhere but on Prospect Hill Road. Carol Mulroy Morton says that "Trying to find a place to park was unbelievable, people parked all over the road. You got smart after a while. If my husband and I were going to go we'd ask another couple to go with us, and sometimes pack six or eight people in a car, because we all knew there was no place to park. You know, you didn't have to have seat belts back then either, so pack 'em in."

Nick Kanakis says that people parked "All up and down the road," though he recalls a small field to the right of Conrad Manor that people used for parking. There was also a driveway to the left of The Barn that people would park in.

In addition to Steve Tallarico's various bands, today's old folks remember other notable bands from their youthful nights at The Barn. Bobby Gagnier and an under age Carey Rush saw The Ham Sandwich, with Ken Aldrich, Dan Morgenroth, and Skip Truman. Bobby says, "I saw Steve Tallarico drumming there for the first time with Thee Strangeurs, but a second fine drummer I saw there was Skip Truman of Ham Sandwich."

Bobby, Jim Goodrum and Peter Yanofsky also played at The Barn in two of their bands, The Invaders and The Other Man's Grass.

A very popular band was The Acoustics. A.J. Maranville played keyboard, Frank Baxter and Johnny Carton switched off on the guitar and bass, and there were several drummers: Hayden Grant, George Bellisimo, Doug Falzarrano and Mike Mulroy. Rick Davis calls The Acoustics "The founding fathers of rock in the Claremont/Sunapee area. They played the pop hits of the early '60s, and played throughout that decade at The Barn." Bobby Gagnier recalls that "Johnny played a twelve-string on The Byrds' 'Eight Miles High.' Very cool for the time."

According to Carol Mulroy Morton, A.J. had another role in the area's music scene. "His mom and dad founded the Music Box, a music store in Claremont, and they got the franchise for Vox. A.J. would go out on the road with equipment and set up for the big acts."

Carol's brother, Mike Mulroy (later the drummer for Stone Cross), played The Barn as a member of The Links, with Rick and Jeff Davis, and Nate and Chris Thompson, in addition to playing there with The Acoustics. Carol remembers another group called The Deadbeats that was very big in the area. Like many bands in the '60s, they drove around in a hearse.

Virgil and the Poets was also a homegrown band, with John Maxfield on bass, Donny Dorr on lead guitar, Jimmy Parker on keyboards, and Pete Shackett on drums. The band's play list included such mid-Sixties staples as "Louie, Louie," "Good Lovin'," "G-L-O-R-I-A," "Midnight Hour," and The Stones' "Satisfaction." Shackett recollects that "The Barn had an upstairs where the audience could sit and look down at the band. I used to play drums and I'd find myself looking up the girls' dresses. I kinda didn't keep such good time at those times! Also, we'd get drinks spilled or thrown on us every once in a while."

Later in the band's existence the former high school buddies, then college students, changed their name to The Hobbits and spent the summer of 1966 on Long Island. John and Pete would subsequently spend time together in the band Birth, and then three years in one of the best bands to come out of the nexus, Gunnison Brook.

Another Sunapee area group that played frequently at The Barn was the Jam Band with Joe Perry and Tom Hamilton. Pete Shackett remembers Joe Perry's distinctive "swinging arm style" of guitar playing, à la Pete Townshend. Pete Merrigan, who grew up in Goshen, NH, recalls that "I played drums for Joe Perry and Tom Hamilton in the early Jam Band for two gigs at The Barn that their drummer, Dave 'Pudge' Scott, couldn't make. He was in summer school. They asked me if I wanted to stay on but I had my own band and declined. I liked Joe and Tom and their harp player/singer John McGuire, but I was pretty happy with my own band."

Peter Wonson

Anyone who ever spent an evening at The Barn remembers the two policemen who patrolled it, Rodney Chandler and Bernie Ross. One long-time patron says of the two cops, "Rodney was just the opposite of Bernie. He had a way with the kids, he could handle us. Rodney was an older guy, he was very relaxed, his body language was completely non-threatening, like you're getting a lecture from your dad.

"Bernie Ross was a short, stocky guy, he used to carry around a nightstick. Actually it was a riot stick, longer than the usual stick. He hated The Barn, hated the noise, hated the traffic, he lived just up the road. One night he was walking around The Barn just slapping his nightstick into his hand, staring at everyone, like, don't make eye contact. For whatever reason, this particular night the third floor was open, and we were on the third floor. Bernie was on the second floor, leaning over the railing, looking to spot any transgression he could."

"My buddy, Terry Morgan, said, 'I'm going down and I'm gonna pour beer in Bernie's pocket.' I kept saying 'Terry, don't do it, you're gonna get busted.' We had long neck beer bottles, and he said, 'No, I'm gonna do it.' So Bernie was hanging over the railing, right near the old board-type barn door that comes down from the third floor, and the door didn't close all the way. The band was so loud he couldn't hear anyone behind him, and Terry stuck his arm out from behind the door, reached out with this long neck bottle and poured the beer right into Bernie's back pocket. It took Bernie a few seconds to realize that he was getting wet, and by then Terry had run back upstairs and sat down. We were all sitting down and Bernie came charging upstairs with his nightstick. Of course everyone was deep into conversation, like we didn't have a clue what was going on. Oh, he was bullshit, he was on a tear the rest of the evening, couldn't figure out who had poured the beer down his pants."

Nick Kanakis appreciated one aspect of The Barn's layout in regard to the Men's and Ladies' Rooms that were located adjacent to each other. "I don't know if there was metal ductwork there. There was a grate there, an air passage between the Men's and Ladies' Rooms. You know how girls always go in together but when guys are in the Men's Room you don't talk to each other. So there's really not much noise from the Men's Room, but you could hear the girls in the Ladies' Room. If you stood up on something, you could put your mouth right to the ductwork, and you would talk and it would sound like there was a man in the Ladies' Room. And of course we'd always say something stupid like, 'Ohmigod that's the sexiest underwear I've ever seen on a woman,' and they would scream and run out of the restroom. You couldn't see anything, all you could do was hear. It was always pretty innocent, but fun."

After a long, successful run, during which John Conrad shuttered it several times because of trouble with the town, The Barn closed for good in the mid-Seventies.

The Barn, June 2010

In the Summer 2010 edition of *Kearsarge Magazine*, K.M. Hurley wrote, "Today, the large, old, neglected barn is still there, but the vital signs are missing. It's dusty and lifeless inside, and it feels chilly, even on warm days. But you can still stand on what was once the stage. You can see three tiers of dance floors rising up around you sixty feet high. And the decade upon decade of storied past is layered in the wood and the dust. The layering makes the barn, even now, feel more like an amphitheater frozen in time than a simple, unattended New England barn." (2)

On a warm June afternoon in 2010, Pete Merrigan and I met caretaker Richard Hamm at The Barn. From the outside the building looked fine. But inside, clutter and disrepair defined a once vibrant place closed down for many years. Nonetheless, I felt the way I always do whenever I walk into a musical landmark like The Barn. To me such a trip back in time is a sacred undertaking. And if I retreat to a quiet place in my mind, and listen very carefully, I always hear the echoes stirring.

Ed Was an Empire

In the early afternoon of Friday, May 2, 1969, Tracks left Hanover for the Aerodrome in Schenectady, NY. An agent had booked us that weekend with The Brooklyn Bridge, whose hit single, "The Worst That Could Happen," had recently peaked at #3 on the charts. Lead singer Johnny Maestro was also the voice of the huge 1959 hit by The Crests, "16 Candles." Here's a chance, we thought, to show our stuff on the same stage as a nationally famous act, generate some buzz, maybe get discovered.

That same Friday, Ariel left South Hadley, MA, headed for the Aerodrome. They had been contacted by an agent who had booked them that weekend with The Mothers of Invention featuring Frank Zappa. Here's a chance, they thought, to show our stuff on the same stage as a legendary band, generate some buzz, maybe get discovered.

More than four decades later I honestly don't remember that agent's name. I'd tell you if I did! I do know one thing. His name was *not* Ed Malhoit. Now, there were two bands that weekend at the Aerodrome—Ariel and Tracks. Seems the agent had scammed both bands, because The Brooklyn Bridge and The Mothers of Invention were nowhere near Schenectady the first weekend in May 1969.

For Tracks there was a major upside to that disappointing gig. It led to a long-term friendship with some bright and talented young ladies, three of whom (Pamela Brandt, Anne Bowen and Helen Hooke) went on to form The Deadly Nightshade, a Grammy nominated rock/country/bluegrass trio that recorded two albums in the mid-'70s. The Deadly Nightshade also filmed an iconic 1975 segment on *Sesame Street,* performing "Keep on the Sunny Side." Plus, we got to hear a band that put the lie to the myth that "Girls can't play real rock and roll."

Another upside for us was that from that moment forward we worked almost exclusively with Ed Malhoit. We knew he would never pull such a stunt.

Edward Wayne Malhoit was born in 1947 in Woonsocket, RI, lived there until he was thirteen, then moved to Claremont with his mother. Ed says that "Even in Rhode Island, in the fifth and sixth grades we used to go to dances and I started listening to bands. When I moved to Claremont as a young teenager, at that age girls are beginning to be important in your life, and dances are the places where you're gonna get close to the girls. So I went to the dances at St. Mary's Gymnasium. They had a student up there with a tiny stereo playing 45s and I said, 'You've got to be kidding me, I've got a stereo bigger than that in my bedroom!'

"At about the same time a young guy from Philadelphia named Brian Hipwell moved into Claremont and he was facing the same thing. He was in my class, and ended up being one of my good friends. He and I formed a social fraternity, Pi Alpha, and we were determined to bring bands to Claremont and get things happening. That was around 1962, I was fifteen, and I had to hire people to drive me places to see bands. Brian and I decided we were going to get some bands, but we didn't know how to go about it."

You will recall that the first band Ed managed was The Sprites, from Brattleboro. "After I got started with The Sprites, work started coming in leaps and bounds and I got another band and then another band. I was still in high school. My first office was located in my house, and my mother used to answer my calls and do secretarial work and callbacks during the day while I was in school. I called my agency Sprite Promotions. Then shortly afterwards I renamed it Wain Music. The spelling of Wain was different from my name because that's how my girlfriend liked it. [By the way, that girlfriend is Ed's wife today.] It stayed Wain Music for quite a while, then I eventually changed it to The Ed Malhoit Agency, which allowed me to use initials like the bigger agencies did. EMA was better for advertising and logos, that sort of thing."

After high school Ed attended Grahm Junior College in Boston. While he was at Grahm, Ed continued to book bands. However, remembering that this was the mid-'60s, before cell phones, even before telephones in dorm rooms, the Ma Bell aspect of his job was often problematical. Ed's dorm had a pay phone on each of its six floors. So, the ever creative Mr. Malhoit hired someone on each floor to take his calls. Unfortunately for his academic career, Wain Music was growing so rapidly that Ed never made it past his freshman year.

Ed moved back to Claremont, rented a house and set up his office in the basement, which was fine at first. But business continued to grow so fast that he moved onto Pleasant Street in downtown Claremont, above Don Whitcomb's Music Store. Pleasant Street turned out to be an excellent location for both Ed and Don. In one trip bands could meet with their agent and also visit the music store where they bought most of their equipment. The symbiotic relationship lasted for several years, as Ed's agency expanded.

"We had four small rooms and it was comfortable, until we outgrew that space, too. My next location was the top floor of the City Bank Building, as it was called then. It had originally been called the Hotel Moody. We had six good-sized rooms which were for secretaries and the three or four agents I had working for me. One room was for just mailing, logo design, art work, album covers, band photographs, and we also had a conference room for meeting with talent. The linchpin in my office for a number of years was Kathy

(Kasaras) Shull, who I first hired when she was fifteen. When I was away I always felt that things were in good hands, and all the bands liked and trusted her.

L – R: Kathy (Kasaras) Shull, Patty Perrotto, Ed's "Right hand ladies."

"At that time my company was grabbing some real attention and good bands wanted to be with me. That's the key to an agency, your bands. If you have twenty good bands, then everyone is calling, and you have some control, and it's not just for the agent, it's for the bands too."

The rocker who suggested this chapter's title was right on the money. For years Ed was *the* agent in New Hampshire and Vermont. He was our gateway to the big time, the one guy every band knew and most bands worked with.

I once asked Ed if there was any band in the nexus that he didn't work with. His immediate and honest response was a succinct, "No."

Perhaps with the benefit of maturity and forty years of hindsight, many rockers interviewed for this book had lots of nice things to say about our agent. Here is a sampling.

Gardner Berry of the Telstars and Stone Cross: "I always liked the guy, he was always good-natured, and he kept us busy. He seemed to keep good track of things, which couldn't have been easy, as many bands as he represented."

Pete Bover: "Ed Malhoit was central to our bands."

Rick Davis: "The thing about Ed Malhoit was that, number one, he was a businessman. At the time maybe many of us didn't cotton to that, but even at a young age back then some of us realized how important he was for our success."

Cher Mitchell Aubin: "There were all these music venues in Claremont in the late '60s; the junior high, the high school, St. Mary's, the skiway. We could see live music two or three times each weekend. Live music was booming in Claremont, and Ed was instrumental because he booked them *all*."

Earlier, I mentioned maturity and hindsight. Rick Davis hinted at those factors as well. Remember that in the late 1960s and early 1970s most rockers sat solidly in the counterculture, anti-Establishment camp. Every businessman represented "The Man," thus many of our band peers disported a thinly veiled dislike of agents generally, and of Ed Malhoit in specific because he was our agent. As transparently ridiculous as it appears today, forty years ago there was a lot of oil and water going on.

I asked Ed, from his perspective as our agent, for his memories of us callow "rock stars." "Generally I enjoyed working with most people. Each band typically had one guy who was tough to rein in for one reason or the other. Some felt that a band didn't need an agent at all. They didn't stop by my office and see how many people were working to try and keep all the bands booked, the behind-the-scenes work like advertising, answering the phone, creating promotional pictures, drawing up contracts that were legal, etc."

As most people know, Ed was Aerosmith's first agent. He recalls a story from the early days after the band first moved to Boston. "Aerosmith owed me some money, and Steve called me up and said, 'I got a guy who is willing to pay what we owe you.' At the time I wasn't taking commissions from them because I couldn't keep them working. Steve says, 'He's gonna send a limo to pick you up.' So I went down to Boston, and I met Frank Connolly, their original manager. Frankie's the one who paid for their apartment and their rehearsal space, and literally paid for their first album at Intermedia on Newbury Street."

That Aerosmith memory led to a Tracks memory, and some interesting self-assessment. "I always enjoyed Tracks, and working with the band. At the time I wasn't a manager, I was an agent, and I was looking to make you guys more marketable. I look back now, and I could have done some things differently. You know, take Aerosmith off the road, take Tracks off the road, get them ready, pay them a salary, and then present them to the record companies."

Ed Malhoit, 1974

Ed tells another story on himself and his bands. One day in the early Seventies, "I came driving in to my house and there are trucks and cars all over the place, on the street, on the lawn, everywhere. There must have been about ten bands that showed up, and they were there to kick my butt. They had all gotten together and they wanted to know what I was going to do about more bookings, etc. But what could have been a really negative meeting turned out very well. We established new guidelines, I started doing things a little differently, moved into the bigger office, and things got better for both me and the bands. The business had already been growing, but then it really started to take off."

One of Ed's favorite bands was Atlantis, with David Curtin on drums; guitarist Bob Hearne; Sammy DeSantis on the keyboards; Chris Quackenbush on bass; Greg Dame as the initial lead singer and guitarist; and the group's second lead singer, Rick McPherson, who also played guitar, flute, and harmonica. Atlantis was a terrifically talented band, but they also had a unique hook. They were the only band around that had a Mellotron. Ed says, "I still remember the day we drove down to Boston and picked up the Mellotron at Wurlitzer's on Newbury Street, right across from the Intermedia studio. We picked it up and brought it back to the Broken Ski in Killington. That night when they did the Moody Blues—wow!"

Atlantis was a part of a legendary musical event in Claremont, the March of Dimes concert of 1971. Ed recollects that "The March of Dimes concert was sponsored by the local radio station, WTSV, and Pi Alpha Fraternity, the social organization that I founded when I moved to Claremont from Rhode Island. There were six bands in all: Aerosmith, Anvil, Atlantis, The Glad, Gunnison Brook, and one other group whose name escapes me. It turned out to be an incredible success! Having bands share the PA and other equipment was kind of new at the time, and with those six well-known bands the place was mobbed. We had 1500 people stuffed into the gym, the police were there, the fire people were there. It was a great show, the largest musical event ever staged indoors in Claremont."

Atlantis, L – R: Bob Hearne, David Curtin, Greg Dame,
Sammy DeSantis, Chris Quackenbush

After the drinking age in New Hampshire and Vermont reverted to twenty-one in the 1980s, Ed's agency experienced a downturn. "Clubs were falling by the wayside and colleges were trying to get away from the wild parties because of liability laws, etc. We weathered the storm for a few years, but eventually some of my agents went out on their own. I decided to downsize the office and move it into the lower level of a new home that I had built, but the writing was on the wall. Most of the agencies that competed with us were doing the same thing. The days of bands being booked everywhere were going away."

Today Ed still lives in Claremont, and works in the automotive industry. He is proud of how successful his agency was for so many years. "I was often imitated and visited to see how we could possibly do what we did in little Claremont, New Hampshire. Agencies from as far away as Chicago would visit. Also, IBM came in one day to sell me some software to make my business more efficient. After they saw how we did things they admitted that my way was better for everybody involved. Many people don't realize how much work was involved in booking that many bands and locations. Just the logistics of moving dozens of bands all around New England by truck on a Saturday night, that could be nightmarish to say the least. The details were never-ending, but as long as it worked out for the club owners, and the bands, and the agency, then it was worth it."

Ed remains in contact with many of the old band members from the Sixties and Seventies. At two musical events in 2010, I watched guys who had disparaged Ed, when we were "rising rock stars" in our twenties, greet him warmly. Yeah, we did a lot for the man's pocketbook. But, in truth, he did more for us than we did for him. All these years later, it seems we denizens of the counterculture finally get it.

Anvil

Friday afternoon, September 23, 1960, fifth grader Brad French headed home from school the day before his tenth birthday. The young man from Swampscott, MA, was soon to become a standout in youth league football and baseball in a town renowned for its athletic programs. Despite his athletic talent, sports were not the passion in his life.

"I had been begging my parents for two years to buy a guitar and let me have lessons. They always said, 'Let's give it a little time.' As I walked home from school, I figured there would be a little cake and candles the next day. I came through the door, it was a beautiful sunny day, and on the kitchen table was a guitar case. And my mother said, 'Hurry up or you'll be late for your lesson.'

"The guitar was the only instrument that I ever wanted to play, and to this day the only instrument I've ever played. I did well academically at Swampscott High, all honor roll, and was in the college track. During our sophomore year guidance session the counselor says, 'What do you want to do?' I replied, 'I want to play guitar.' 'No, no, no, you want to go to college.' 'No, I want to play guitar.'"

Brad applied to Berklee College of Music when he was a junior. He was accepted, and could have dropped out of high school at age sixteen, but agreed with his parents and stayed to earn his diploma. Then, his first year at Berklee, Brad was recognized as "most outstanding guitarist." Brad recalls that "The head of the guitar department, William Levitt, wanted to meet my parents. He had dinner with us, and at the end of dinner he said to my parents, 'Your son is the finest guitarist that's ever walked through the doors at Berklee.'"

From 1964 to 1967, five high school students in Springfield, VT, pals since junior high, played in two different rock bands. Bill Belden and Bob Hathaway were in an outfit called The Four Dimensions. Bob Gagnier, Jim Goodrum, and Peter Yanofsky played in a group called The Invaders. After a year of college the two bands merged and The Other Man's Grass was born.

The Other Man's Grass featured Belden on guitar; Goodrum on bass; Yanofsky on keyboards; Hathaway as lead singer, percussionist, and sometimes drummer; and Gagnier as the principal drummer and also lead singer. Coincidentally, Belden, Gagnier, and Yanofsky also played trumpet. "In those days we all played two or three different instruments," reports Jim. "We actually did 'Nowhere Man' by The Beatles in a Battle of the Bands with Peter and Bobby playing trumpet. All of us were pretty versatile musicians, especially Bill, who studied at the Hartt School and today is a music teacher."

The band played through their sophomore year in college, the two Bobs in Massachusetts, Peter and Jim at the University of Vermont, and Bill at the University of Hartford's Hartt School. Jim explains, "We'd all go back to Springfield on the weekends, gather on Friday afternoon, load our gear into the van, and then drive to some high school gig or college fraternity party somewhere. We played almost every weekend that year and played UVM's Freshman Mixer that fall, which led to a lot of frat jobs and a loyal fan base at UVM and in Burlington."

The Other Man's Grass found steady work in the summer of 1968, the highlight a five-week gig at the famed Hampton Manor. They shared the stage with a white soul band, Wet Magic, who backed up "Queenie" Lyons on weekends. Fall meant the start of another college year, but the boys' educational plans were soon to be overridden by events.

In the spring of 1969, Brad French was in his second semester at Berklee when he got a phone call from an old Swampscott buddy, Bob Davis, then a UVM student fronting a band called "The Jerome Mystic Movement." Brad recalls Bob's tale of woe. "Bob, who went by the stage name of Jerome Mystic, was not only a good singer, he was an incredible showman. He could get a cripple up out of a wheelchair and dancing. He told me his lead guitar had taken ten tabs of acid and disappeared. He finally surfaced in Colorado. Bob said, 'I've got six gigs for huge money right through UVM graduation and no guitar player. Can you help us?'" Davis offered to pay for everything, transportation, room, etc. Brad said yes, and soon was on his way to Vermont for the first time in his life.

After Friday classes Brad took the MTA to Boston's Logan Airport, flew up to Burlington, and played all weekend. This commute went on for six weeks, into the summer. Then the gigs started to dry up, and Brad started thinking a soul band that featured a horn section maybe wasn't the right place for him to flex his talents.

So Brad did some research, and everyone he asked told him that The Other Man's Grass was the best band around. He called Peter, who remembers that "I went out to hear him play, he had this little Fender. I had never heard him play, but I knew Jerome Mystic. I called Jimmy that same night and said, 'You gotta hear this guy.'"

Jim picks up the story. "We went to his apartment and saw him play. He plugged into a Fender twin reverb and started playing stuff like Jeff Beck and Jimmy Page, including 'Good Times, Bad Times' which became one of our Anvil set openers. I had been noodling around with some of that stuff, so I started playing along with him and he kind of perked up, like, 'Wow, these guys are okay.' Peter and I were blown away. The guy was great."

Peter continues, "We decided right away we wanted to add him to the band, but we didn't want to replace Bill Belden. Bill was not a really strong lead/blues type player, but he was a good rhythm guitarist and a true musician. So we went to the guys and said we found this guitar player and he's gonna knock your socks off. Bill took immediate offense, which of course was not what we hoped for. We thought a six-piece, two-guitar band would be a leg up, when you look at bands like the Allman Brothers.

"Bill was really opposed to two guitars, but I held my ground because I couldn't let this guy get away. I knew we were the perfect situation for him, and I knew what he could do for us. Well, the band literally broke up over night. Then, one by one, the other guys all came around to my parents' house where I was staying and said, 'I'll stay.' I had hopes that we could talk Bill into staying, but even Bobby H., who had been in his old band, couldn't talk him into it. That was sad because we'd known each other since elementary school."

The four remaining members of The Other Man's Grass and Brad began rehearsing in earnest at the Community Center in Springfield. Jim says, "We learned a lot of the original sets of music that we used; that's where we crafted the Santana medley we became known for." Peter adds, "We had two or three weeks to learn a new repertoire, forty or forty-five songs, and it was all new to us and to Brad. We worked from morning to night. The guy who ran the place gave us the back room to use and we practiced forever. It was grueling for Brad but he knew we had to muscle up. We never did that again!"

During this time the band picked its new name, though no one recalls how Anvil rose to the top of the list. Peter docs remember one name that didn't make the cut. "I always got outvoted during the times we talked about naming the band. I wanted to name it 'Free Beer and Naked Women.' My motivation was purely short-term profit driven. I figured any club with a sign outside that read "Tonight Only! Free Beer and Naked Women!' was assured of a packed house even if there might be a problem or two with angry patrons after the first set. True story!"

Front, L – R: Peter Yanofsky, Bob Gagnier; Rear, L – R: Bob Hathaway, Brad French, Will Tracy, John O'Hara, Len Warner, Jim Goodrum

Once Anvil started playing out regularly the band almost never rehearsed. Instead, arrangements would evolve out of jams. One example is "Ain't Supersititious." Jim says, "Brad loved Jeff Beck, and really could play like Beck. We started out with the version off the album, which was a seven-minute song, and it became a thirty-five minute song. Parts would just come up. I'd add something, Brad would add something, Peter would add something, a lot of our songs were like that. We would cover the first couple minutes of a song like the crowds were used to hearing it, then we would go off on our thing, and then return to the cover type thing at the end. Some of that happened because when you're playing five sets a night you gotta do something to stay fresh."

Although the band practiced a lot less than most fans would have imagined, Bob H. was always singing. Not so much to exercise his chops, but because he just loved to sing. Peter recalls that when Bobby would drop him off at his home in Springfield, on a street where over ninety percent of the residents were of Polish descent, Bobby would sing Elvis's "In the Ghetto" as the car pulled up. Conversely, when Peter would drop Bobby off at his home in a World War II public housing development known as "The Projects," Bobby would launch into Johnny Rivers' classic, "Poor Side of Town." The ritual always made them both laugh.

Peter says that "Two things about Anvil made us as good as we were. First, we knew each other so well. The four of us from Springfield, we had known each other so long that we were really tight, as friends and as band mates. On stage we just kinda knew where we were going because we had played so long together. Plus, having combined two bands to form The Other Man's Grass, we had two drummers who were so strong and so versatile.

"The second thing was Brad's skill on the guitar. It was rare that people could hear someone play guitar like Beck or Hendrix, but Brad could do it. Brad is the best guitar player I ever heard, and I heard Beck and Clapton live. On any given night he was unbelievable, he would awe people. He was so talented he intimidated other guitar players."

One Anvil fan who remembers the Jeff Beck songs is Carey Rush, who saw the band for the first time at the Springfield Community Center. "They bring the lights down, the curtain opens and I see this gold top Les Paul. I hear the click of the amplifier switch, and a little bit of hum, and I direct my gaze toward the stage. They started with 'Situation' by Jeff Beck. At that time *Rough and Ready* was the consummate album for me. Here I am a teenager seeing a band that can pull this off, and I'm like, wow! They had me from the first note."

Brad French and his gold top Les Paul

Anvil's reputation grew quickly throughout upper New England and New York. One reason, in addition to the band's talent, was the amazing amount of equipment they put on stage. On bass, Jim Goodrum had two full sets of Ampeg SVTs, four boxes! Brad had a Marshall amp and custom-made E.U. Wurlitzer cabinets with eight EV SRO speakers. According to Jim, "Brad had to really crank them up to get them to produce that Marshall 'distortion' sound. They were just overpowering." Peter Yanofsky had a 1939 Model D Hammond organ he had bought from a church in Springfield, two Leslies, and an Ampeg SST with eight 12" speakers to power his mic'd Leslies and piano. Bobby G. had a full double bass drum set, and to ensure their ability to showcase the vocal talents and showmanship of their front man, Bobby Hathaway, the group had eight Altec Lansing

Voice of the Theatre boxes for its PA. Peter says, "At some of the clubs we played, like the Blue Tooth in Burlington, we'd set up just *half* the gear and the whole room would be pulsating, like the support beams were gonna come down."

Exactly how much gear did Anvil bring to the stage? This story should clue you in. The band was at its house in Salisbury, VT, when Will Tracy, one of the road crew who was also the band's manager, fielded a phone call from a guy at UVM who sounded desperate. "We're in big trouble. The Allman Brothers are playing here tonight and their truck is stuck somewhere. You guys are the only band we know that has the kind of equipment they need. Is there any possibility they could use your stuff?" Since the band wasn't playing that night the roadies went up with the truck, and set up all of Anvil's equipment in Patrick Gymnasium for Duane and Gregg and the boys. Peter recalls that "Gregg played my Hammond that night, but we were so jaded—or something—that the band members didn't even go. Our roadies got to meet the whole band and hang with them."

Anvil's play list, according to Bobby G., featured "a lot of Jeff Beck, select Led Zeppelin numbers, Santana, English blues by John Mayall, the Yardbirds, Cream," and, adds Peter, "any Hendrix tune you could imagine. My favorite was 'Voodoo Child.'" There was also Anvil's lone original tune, written about a friend of a friend and his penchant for providing substances, "A Man from Afghanistan."

One of Anvil's crowd favorites was its Santana medley. It showcased the band's percussion talents, with a partial drum kit out front on which lead singer Bob H. accompanied drummer Bobby G. The medley started with "Jingo" and ended with "Soul Sacrifice." Jim says, "'Soul Sacrifice' was a great way to finish. The song stops, then starts again, but when it first stopped the crowd would always scream, and then we'd go back in and it was like a double ending."

Despite their eminently danceable music, Anvil encouraged its audiences to enjoy a show as if it were a concert. This unusual approach perhaps had its genesis in Canada, where, according to Jim, "The crowd would not dance when the band was playing. They considered it a concert so they'd watch, then as soon as we went on break the jukebox would come on and they'd all start to dance. When you would do solos, there was applause after each solo. People who knew us would say to others in the audience, 'Sit down. If you want to dance put on a record.' Everything we did was geared to a concert set up."

Anvil played throughout Vermont and New Hampshire, on what we in bands referred to as "the Malhoit Circuit," but they were more a northern Vermont, Upstate New York, Montreal and Quebec band. Bobby G. says that "We did play Malhoit gigs, and a lot of shows at Dartmouth, but we didn't play that circuit as much because one of our roadies was also our manager. Will Tracy was an incredible smooth talker, and he got us a lot of our own gigs." Tracy was also from Springfield, and attended the same junior high school as the other guys in the band. He was one of three road men for Anvil, with John O'Hara and Lenny Warner, who, says Peter, "was a great athlete and as good-looking a guy as there was in the band."

The band played often in the Burlington area. At The Blue Tooth in particular Anvil was so popular that there would be lines all the way around past the Flynn Theater with people waiting to get in.

In New York the band worked the Hampton Manor, the Whitehall and Glens Falls area, Albany, The Aerodrome in Schenectady, and The Egg and Machine Shop in Plattsburgh. The Egg and Machine Shop was a favorite destination. The crowd loved the band and, says Jim, "The owners were all in their forties, all having their mid-life crises. One was a judge, one was a professor at SUNY-Plattsburgh, they thought we were the coolest thing going, and they wanted to hang with us. It was the cool thing to be able to get Anvil to stay at your house when we were playing there, and we stayed at the professor's house a lot."

Perhaps the band's favorite Canadian nightspot was the "Boulevard de Paris" on Sainte-Catherine Street in Montreal. Jim recalls that "We used to call that club the 'TV dinner' because the walls were all tinfoil, the ceiling was tinfoil, and somebody said 'This is like playing inside a TV dinner.' They had this big bar, and beside the bar was a raised platform area with tables. The first time we played there, as the night went on all these girls started congregating in that area. We got two or three sets into the night and one of the bartenders says, 'Don't you like girls?' We said, 'Well, we don't know any girls up here.' He said, 'All of those girls are for you.' The girls at that club, if they wanted to meet the band, they would go sit at those tables."

Bobby G. remembers the time the judge from Plattsburgh traveled with Anvil to a gig on Sainte-Catherine Street. "He came with us to Montreal, and after the show he left the club with us and his mind is quite altered, let's say. He goes to get in his custom Jaguar XKE and drive back to New York and he can't find it. He figures it's because he is so altered, but after a while he realizes it's been stolen. So he spends the entire night riding around the city with the Montreal police, tripping, trying to find his car. They eventually find his New York plates on an Aston-Martin that was heading out of the country the next day. The police determined some big-time theft ring took his car, and he never did find it."

Anvil opened regularly for big-name acts, solid evidence of the band's talent and popularity. Among those big names: The J. Geils Band, Mountain, Edgar Winter's White Trash, and Richie Havens.

Peter: "At the Mountain concert we went on before them and opened with our Santana medley. Later on it became clear to us that they were sitting in the back somewhere listening, and they had to have heard this thunderous, percussive noise coming from the stage. Well, somehow that either pissed off or intimidated Corky Laing, because when they did their set he kept messing up and breaking sticks, and Leslie West and Felix Pappalardi were shooting him dirty looks. What Corky had heard, but never saw, was our second drum kit out front, because it had been taken down before they came on stage."

Peter also recalls with some amusement the Richie Havens concert. "We set up our stuff to play before him, and his manager walked in and said, 'These guys can absolutely not go on first. If they do, everyone will leave before Richie plays.' The guy had come in and seen the stacks of Marshalls and Ampegs and the eight Voice of the Theatre boxes and thought, 'No way.'" So the backup band went second that night. "Richie went out first and we're thinking 'Oh shit, everybody's gonna leave.' But we went out there, not a soul had moved, the place was jammed, and they give us this huge standing ovation."

How does such a talented group, truly a band of brothers, come to the end of the road? Slowly and, it turns out, painfully. Jim remembers that "Early in 1972 we were living in 'Bummerville,' our second band house in Salisbury. Len Warner came up with the name for a couple of reasons, one being that in a band with eight guys you aren't gonna get along with everybody." Brad adds, "One of the things that brought the band down was the fact that we were together too much. When you try to put a whole band into a house, and you have all these different personalities, trying to cook and clean house and all…. Toward the end people who were best of friends since elementary school started bickering over stupid stuff like, 'You left your hairbrush on the sink,' or the toothpaste tube. We were together seven days a week, and after a while we started wearing on each other's nerves."

About that time, says Jim, "The majority of us wanted to add Kip Meeker, another great guitar player, to the band, and Kip wanted to bring his own drummer, Steve Arey. Bobby G. left, and also two of our road crew. It was very painful." Anvil played as a six-piece band for four months, and to this day people still talk about Brad and Kip in the same band, about how fluid and phenomenal they were together. Jimi Slate remembers that "Meeker and French were awesome, the double lead guitars were amazing!" But soon Bob Hathaway and Peter Yanofsky had also had enough, and they, too, departed after those four months.

The band played on as a foursome—bass, drums, and two guitars. Jim says that "We started playing for some agents in Massachusetts, but clearly the most successful incarnation of Anvil was the first one. Brad adds, "Kip was phenomenally talented, the best singer I ever heard in my life to this day, and when the band sounded good we were very good. But much of the time it didn't sound like Anvil. It just was not Anvil, and it didn't take long."

Two months later, "I'll never forget the day," laments Jim. "I called up my girlfriend, who is now my wife, and I said, 'Come and get me, I'm quitting the band.'"

Chemistry is a funny thing. It can be an incredibly powerful bond, yet it is so delicate. Jim offers this insight. "I used to say that if it was just about being on the stage, it would have been really easy. But you had to get along with guys off the stage as well." Brad's requiem for Anvil: "The chemistry changed, the magic was gone, and we were burned out. A couple of big waves washed over the band and, like castles made of sand, it just dissolved."

Kemeny's Lemon

By Pete Merrigan
Reprinted with permission

Protests against the war in Viet Nam were reaching a fevered pitch in the spring of 1970. There was a sense of community and commonality of purpose throughout the university systems not only in this country, but around the world. Anyone with a shred of sanity and decency knew that there wasn't a shred of either in what was going on in Southeast Asia at the behest of Nixon, Kissinger, and the rest of the gang in the Pentagon and the White House. Body bags were everywhere and almost everyone had a friend or loved one who was either in one or still entrenched in the jungles of Viet Nam.

Our little five-piece rock 'n' roll band called Birth played at a few fund raisers for anti-war causes, but for the most part we were doing our commercial gigs without too much interruption from the war.

The band, at that time, consisted of three Dartmouth College students, John Maxfield, Oliver Hess, and Andy Raymond, Pete Shackett who was at Plymouth State, and me. I was enrolled at the University of New Hampshire. Every weekend we'd convene to play two or three gigs, usually high school dances, fraternity parties, or nightclubs. We got a lot of work at Dartmouth fraternities thanks to an energetic student agent who was a friend of Oliver and Andy's.

In May of 1970, as "Green Key" weekend approached, we were looking forward to the most lucrative and fun three days of the year. Three one-night stands at different fraternities would make us a few hundred dollars apiece. In those days, that was a lot of cabbage for twenty-somethings to be making on weekends.

Of course, to us, the money was not nearly as important as the status and excitement of being "the band" at some of the wildest parties we'd ever seen. The movie *Animal House* was written by a Dartmouth grad, and those big screen shenanigans were often played out in real life on fraternity row. The atmosphere at Dartmouth on weekends such as homecoming and Green Key—whatever Green Key meant, I never knew—was one of Mardi Gras-like indulgence and uninhibited saturnalia.

Bleary-eyed students meandered through the ordinarily somnolent town of Hanover, NH, stumbling or dancing their way from party to party. Even in those days, they were intoxicated primarily on beer, although a growing number would be doing acid, speeding, or smoking hash or pot.

On any one of these major weekends, fifteen or twenty different bands might be rocking various fraternity houses. Every frat tried to outdo the others by getting the hottest band, the loosest women, and apparently seeing which brother could vomit the most without actually dying.

So, you can imagine my disappointment when I got the call saying that all three of our Green Key frat party gigs had been cancelled.

On May 4, 1970, the entire world was horrified by the news that a National Guard unit had opened fire on a group of students at Kent State University in Ohio who were protesting the war. Four students had been killed, many were injured. Nixon had gone too far this time. Surely this was the start of the revolution!

It was one of those events about which we think, "Well, shouldn't everything stop now?" From Wall Street to Pennsylvania Avenue, from Hollywood to Viet Nam, business as usual went on; not much changed. But colleges and universities across the nation and around the world were, in fact, coming to a standstill. Many of them were going on strike to protest this God-awful, undeclared war raging under the term "conflict." How had it gotten this far? How had things gone so horribly wrong that now our own National Guardsmen were firing on U.S. citizens! College kids!

Even realizing the enormity of the event, it didn't occur to me that the fraternity parties would be cancelled. Once I got the call, I thought, well, of course. What was I thinking? They aren't going to be having parties all weekend with this kind of shit hitting the fan.

At UNH there were rallies demanding that the University System shut down in solidarity with the Kent State students. No such action will be taking place just yet, the administration announced, but they did say they were considering what action they should take. That was typical of conservative UNH. "We're thinking about what we ought to do…but we aren't doing anything."

Then I got a second call from Dartmouth. Maxfield said that Dartmouth was going to officially strike and it would be announced by College President John Kemeny sometime that weekend. Our agent had called the three fraternity houses where we had been booked and, in a maneuver worthy of uber-agent Irving Azoff (who was also still in college at the time), had convinced them to donate the money they would have paid us to the College strike fund. In return, we would agree to play at the only function not cancelled that weekend, the concert at the Leverone Field House.

We would be opening for Jesse Colin Young and The Youngbloods. The Youngbloods were a nationally-known act, and extremely hip. The epitome of cool. Would we agree to do that? We would have traded three frat parties for a concert like that any day, anywhere. Free! In a heartbeat!

It was relatively quiet in the field house as we hauled our gear onto the stage. It was a cavernous building; certainly the biggest venue we'd ever played. There were crew and staff members, mostly students, busily moving chairs, setting up lights, and milling around. The floor was cold, bare ground, but very level.

I remember being quite surprised when Jesse Colin Young drove in with the roadies in the passenger seat of the equipment truck. Surprised, too, that he looked so normal. Faded jeans, an unremarkable t-shirt that was also well-worn and road weary, and his mustache, which looked just like it did on the record jacket, surrounded by week-old stubble. After wandering around and scoping out the situation, he sat down next to me on the front edge of the stage and pulled out a joint. A faint brume of patchouli enveloped him.

I should pause here to tell you that I *loved* the Youngbloods! I wouldn't say I idolized them, but I thought they were one of the coolest groups in the world. I had that album with "Get Together" on it and played it until the vinyl was thin.

And here I was, sitting next to Jesse Colin Young as if he were one of the guys in my band. "Wanna get high?" he asked, as he lit up. "No thanks," I said. "I don't get stoned before I play." Wow. I felt so square. *So* square. But it was true. If I'd smoked that joint with him, all I'd want to do is eat some Oreos and listen to somebody else play music. No, we were into Dexedrine and coffee when we played. Speed, man. High octane energy! Smoke some weed *after* the gig. Mellow out with some beer and joints. Maybe some wine.

"Is that all the equipment you've got?" he asked, cocking his head back towards our stage gear. "Yeah," I said, immediately feeling inferior to this California recording star. "That's all we have. It's plenty for most of the places we play. We don't usually play places this big. We're only here because of the strike."

It didn't occur to me how much he was winding me up until later, when they had all their gear set up. Their amps were much smaller than ours, their drum set less elaborate. Their only keyboard was a simple little Wurlitzer piano with a sunny pastoral scene painted on the front of it. And Jesse would play those great songs on it, songs which decades beyond would epitomize a generation. I recognized the piano instantly as the one on the cover of that classic album.

So here's how it went that night. As a few thousand Dartmouth students poured into the field house, Birth took the stage. We played a set of about an hour. I wish I could, but I can't, remember the details or the songs we played.

When we finished, someone introduced President Kemeny. Dr. John G. Kemeny, born in Budapest in 1926, had just become Dartmouth's top dog that year. Kemeny was a well-respected, perhaps even revered, member of the intelligentsia, an erstwhile student of Albert Einstein, and besides all that, a very well-liked and down-to-earth man. Well-liked, it seemed, by everyone except William Loeb of New Hampshire's infamous right-wing newspaper, the *Manchester Union-Leader*.

That morning's edition of the paper had vilified Kemeny for his unequivocal anti-war stance. Loeb ranted that Dartmouth had picked a lemon for its new president. This same newspaper had, some weeks before, run an editorial on its front page in red ink, denouncing Earth Day as a communist plot because it was going to coincide with the well-known communist holiday, May Day. I had attended a public bonfire for the burning of that edition at UNH.

Unfortunately, the *Manchester Union-Leader* was the only state-wide newspaper in New Hampshire so it carried then, and still does today, considerable clout with the citizenry.

I was sitting backstage when Kemeny walked to the podium. He received a warm, rousing ovation. But it paled in comparison to the thunderous cheer that went up when he announced, "Dartmouth College is now officially on strike!" I got goose bumps. It was one of those rare moments when you know history is being made and instead of watching it on television or in a movie, you are part of it. You're in the freakin' movie.

I don't recall the exact words of his impassioned speech that night, but I will never forget its conclusion. Dr. Kemeny came out from behind the podium and pulled a bright yellow lemon from the pocket of his tweed jacket, holding it high for the whole assembled lot to see. Then, in his wonderful, still slightly Hungarian accent he said, "And William Loeb, *this* is for you!" and heaved the lemon into the audience. The crowd erupted in such a tumultuous, primordial roar, that even in Manchester, NH, some sixty miles away, William Loeb must have felt it, deep down in the abyss where his commie-tormented soul festered.

And the death grip in which Richard Nixon and his zealous cronies held the youth of America and the people of Southeast Asia loosened just a little bit that night.

Can't Get Theah from Heah

Many of you, certainly the majority of you who have lived in New England, are familiar with Marshall Dodge and Bob Bryant, though you probably won't recognize their given names. Dodge and Bryant portrayed Bert and the Narrator in the beloved radio, television and LP record album stories of "Bert and I," originally from the 1950s and 1960s. Two of the best-known Bert and I tales, "Which Way to Millinocket?" and "Which Way to East Vassalboro?" trade on the rural New England legend of the curmudgeonly native and the unsuspecting tourist from the city. The following incident demonstrates the staying power of our myths and their basis in fact.

My brother Mitch lives "upta" the "Natheast" Kingdom in Holland, Vermont. A fellow Minnesotan and Dartmouth grad, he lives in glorious semi-isolation on a scenic dirt road. I say semi-isolation because, while his road is unpaved, it passes for a main road in Holland.

One fall day not so long ago Mitch was hiking along the road and heard a car in the distance. I'll let him tell the story.

"The rumbling announced the vehicle's approach about a minute or so before it hove into view, and I moved slowly to the side of the road. Unsurprisingly, given the fall foliage season, a white Caddy with out-of-state plates rolled around the curve, stopped alongside, and, as the window descended, revealed a bewildered middle-aged couple.

"Assuming I was a native from the facts that I was bearded, scruffy, and on foot, the driver tentatively inquired, 'Does this road go straight?'

"Pausing ponderously, while peering in at the two, I adopted my best approximation of a severe rural New England accent and responded, 'It do foah a biht.'

"Somewhat taken back by my lack of clarification, he looked at me with an expression one sees on 'flatlanders' bethumped by the multitudinous twists, turns, ups, downs, and lack of consistent direction of the Kingdom's road system and wearily stated, 'We're trying to get to East Charleston.' Dismayed by the silence after my response of 'Ay Yuhp,' he followed with an actual question. 'Can we get there from here?'

"With glee in my heart, I turned in the direction they were facing, made a few gestures with my hands as if mentally driving the roads ahead, paused, shook my head in a negative fashion, looked into the car, and queried, 'Eeeast? Challstun?' At his positive response, I turned to the rear of the Caddy, and repeated the hand gestures and head shaking. Turning back, their expectant countenances fell as I replied, 'You cahn't get theah from heah.'

"With a solicitous voice, but decidedly less solicitous intent, I inquired where they had started and if they could return to that point. As tears seemed to well in her eyes and befuddled fear dominated his expression, I relented. Using my most precise oratorical diction I enunciated the directions that would indeed take them to East Charleston. Unamused, they sped south while I continued north accompanied by a monstrous grin and occasional chortle."

Mitch has always reveled in twisting the lion's tail. Knowing how folks in the Kingdom feel about "flatlandahs," however, and having employed the same accent with the same intended effect at times in my past, I am afraid I can freely admit to wishing it had been me that day out on his dirt road, and not my facetious little "brothah."

I love the rural accent of upper New England, though it is disappearing, as are regional dialects all across our country. I loved it the first time I heard it; love hearing it fifty years on. I hear that accent today and am instantly transported back to my rock and roll years, and visions of memorable excursions to and from paying engagements along the highways and byways of Vermont and New Hampshire.

Ammonoosuc River, south of Littleton, NH

It was not at all unusual for a band to spend more time on the road getting to and from a show than in actual performance. While the back entrances to auditoriums and clubs and gyms all looked mind-numbingly and grubbily the same, the roads we traveled were, and are, among the most beautiful in the country. Some favorites: coasting alongside the Ammonoosuc River on NH Route 302 between Lisbon and Littleton; rolling east along NH Route 2, headed to Berlin, past the awesome beauty of Mount Washington and the other Presidentials; winding along VT Route 4 up the flanks of the

Green Mountains past Killington and Pico Peak; and motoring along the flat, field-lined stretch of NH Route 118 between Canaan and Dorchester, with cows standing so close to the road you felt you could reach out the car window and touch them.

I won't speak for other bands or other rockers, but for me one part of what was memorable, in addition to gorgeous countryside and pastoral tranquility, was not comfortable. It was, as that hapless couple who had the misfortune to run into my brother felt, the incipient dread of wondering whether we were really on the road to East Overshoe High School, or, rather, the Road of No Return. When Tracks first drove VT Route 125 west toward Middlebury College in the dying twilight of a winter's afternoon, I found myself thinking, "We may be going the right way, but we are never getting home again. Kenny, watch that curve! Wait, are there Yeti in Vermont!!"

I have to believe there were times when every band experienced the same disquiet. The first time any band journeyed to Newell's Casino in Whitefield, NH, turned off NH Route 116 and headed into the woods, no doubt the thought crept in, "Where the hell are we?"

Don Coulombe of Fox and Company remembers a bitter cold winter's night in northern New Hampshire. "Of the many road adventures we had, the one I remember most was breaking down in 1968, coming back from a gig in North Conway, NH. Our bus broke down at two o'clock in the morning at Pinkham Notch. We were twenty-five miles from the nearest gas station; it was fifteen degrees below zero. An hour passed before someone stopped to give me a ride to Gorham to get some gas. When I returned, all the band members had jumped into the sleeping bags on the bus, so they wouldn't freeze to death. At 5:00 a.m. we were finally gassed up and ready to go. I've never been so cold in all my life! It took me all day just to get warm again. That was only one of many breakdowns we had in the early days of rock and roll. Got to love the New England weather!"

Dave Cross, drummer for Dream Engine and Ragweed, recalls a night returning from a gig at Bennington College, in the southwestern corner of Vermont. Dream Engine had appeared with the Apple Pie Motherhood Band, whose keyboard player, Jeff Labes, is best known for his work with Van Morrison, Jonathan Edwards, and Bonnie Raitt.

The band had two options for its return trip to Hanover. Take VT Route 9, a main road, east across the southern edge of the state, then head due north up I-91 to Hanover. Or, cut the hypotenuse diagonally across Vermont on narrow back roads frequented after midnight only by deer, polecats, and other varmints.

"Dave Gilliatt was driving and I was the only passenger. Where the other guys were I have no idea. It was so foggy on the back roads we were traveling that we couldn't even see the end of the hood the entire way. I remember leaning forward, practically pressing my face against the windshield as if that would somehow bring the road into view. It took us forever to get to Hanover and we were—at least I was—so drained, mainly from the tension of traveling blind, that I slept most of the next day. How we made it back safely, or even alive, I'll never know. Why we even tried can only be chalked up to youthful illusions of immortality."

One winter afternoon John Maxfield was driving the Gunnison Brook equipment van to a gig after a visit with a friend in Montpelier, VT. John recalls, "I had just picked up a hitchhiker, who didn't know about my legendary driving record, although he was soon to learn. We were heading south in a blizzard down I-91 when the van just decided it wanted to try the median strip. This was one of those deep valleys that characterize much of Vermont's median strips. The van rolled over, I steadied myself with the steering wheel, but the hitchhiker didn't fare as well, crawling out of the vehicle wracked with back pain.

"By coincidence, we were only a few miles from Claremont, NH, and my father's office. He was an osteopath, so I thought he might be able to help. I sent my unfortunate passenger via taxi to see my father while I had the van towed and transferred the equipment into a rental truck. I headed back up onto the highway and who should be standing there hitchhiking but the same guy. He got in! Twenty-five years later my father received a letter from a man in Mississippi demanding $25,000 restitution for back pain sustained in an accident with his son. My father didn't write back."

Pete Shackett often eschewed the comfort of a roof over his head, instead riding his motorcycle to gigs. Pete earned his Rodney Diamond and the Studs *nom de guerre*, "Motorhead Red," honestly. One particular trip is lodged in Pete's brain.

"I was in Gunnison Brook and headed to Mother's in Lake George, NY, or maybe a gig in Whitehall, NY. I decided to go overland and I was on VT 103. Once up in the Green Mountains, it began to rain so freakin' hard that I literally could not see the road in front of me. It was just sheets of water on my helmet mask. I stopped the bike at what seemed to be the top of the hill I was going up (ever so slowly) and got off to feel the side of the pavement. I found it and pushed my bike well off to the side so that, hopefully, someone else coming along wouldn't wipe out me and the bike. I huddled down beside my bike to wait out the storm. When the rain let up, I looked around and three feet to my right was about a hundred foot drop off. That was an interesting wake-up call...creeped me out!"

All that time on the road had one sublime compensation. I know every band experienced it, because every band played 9:00 to 1:00 shows far from home, then had to break down the equipment, load the truck, and head back to the old homestead. After a stop for some early morning breakfast, hopefully sans harassment by the locals, we would pull into our home base, dog-tired, around 5:30 a.m.

In the summertime, when Tracks returned to Hanover in the early morning hours from a gig in Vermont, we often crossed the Connecticut River as the sun was coming up. There were times when a thick fog hung over the entire breadth of the river itself, rising to about ten feet, the rest of the landscape free of fog. What a magnificent sight that was! And even though it was 5:30 in the morning after a sleepless night, even though I was completely blown out, that scene never failed to amaze and inspire me. All these years later that fog on that river is burned in my brain. When it rises in my mind's eye I am inspired anew, as I recall how much I felt at one with the planet as we drove across the bridge that spanned the Connecticut.

Ragweed

In the summer of 1970, shortly after the Green Key concert with The Youngbloods, Birth split up. Andy Raymond, Oliver Hess, and John Maxfield decided they wanted to move their music toward the blues. That left the two Petes holding the bag, although they rebounded spectacularly within a few weeks, forming a band that would make a huge name for itself throughout northern New England over the next three years.

Ragweed was a reincarnation of the Dartmouth College band Dream Engine, which suffered the fate of many campus bands when graduation reduced it to rubble. Degree in hand, Peter Christenson had returned to the Pacific Northwest. John Maxfield started teaching science at Henniker, NH, High School, though he continued to rock out on the weekends with students Shackett, Merrigan, Hess, and Raymond. Dave Cross became a junior high art teacher in Albany, NY.

Dream Engine had been a pretty progressive band in its Dartmouth days. While they did play the requisite popular dance songs, the guys favored blues, jazz, and esoteric rock covers. Rehearsals and even gigs often contained sprawling, periphrastic jams and solos. The urge to return to these "roots" is likely what prompted Oliver, Andy, and John to re-form the old band under a new name.

Calls went out to New York and Oregon, attempts to entice two former mates back into the fold. Dave Cross was convinced to return from his teaching job in Albany. Next, since, as John Maxfield put it, "None of us could sing very well, as evidenced by my being the lead singer," the band lured Peter Christenson back from Oregon. Peter remembers that "Andy called me on the phone and asked would I like to come East and front the band. They had rented a house in southern Vermont and they were going to get serious. I had nothing to lose, my student deferment having run out, and so off I went to Vermont."

The Ragweed band house hid in the woods of rural Windsor, Vermont, a two-story affair with bedrooms for five band members, one with a girlfriend. Space was tight, a fact celebrated in Peter's original tune, "Close Quarters." John Maxfield recalls that "The lower floor was a basement with three sides underground, opening on the front of the house onto the termination of a dirt/grass driveway that was always covered with leaves."

Dave Cross maintains that "There was remarkably little friction in terms of who sweeps up today and who cooks today. I recall we had a schedule for cooking dinner. Breakfast and lunch were on your own, and there was a cleanup schedule also. Responsibilities were laid out, and we had very few disagreements about that 'as I recall'—the all-purpose disclaimer!"

The band rehearsed relentlessly. They spent hours in a semi-finished basement recording studio that was, as one of the guys recollects, "Very homemade...we used somebody's tape player, but it was not even close to top of the line."

Like its progenitor, Dream Engine, Ragweed's play list was diverse. Songs included several originals; tunes by The Paul Butterfield Blues Band; "Hitchcock Railway" by Joe Cocker; "Beautiful" by The Youngbloods; The Band's "Chest Fever" and "The Night They Drove Old Dixie Down;" "Well All Right" by Blind Faith; songwriter oriented numbers by Buffalo Springfield, Nazz, and Traffic; and Van Morrison's bouncy "Domino." Of the Van Morrison number and Ragweed's two trumpets, Peter says, "Listening to our version of 'Domino,' I think we were very good when both horns were deployed."

The sixth member of the band while they were living in Windsor was Blitz, who was innately skilled at playing dog. By way of example, there was the day Peter took Blitz, an unneutered male, for a walk. They met a female dog along the way and, in a moment of enthusiasm, well...let's just say it took Blitz a long time to extricate himself from the lovely young lady. Gentle reader, that's as close to a "dogs, sex, and rock and roll" moment as you will get in this book.

Besides the usual circuit of bars, dance clubs, college fraternities, and high school gyms, Ragweed played one gig that stands out for its unusual surroundings. The story begins at the Crescent Beach Motor Inn in Mascoma Lake, NH, in early summer 1970, where a guy named Sherry Snyder booked the band to play a party at the U.S. Open Tennis Tournament in Forest Hills, NY, later that summer. Dave Cross remembers "An audience member at that show walking back and forth in front of and around the sides of the stage area, scanning our gear as if he expected to find the Holy Grail hidden among the amplifiers and speakers. At a break he asked where the tape player was, not believing that we were playing all the music live!"

Ragweed's diverse repertoire meant extra equipment. And sometimes the extra equipment could turn into an annoyance when it was lightly used, say for only one or two songs. Here's how the boys in Ragweed handled a unique piece of equipment with some extra muscle, a dash of aplomb, and the punny humor that was a trademark of many bands.

One afternoon the guys loaded the van in Windsor for a gig, but forgot to include the cello Andy would be playing for the first time that night on Chicago's "Color My World." The van was already filled to capacity, yet after endless shuffling,

113

unloading and reloading, grunting and groaning, pinching of appendages, plus foul language, the cello went in, prompting Andy to declare, triumphantly, "See, there's always room for cello!"

The instrument that bedeviled virtually every band, that had band members and roadies swearing every time they moved it, was the mighty Hammond organ. John Maxfield says that "mine was a Hammond C-something, huge thing. In its former life it had been a church organ. It was just what the doctor ordered for 'Chest Fever.'"

Peter Christenson's "memories are of a feel, a flow. Loading the Hammond and the Leslie onto the van...then off the van. One time we were playing a high school dance somewhere, Mapes and I were trying to get the organ up a flight of stairs, and somebody dropped that six-hundred-pound monster on my shin. 'All in a day's work,' Mapes said. And there was something about our ongoing love (because of the sound)/hate (because of the hassle and resultant bruised shins, etc.) relationship with the Leslie. I seem to remember that at one point we referred to it familiarly as 'Les' and then, later, as 'Les Morceau' after Mapes meant to say something like 'less so' and it came out 'less moreso.'"

You may be wondering who "Mapes" was? A roadie? Nope, it was Maxfield's nickname, coined because of his love for maple syrup.

In the fall of 1970, Peter lobbied the band to pack up and head west to his native Oregon to seek its fortune. The band members were not necessarily opposed to moving to the West Coast, but one Ragweeder wondered, "Why move three thousand miles to find ourselves in the same situation we were in already, plus not near Boston and New York City, big music and media centers? Plus, we would have to rebuild whatever reputation we had been building. Portland was hardly a show business nexus, and Seattle was another four or five hours north."

The guys found the concept intriguing, and agreed that Portland sounded nice. Finally, decision day arrived. The band took a vote: three to move, two to stay, none to quit.

Peter had persuaded his mates to abandon their palace in Vermont for moister environs. They hadn't even stayed in the woods long enough to enjoy digging themselves out of the snow.

Ragweed/Galadriel, Windsor, VT, Fall of 1970, L – R: Dave Cross, Blitz, Andy Raymond, Oliver Hess, John Maxfield, Peter Christenson

On the long road trip the band had plenty of time to consider a new name. Keith Osborne, the agent in Portland who booked the band's first few West Coast gigs, thought Ragweed made the guys sound like hayseeds. This from a supposedly hip Oregonian, who clearly missed the drug double entendre so popular with '60s and '70s rock bands. Bet he didn't last long as an agent!

Peter explains, "There was much disputation on the name change. We chose Galadriel before we left Vermont, a name which made sense from a marketing point of view since J.R.R. Tolkien's trilogy was so popular then. But on the road we talked through another name change and in the end settled on Fred. Not a good choice, in my view, and I think its selection accounted in part for our failure to make it big."

The band hit the road in early December, not smart weatherwise. But they had to roll because agent Osborne had booked them for a December 11 performance.

En route to Oregon the band had a near-death experience in more than one sense. Someone had the bright idea of driving straight through, and in freezing rain outside Cleveland in the dead of night the van had a flat tire. The Ragweed mobile was stuffed to the gills with rock 'n' roll equipment and all the band's worldly belongings, and the spare was located just behind the front seat. Five miserable Men of Dartmouth immediately saw the implication and set about the grim task "with the granite of New Hampshire in their muscles and their brains." They unloaded the entire van onto the icy pavement in their quest for said tire. On the side of I-90, with semis "slipping by" mere feet from where they worked, the guys accomplished the task. Says John, "This was performed in complete silence. Had there been a single utterance, and had our lead guitarist, not known for a placid acceptance of adversity, had a gun, the morning commuters would have been treated to the sight of four dead Ragweedians decorating the southern shore of Lake Erie. Fortunately there was no gun."

The tire incident aside, the trip out was hurried, though there was an air of expectancy. Osborne had booked the band for six performances in December, including the day after Christmas in Seaside, Oregon, at the Pypo Club, which in its day was one of the top Pacific Northwest clubs. All the leading Northwest bands played there. When Ragweed arrived in town they all went to a meeting at their new agent's apartment. One of the boys remembers thinking "He looked like what you would imagine the typical second- or third-rate booking agent for a local band to look like. He had the hair all in place and the apartment was modern-ish but appointed cheaply."

Oliver "where's my gun" Hess, 1969

The Pypo Club turned out to be memorable, mostly for the wrong reasons. Peter was driving the van with all the equipment in it. Dave had bought a car, and had two flat tires on the way to the gig. There was some kind of grit on the road because the weather was foul, chunks of gravel or something similar, and it blew the tires. Dave had, of course, only one spare, so Peter had to drive off and look for a place to buy another tire.

To get to Seaside from Portland one has to go over the Coast Range. It was the day after Christmas, and the band thought, "This is a huge gig, we aren't gonna make it, and what's gonna happen?" Eventually Peter came back with a tire and the guys put it on the car. Shades of Cleveland, still no gun. They arrived late at a packed Pypo Club, soaking wet and sweaty. Dave's recollection is that, "While I don't know for sure how we played I remember feeling like we were pretty awful. We were distracted, none of us was prepared, and generally it was a pretty unpleasant experience."

In Portland the band did what they had done in Vermont; rehearsed every day. They rented a house in a nice neighborhood, and no doubt the folks next door felt invaded. There weren't any complaints, however, perhaps because Dave ("our adult," says Peter) was such a good diplomat. Peter adds, "I know that I would raise holy hell now if my suburban calm was interrupted by a bunch of hippies playing rock music." The band also did some recording in Portland, at the Portland State University radio station studios, a slightly better set up than the basement studio in Windsor.

As the band settled in they discovered that Portland was indeed a great town with plenty of places to play. At the same time it was like starting all over again. There were armory gigs, all the way to Eastern Oregon, shows at the coast, and some performances in local clubs. And yet, despite the burst of activity in December, the cross-country move simply didn't take.

John says that, "Although the band was pretty talented, it was not sufficiently successful to keep us in food and clothing. I was tired of cheese and rice and holes in my shoes, especially in rainy Oregon. I heard from my other band mates in Birth, Pete Shackett and Pete Merrigan, who had formed a new band and wanted a second keyboard player, so I deserted my comrades and left for New Hampshire." Oliver also said enough, I'm tired of eating brown rice, I'm going back to school. And so it went. Ragweed had driven to Oregon in December of 1970. Three months later the band was running on empty.

Still, some very good things came from that ill-fated trip west. Four band members still live on the Left Coast today. Peter remains in his home state of Oregon. Dave, a native New Yorker, lives in Tacoma, Washington. Oliver, originally from Pennsylvania, calls Ojai, California, home. Andy from Illinois is in Los Angeles. Lemonade after all.

Gunnison Brook

The last time we saw our heroes, Pete and RePete were left, apparently, holding the bag. The blues triplets—Andy Raymond, John Maxfield, and Oliver Hess—were departing Birth to return to the likes of Paul Butterfield and Allen Toussaint. Shackett and Merrigan were without a band.

Before Andy, John, and Oliver could start playing out with their band, Ragweed, Birth was contractually obligated to a few last gigs, including one at the Chopping Block in Proctorsville, VT. Pete Merrigan recalls that, "By some serendipitous coincidence, my cousin Nancy from Montclair, NJ, whose husband was a musician, had run into a seventeen-year-old bassist in New Jersey named Mario Casella. Nancy knew we were in the midst of forming a band and needed a good bass player. Nancy told Mario about us, and he decided to accept a ride to New Hampshire to meet us and audition.

"We invited Mario to the Chopping Block to hear Birth perform. He had to find out, maybe even more than we did with him, if we were players he wanted to set sail with. He was impressed enough to audition, so we set it up for him to do some playing with us the next afternoon at the club. To help us in our assessment of Mario's abilities, we asked Ollie and Andy and John to observe. In fact, John and Ollie probably played while Andy, the bass player, sat out.

"There was no disguising the fact that everyone was impressed with Mario's ability. I remember Andy flashing me a big grin and nodding 'Yes,' as in, 'Grab this guy!' I was no judge of great bass playing, but I knew instantly that this was a performer who was going to give us 100%. His stage presence was phenomenal, especially considering that he was 250 miles from home, seventeen years old, and auditioning for guys who were older and more experienced. Talent is talent, though, and knows no age."

Pete Shackett thinks, peering back through the mists of time, that John Maxfield suggested his Dartmouth buddy, Alan MacIntosh, to Pete Merrigan. Pete M. remembers that "We quickly asked him to join the band, having heard great things about his musical ability from fellow Dartmouth men Oliver, Andy, and John. It was a bit of a coup that several months later we ended up with both John and Al in the band. John had great respect for Al, and after a short West Coast outing with Ragweed returned to New Hampshire and joined us."

Gunnison Brook's original guitarist was Bill Kendall, replaced after just a few gigs by Dan Sibley. Pete S. says, "Again, I don't remember precisely how we got Dan's name, but we went to see him play somewhere. Maybe the connection was Glenn Jordan, who co-wrote Gunnison Brook original 'Old Dear Friend' with Alan."

Pete M. was the lead singer, and also played harp and percussion. Pete S. sang and played the drums, but also chipped in with some rhythm guitar. Mario handled the bass, occasional lead vocals, and provided high harmonies. Alan (keyboards) and John (keyboards and trumpet) also sang, and Dan was the lead guitarist. The full cast of multi-talented multi-instrumentalists was finally assembled, and Gunnison Brook took flight.

The band's home base was Pete Merrigan's family home, Gunnison Manor, in Goshen, NH. Alan recalls that "Everyone, including the roadies, lived there at one time or another. It was our place to live, learn, rehearse, write songs, and co-exist, for which we will always be grateful to Peter. Peter and his house were the core of Gunnison Brook, brought the band together physically and creatively, and provided a venue for our music to flourish."

Wells, Maine, 1972, L – R: Pete Shackett, Alan MacIntosh, Pete Merrigan, John Maxfield, Mario Casella, Dan Sibley

Pete's mother had passed away in the spring of 1970. With permission from his brother and sister, Gunnison Brook moved into the house that summer, constructed the band's foundation, and built a song list. Pete M. recollects that, "Oddly, it was a time of both great discipline and reckless abandon, of both strict regimen and easy permissiveness. Still, we had a strong desire to hone our abilities as a band and to come from nowhere onto the scene as the best possible band we could be. At a time when there were some serious competitors, we buckled down and practiced diligently that summer.

"Every morning we were up early getting breakfast and talking over what we'd done the day before, what we might do that day, and getting ready to start rehearsal. By 10:00 a.m., after taking care of individual routines or chores, we began the group rehearsal. Al was usually the 'director,' and in the beginning was the only one contributing original material. John was our second-in-command, having as much musical training as, if not more than, Al. Both played keyboards and had mutually agreed that John typically would play the Hammond, while Al would play piano. Al used a Wurlitzer, which had a trademark sound generally considered to be quite hip. The Youngbloods, among others, were known for that Wurlitzer sound."

Gunnison Brook's first gig took place in the early fall of 1970 at a club in Portsmouth, NH, that became a favorite band destination. It was also the last place Gunnison Brook ever played, but more on that later.

Ladd's was a restaurant with a nightclub attached, located on the outskirts of Portsmouth near the Atlantic shore. The restaurant was open all day, and dinner was still being served when the club opened. At some point in the evening the restaurant would close and the club would shift into high gear. Ladd's was a one-floor building, and it had the typical small stage that bands were used to in clubs. There were tables up front abutting the stage, the dance floor was behind those front tables with other tables on either side of the dance floor, and the bar was at the back of the room.

Alan confirms that Ladd's was a favored venue. "We played there a lot, and developed a very large and devoted following that would fill the place even on weekdays. There was excitement in the air each night in anticipation of our first set, and the fans adored our show, especially Merrigan's strong and personable front man performance and Mario's unique, musical persona. Maybe the best part of playing there was that while the crowd loved to dance to the chart toppers we covered, they also were thrilled to listen to our original material. Our originals were not geared to dancing, rather they reflected our more intimate side. We developed many friendships with the staff at Ladd's, and with the local people, who always seemed eager to spend time with us."

One of the band's best friends at Ladd's was Grant Laber, who, according to Alan, "Was an old-schooler who knew the hospitality business, knew that his customers were 'creatures of habit,' as he often said, and knew how to accommodate them gracefully." Dan adds, "One person I remember in particular was Grant, the head bartender, who was always really nice to us."

Gunnison Brook's repertoire was eclectic and, truth to tell, some of it was downright astonishing. As Alan noted above, the band played a lot of popular dance material. Covers of The Youngbloods, The Beatles, The Stones, the Paul Butterfield Blues Band, Joe Cocker and others were well-known and well-received. Dan points out that, "We took pride in playing the covers as verbatim as possible. Pete did a great Joe Cocker!"

Then there were other, more obscure covers, like "Time to Kill" by The Band, "Peaches en Regalia" by Frank Zappa, and "Song of Job" by Seatrain (Pete M. wonders, "How many bar bands were covering that?"). Oh, and of course no one can ever forget Gunnison Brook's alter egos, Rodney Diamond and the Studs, but that side project is for another chapter. Still, of all the numbers in its repertoire, Gunnison Brook was best known for its performances of the second side of *Abbey Road*; a medley of Rolling Stones songs; and almost twenty high quality originals.

Among its many musical talents, perhaps what Gunnison Brook was best known for was its vocals. Pete Merrigan says, "We had stunning vocal capability in that five of the six of us sang. Most of us were taking lessons once a week in Boston from an Italian opera singer by the name of Dante Pavone. We heard about him from our piano player, Al MacIntosh. Al, being our de facto musical director, had recommended strongly that we all at least try a lesson or two with Dante. Most of us continued for several years with him. Dante took our already strong vocals and helped us raise them to another level."

Those vocals certainly came into play in the band's virtuoso effort on *Abbey Road*. I remember long afternoons on the stage of The Rusty Nail rehearsing with Tracks. Our band labored with the songs from *Abbey Road*, trying to master them or at least get them to the point at which we could perform them live and not embarrass ourselves. Finally, we gave up; we just didn't think they sounded good enough. But Gunnison Brook grabbed the brass ring. Both our bands played The Stones, but Gunny Brook also had the stones to do what we chose not to.

Eric Van Leuven, a Dartmouth music major who at age ten played a piano recital at Carnegie Hall, remembers hearing Gunnison Brook's rendition of *Abbey Road* on more than one occasion. "People would wait all night for that. There was lots of non-dance music on that side, but people listened all the way through. It was amazing that they could re-create some of that music, and audiences loved it."

The Rolling Stones medley; wow, I had fun mining the Gunny boys' memories on this one! I never heard the band perform their medley, but, based on a couple of medleys Tracks did, my guess is Gunnison Brook's Stones medley contained five or six songs. However, when I asked all six guys to weigh in on which Stones tunes were included, here's what I got back: "Sympathy for the Devil," "Let It Bleed," "Live with Me," "Monkey Man," "Ruby Tuesday," "You Can't Always Get What You Want," "She's a Rainbow," "Brown Sugar," "Honky Tonk Women," "Love in Vain," Jumpin' Jack Flash," and "Dead Flowers."

Huh. Some of those songs Gunnison Brook no doubt performed stand-alone, but there is no way that Stones adventure had twelve songs in it. That's what you get for asking sixty-something fellas to remember back forty years! Still, regardless of which songs were in that medley, there is no disagreement from fans or band members as to how popular it was.

Unfortunately, there was a downside to one of those Stones tunes. Mario Casella offers this commentary on "Sympathy for the Devil." "Some of the worst fights I have ever seen anywhere occurred during that song. One time we were playing a club in Rhode Island and on our first night there a terrible fight broke out during that song. It was not just a fight, it was an out-and-out brawl involving twenty people or more. Tables were thrown, a plate glass window was smashed, the club was basically destroyed. We were booked there for three nights, but after that incident the club was closed down. We lost the rest of the gig, packed up, and went back to New Hampshire."

Then there were the Gunnison Brook originals. Alan MacIntosh was the primary writer in the group, although Mario Casella contributed to an extensive catalog of original songs. The list of almost twenty songs the band played live follows: "Steppingstone;" "Old Cat Lady;" "Down On The Farm;" "Late Late Show;" "Old Dear Friend" (co-written by Glenn Jordan); "Reap What You Sow;" "Don't Tell Me Tomorrow;" "Humble Pie;" "Lonesome Me and My Dog;" Long Term Wrong Turn Blues;" "Ninety Nine Percent;" "Only At Your Convenience;" "Guiding Hand;" "Wailin';" "Can't Wait to Get Back Home;" "Took A Vacation;" "Lazy Living;" and "Marmalady."

These originals are often lilting, light and airy. Many are musically intricate, fun to listen to (even those with serious subjects), and reminiscent of a certain Liverpool duo. On live tapes from 1972 and 1973, you'll hear really solid musicianship, vocals, and songwriting. Gunnison Brook's songs are, simply, very impressive. The band's fans clearly would apply the same adjective, and cite this as one of the factors that made Gunnison Brook so popular with such a broad audience.

Eric Van Leuven recalls hearing Gunnison Brook several times. "I just couldn't believe the show and the music. With Gunnison Brook I could count on hearing fantastic music played fantastically. The music was clean, practiced, and just incredibly impressive."

Allen Atkins, a Dartmouth student and co-founder of Eleazar's in White River Junction, says, "Gunnison Brook played at Eleazar's a number of times, and they were just a very good band. You could almost measure how good a band was by the crowd size, how many people showed up. We couldn't have a great band every weekend because it cost more and it didn't fit the budget, but when we had a really good band we got hyped up for a good weekend. Gunnison Brook was one of those really good bands."

Joy Moffat praises Gunnison Brook for being "very down to earth. No song was beneath them. Almost all of them were multi-instrumentalists, they had great chemistry, and they were so tight it seemed like it was in their bones."

Like every band, Gunnison Brook has hundreds of stories from its time together. Here's one that's unusual for a rock group. It happened in the Henniker, NH, High School auditorium, where "Reap What You Sow" by Alan MacIntosh was played at graduation after being chosen as the senior class song. John Maxfield, a former science teacher at the school, was the graduation speaker, and delivered what he calls, "A very embarrassing left-wing diatribe." One parent walked out muttering, "Every chance they get." More than forty years later, John offers this opinion: "The man should have thrown a tomato."

Mario Casella tells this story straight out of The Beatles' *A Hard Day's Night*. "We were playing up north in Berlin, NH, and before the show we were out walking around the town. The promoters must have put up some posters of the band, because this group of girls passed us on the sidewalk and one of them said, 'Isn't that Gunnison Brook?'

"We kept on walking, and they turned around and started running at us. I remember Pete Merrigan and myself just being completely caught off guard by these girls running at us, and we lit out. I mean, we were actually running away from them, and it was so odd because we weren't anywhere near famous enough to deserve that sort of thing. That kind of attention, you know, pandemonium I guess you would say, maybe was typical of what you would expect to find in a very small, celebrity-starved town."

Remember John Maxfield's visit with the median strip a couple chapters back? Dan Sibley calls up a memory from that same day. "We had a gig that night at the Round House in Manchester, VT, on the western border of the state. Amazingly, none of the gear in the van was harmed, except for John's Leslie. The damage it sustained caused it to distort, so that everything John played that night sounded really ballsy, the way the organists in such bands as Procol Harum or Deep Purple sounded. I loved it!"

Finally, this wild ride from the night Gunnison Brook played a senior class dance at Stevens High School in Claremont. The band was one of the most sought-after acts on the New England circuit and, according to Pete Merrigan, "We were very full of ourselves. Like many of our rock and roll peers, we had a righteous sense of anarchy. Bottles of beer and Boone's Farm in the dressing room, a high school locker room, prior to the show? Never mind that Mario was only nineteen. So what! Hey, we're in the band!"

Approaching the end of the dance, the band launched into its Rolling Stones medley, which often closed a show. Two hundred high school seniors had stuck around for the medley. It started with "Honky Tonk Women," rose and fell through sections of "Sympathy for the Devil" and other Stones staples, and climaxed with "Jumpin' Jack Flash." Pete recalls his focus was on the fevered fans four or five deep at the edge of the stage, and on giving them his best Mick Jagger imitation.

"Just as the medley reached its climax," Pete remembers, "the janitor came up on stage, went to the breaker panel and snapped on the house lights. As he left the stage I walked over to the breaker panel and shut the lights off again. The band never stopped playing. The janitor stormed back onto the stage and once again switched the lights on. This time, as he neared the edge of the stage, I told him, 'Leave the damn lights alone,' and gave him a swift kick in the butt to help him off the stage. He glared at me and charged off in the direction of the police officers on duty out at the front of the building.

"About a minute later, across the mass of teenagers, I saw the janitor and two uniformed cops headed for the stage. I knew if I stuck around I'd be arrested, so I did what any self-respecting rock star would do. I bolted. Ran off the stage, out the rear stage door and up the street, 'Jumpin' Jack Flash' still echoing through the night air. Three of the band's girlfriends were just driving back toward the gym in my car. I flagged them down, jumped in and said, 'Don't go to the gym, head back to Goshen!' On our ride out of town we saw several cruisers, blue lights flashing and sirens blaring, heading toward the high school.

"I didn't know until later that night when the band filled me in that my good pal Ron Grace had come up on stage after I'd fled and rallied the audience into a near riot while 'Jumpin' Jack Flash' played out. Since the cops couldn't find me, they arrested him instead.

"There I was, back home at the Manor, with Ron in the slammer. I began to feel guilty, and decided it would be great fun to go bail out Ronnie dressed as my greaser band alter ego, Rodney Diamond. Had I gone as Pete Merrigan, the cops would have thrown me in the cell with Ron. With a sober driver, I returned to Claremont in full disguise and bailed Ron out with cash. There was never any question about who I was. I *was* Mr. Rodney Diamond and I was there to bail out Mr. Ron Grace. I signed the papers— 'Rodney Diamond'—and we left."

Gunnison Brook's final performance took place on April 2, 1973, at Ladd's. The band's #1 fan, Joy Moffat, was there. Members of the band Stone Cross were also there. The show was laden with original tunes penned by Alan MacIntosh and Mario Casella. The last song of the evening was scheduled to be "All Over the World" by The Youngbloods (also known as the "La La" song). "All Over the World," not coincidentally, was the very first song Gunnison Brook ever played before a live audience, also at Ladd's.

Alan MacIntosh remembers "us discussing what song to end with, and Pete Merrigan coming up with the tidy idea of going out by completing the circle. Just before we counted off Pete said, 'We're gonna finish out with the one we started here with two-and-a-half-years ago, go out like we came in.'

"But then we did an encore song, the actual final song, which was 'Ninety Nine Percent.' I don't recall if it was intentional, but if not intentional the selection of that song certainly was ironic, given that it was the last song Gunnison Brook would ever play together. 'Ninety Nine Percent' was a song I wrote about death, sung from the perspective of a corpse in a casket as the casket descends into the grave.

"To introduce the song Pete said, 'Before we end this thing, I'd like to show you all that the feelings are mutual. I'd like the band to give the audiences that we've had everywhere in the whole world a big round of applause. All right, audience! Here's a thing we wrote called 'Ninety Nine Percent.'' Then we played 'Ninety Nine Percent,' and Pete said, 'Thanks a lot.' And that was it."

Original 1972 Gunnison Brook poster by Rick Hunt

Home Is Where the Band House Is

It's 4:15 in the morning, still pitch black, even today on the summer solstice. You mumble quiet thanks to the steering wheel, the dashboard, and your band mate sleeping shotgun next to you. At least you aren't driving in the whiteout of a New England blizzard, or into a torrent of rain, or through the ubiquitous morning fog that clamps down on the back roads of New Hampshire and Vermont, including the one you are navigating.

But you also aren't driving the sort of vehicle suited for such a narrow, hilly, winding road, like the Porsche you saw in this month's *Rolling Stone*. You're driving a 1957 hearse, loaded with the band's equipment. Or maybe it's a 1969 Buick Electra with a U-Haul trailer lashed to the back, or a twelve-foot truck.

You left home at 3:00 the previous afternoon, drove two and a half hours, set up and did your sound check, then found a diner for a burger before the gig started at 9:00. 1:00 a.m., the show over, you broke down the equipment, bone-weary, after using up what you thought was every ounce of your energy during the previous four hours. 2:00 a.m., you're back on the road, with no place to stop for a bite on this return trip.

As you push on toward 4:30, you chuckle to yourself as a line from Robert Frost's poem, "The Death of the Hired Man," insinuates itself into your consciousness: "Home is the place where, when you go there, they have to take you in." The line fits your mood as you squeeze the steering wheel hard, hoping the jolt of pain will keep you awake a few more minutes.

Finally, you round the last curve, and there it is. Some mornings you stumble into the house and fall asleep the instant your head hits the pillow. Other mornings you are so tired sleep won't come. Those are the mornings you greet the sun with a cup of coffee and some weary, though usually insightful, conversation with the Sandman's other exiles. Those also are the kinds of mornings, astonishingly enough, when the band's best music has a knack for speaking to you and being written.

The band house—what a fine place to wake up early in the afternoon on a warm New England Sunday. If you don't have a gig, Sunday is your day off, so you also don't have rehearsal. What'll it be? Sit in the rocking chair on the porch and have a smoke; take a hike up the mountain, or a walk down by the creek; toss the Frisbee; romp with the dog? It's hard to go wrong with any of those options.

I never saw a band house that could be described as elegant, though some were nicer than others. Comfortable, maybe; ramshackle, quite often; and sometimes downright, aaah….

Gunnison Manor was located on Brook Road between NH Routes 10 and 103 in the township of Goshen, NH. The house had been Pete Merrigan's family home. His parents moved up from New Jersey in 1950 when Pete was six months old and bought "Skyholm," as it was called, from people who had run it as a sort of ski lodge. It was a big place, with six bedrooms, three baths, a large living room and a dining room.

Pete's mother died in 1970 and left the house to her three children. Pete and his older brother had moved out upon graduating from high school, and in the last two years of his mother's life only she and her high school-aged daughter lived in the house. The upkeep of the place began to decline, and the fact that none of the band members had a clue about home maintenance only accelerated the decline once the band moved in.

Pete Shackett says, "The Manor was open, drafty, hot in the summer, cold as ice in the winter. Toward the end of Gunnison Brook, there just were so many things wrong with the house. In the winter, the heat would go on the fritz, and snow actually used to blow into the upstairs hallway due to an end door that never got fixed. The only shower in the house was in the only bathroom in the house [two had fallen into disrepair and were "out of order"], which was down at that end of the hallway. Freakin' freezing, taking a shower and trying to stay warm.

"In some ways, our band home really sucked. But it always felt great getting back from the road to a familiar, welcoming place that, regardless of what shambles it was in, was still at least five magnitudes better than the digs you stayed at while playing a week-long gig at a distant club.

"The band house was also a sanctuary. You could write, practice, plink around just looking for a different direction, bounce ideas off other musicians, talk shop forever. Plus, at times when not many people were around it also provided a needed source of introspection and reverent silence."

Tracks had two band houses. The first sat on a side street in "downtown" Hanover. 4 South College Street was a small house, long on disadvantages and short on upkeep. Three upstairs bedrooms, one grungy little bathroom at the back of the first floor, an antiquated kitchen. The house wasn't big enough for any stretching out, particularly since we rehearsed in the living room and turned the first floor dining room into a fourth bedroom. Even after converting the dining room the house was not big enough to sleep all the band members, so Jeff Wilkes decided to turn the unfinished, unheated basement into his living quarters. This feat of architectural legerdemain was cut short by his contracting pneumonia brought on by all the cold, damp hours he spent fixing up his subterranean digs. The move to the second band house on Watkins Road, out in the country in North Hartland, VT, was greeted by all as a welcome improvement.

Tracks band house, North Hartland, VT

Ragweed rented a two-story ranch-style dwelling in the woods in rural Windsor, VT, a house built for skiers to rent in season. Dave Cross remembers that, "We sometimes woke to the bells worn by the cows belonging to the neighboring farmer, cows who seemed to enjoy escaping their pasture and wandering up the road to our house. My first cowbell, in fact, was removed from the neck of one of those cows. Do you suppose that her owner, when visiting the local Agway a few days later, was the first person to utter, 'More cowbell?'"

Peter Christenson notes that with all the band members living in the house, "the quarters were close. I wrote a song called 'Close Quarters' about our all-too-intimate living situation, and I think it was maybe the best I ever wrote. We practiced religiously every day and became very tight. There was a television in the house, though; we were there for the first season of Monday Night Football in 1970, and we used to carry on about what an asshole Howard Cosell was."

Bands also visited each other's houses. Pete Merrigan recalls a visit made to the Manor by members of Aerosmith. "Our gear was usually set up in the living room when we weren't on the road and the guys often stopped in to party and jam. One afternoon Joe and Steve stopped by and Steve played an unfinished version of 'Dream On' for us on my old, beat-up tack piano. He said something like, 'This is it...this is my hit song that's going to sell a million.' That moment was so prescient, it was akin to Babe Ruth's pointing to where he was going to hit the home run for the little boy in the hospital. He was so certain that song was going to launch their careers and make them famous. I wish now I'd paid more attention and thought to switch on the half-shoebox size cassette player with the big pushbuttons we all had."

Food played a significant role in determining how broad a comfort zone existed in a band house. Sometimes it was a positive factor, sometimes things didn't work out so well.

Ariel, a kickass band of ladies from Smith and Mount Holyoke, was the house band for the summer of 1969 at Fat City in Wilmington, VT, near Mt. Snow. The club had a "house" for its bands, although the house appeared to have been some sort of barn or outbuilding in an earlier life. One day guitarist Beverly Rogers and her boyfriend came home with what seemed like bushels of corn they had stolen out of a field. The band at first tried eating it as corn on the cob, only to discover that their bonanza was cow corn.

At that point Pamela Brandt decided to scrape most of what remained off the cob and into a pot. She added "a ton" of heavy cream and multiple sticks of butter. Pam says that "Anne Bowen had this rule that no matter how poor we were we absolutely could not use margarine, we had to use butter. So I used real butter and made a pretty decent corn chowder. To this day I make a mean corn chowder! We ended up with a big vat, and we and our boyfriends and all the other bands in the neighborhood came and ate that chowder. It was a really nice, homey experience."

On the flip side of the food ledger was the night at the first Anvil band house in Jerusalem, VT, when Peter Yanofsky led "the revolt of the meat eaters against the vegan." Brad French's girlfriend, Janet, was a committed vegetarian. She made the band grow a garden (which never sprouted anything but radishes), and she ruled the culinary roost. Every meal was a sit-down affair at the big dining room table, and it was always a lot of brown rice and vegetables.

Peter remembers that "One day we said, 'what's cooking,' and it was some ridiculous crunchy combo of things and I got so fed up I said, 'That's it.' I took off down the hill to Hinesburg to some store, I bought every bag of potato chips, beer, soda, ham and turkey to make sandwiches and all sorts of other junk food. We had just split the money from our most recent gig, and I spent my entire share on food that would make Janet just cringe. I brought it home and everybody was so happy!" Jim Goodrum recalls that "We just sat there eating chips and drinking coke and beer, and Janet was so horrified she ran upstairs and hid in her room."

Lots of bands did, or tried to do, the vegetarian thing. Here's an interesting variation. Jeff Wilkes and Dan Morgenroth were living in the Tracks band house in 1974 and, as Jeff puts it, "That was the time the whole macrobiotic thing came out, you know, eating basically beans and rice and you combine the proteins and it's all very healthful. We were both really into that in a big way. We would make ourselves beans and rice, and that was what you were supposed to eat all the time. Turned out it wasn't quite what we had in mind. So we would slice up frankfurters and put them in the beans and rice. In the midst of all this healthy organic brown rice and Azuki beans we were dropping in Oscar Meyer franks. You know, homemade Beanie Weenies."

I'll bet you didn't know this: according to the Save Vermont Barns Project the state has more than 12,000 historic barns, and loses about 100 of those barns every year. In other words, every three or four days a Vermont barn collapses in on itself. Not that they were badly built; there are just a lot of old, derelict nineteenth-century barns in the state. Remember this interesting fact in the following story, told anonymously at the request of the guilty.

One day a band was rehearsing in its band room, from which one could see out a window to the driveway. The guys had all been smoking a "bit" of pot and the air in the house was redolent of reefer. All of a sudden someone looked out the window and said, "Jesus, a state cop car just pulled into the driveway." Panic ensued—there was a lot of pot in the house, in the air, in the band members. "Holy shit, what're we gonna do?"

One of the fellas recalls that, "We all started to freak, ohmigod, everybody go grab your stash, we gotta hide everything, everything, pipes and reefer. We're all trembling, and the cop is sitting in the driveway, everybody dashing around, where do we hide it!" Then the cop pulls out and on down the driveway.

Huge sigh of relief…but only momentarily. Then somebody said, "What if he's just going to get reinforcements? They may come back with two or three cars and kick the door down. Holy shit, what're we gonna do? We gotta get rid of the stuff." So the band rounded up all the pot in the house, along with one member's extensive pipe collection: Meerschaums, Briars, some really quality pipes. There was an abandoned barn located directly across the street, and they ran the contraband across the street and buried it by the edge of the barn out of sight of the road.

They returned to the house and waited breathlessly, but the cops never returned. Turns out the state trooper just pulled into the driveway to turn around. By the time they were certain things were safe, it was dark, so they agreed to go dig it all up in the morning.

If you remember the aforementioned "interesting fact," you know where this story is going. That night the barn collapsed. Four decades hence there is disagreement as to whether the stash was ever recovered. There is unanimity that the pipe collection was never found.

In the pantheon of band house lore, nothing rivals the Gunnison Manor house party of August 1972. The band threw a summer party in 1970, 1971, and 1972. The first year was very small, and in fact the Gunnison Brook boys supplied a couple of cases of cheap wine, Boones Farm and Night Train, handing it out to the audience of maybe two dozen. The next year it was a little bigger.

Pete Merrigan says, "The third party was the one 'for the books' that everyone still talks about. We began talking about it from the stage months ahead of time and inviting people wherever we played, Newport, RI, to Burlington, VT, and all points in between. We knew we had a big party on our hands when people began showing up to camp out two days early. Maybe half a dozen came on Friday and some more on Saturday for the party on Sunday, August 6th. When the party got going, people at Mt. Sunapee's

Craftsmen's Fair told us they could hear the music there, five miles away on the other side of the mountain.

"Steven called a couple of times that morning from Boston saying Aerosmith really wanted to come play but they were trying to track down Joe Perry. Joe had been out with Judy Carne [of *Rowan & Martin's Laugh-In*] the night before. They eventually showed up sometime in the early afternoon. They were the last band to go on, right after Gunnison Brook. Daylight was fading and we had minimal lighting so the party began to break up after their set.

"By early that Sunday afternoon, we had what the papers estimated to be a crowd of five hundred to a thousand people. Cars were lined up and down both sides of the road, a couple of miles north and south of the house. We had five bands that year including American Stone; Spice; Stop, Look, and Listen; Aerosmith; and Gunnison Brook. The bands all played on our back porch, which made a natural stage as it was about four feet off the ground and ran the length of the south and east sides of the house. We faced south and most of the audience was on the lawn. In reality, they were on all sides of the house, including across the road, in the woods...everywhere!"

Rick Hunt, who had become friends with Mario Casella and did some art work for Gunnison Brook, came down from Littleton, NH, for the party. "I was upstairs sitting in Mario's room just drawing, I had my sketch book out, sitting there on the bed, and the door opens and Steven Tyler comes in. He sat down on the edge of the bed, and there was a mirror on the wall, and he was putting red glitter on his eyes. Then he started singing 'dream on' (I hadn't heard the song before) and I remember sitting there thinking, 'Yeah, that's a catchy tune.' And I was sitting there with my head cocked kind of like the RCA Victor dog and I'm like, huh, well that's kind of different, that's kind of catchy. We were just sitting there sharing the same space, didn't have a conversation, Steven just acknowledged my presence and I kept drawing. That was a Forrest Gump moment."

Gunnison Manor House Party, August 1972

Rick Davis of Davis Brothers Garage remembers the scene as Aerosmith took the stage. "Steven went up on stage first and tuned all the instruments up. Then the band came on and played a set that blew everybody away. It turned out it was most of their first album that they began recording two months later in Boston."

The Tuesday after the party the proprietors of the Goshen Country Store, located at the end of Brook Road, told the band to come by the store and gave them a case of Michelob. The store had sold out of beer and many other items the day of the party, by far the best sales day in its history. The police also stopped by the Manor and asked the band to please let them know in advance the next time it planned on throwing a party that big. Pete Merrigan agreed, but there would be no "next time." By the summer of 1973, Gunnison Brook had disbanded.

Rodney Diamond and the Studs

One of the great bands that formed in the nexus was not from New Hampshire or Vermont, it was from New Jersey. And it wasn't even a real band, but a figment of Gunnison Brook's imagination. Among the tallest tales in this saga is the genesis of the fictional group, Rodney Diamond and the Studs. 'Tis a tale best told by someone who was present at the birth, the inimitable Rodney (Pete Merrigan), himself.

* * * * *

When Dwight Aiken, the manager of Killington's Wobbly Barn, called a meeting to ask us if we would play Sundays in addition to the six nights we were already doing, we didn't know what to say. We were exhausted by the time Sunday rolled around and really counted on that day to unwind.

The club's restaurant got very busy with the après ski crowd after the lifts closed. Like clockwork we'd be awakened from afternoon siestas by the folk singer starting his solo acoustic gig there at 4:00 p.m. Now, Dwight wanted *us* to perform on the main stage at 4:00 p.m. on Sundays. On the one hand, we were flattered to be asked to play the Sunday matinee. It was great that they liked us enough to plug us into that additional spot. On the other hand, with six more weeks to play in a nine-week engagement, we worried about burning out playing seven days a week. Forty-two days in a row. No day off. Same old sets.

"What if we do something completely different?" I don't recall whose suggestion it was but we started bandying it about and before we knew it, Rodney Diamond and the Studs from Hackensack, NJ, became our alter egos. We'd have to be careful not to be too much of a Sha Na Na rip-off, but we were inspired by their energy, by the fact that what they did looked like so much fun, and especially by how the audience reacted to that kind of '50s and early '60s material.

We told Dwight we would do the seventh day if he would give us the artistic freedom to do something totally different from our regular show. We would play one set, then introduce our good friends from Hackensack and he would just have to trust us that Rodney Diamond and the Studs would be an act he would be proud to have in his club.

Dwight agreed to our plan and we began to rehearse classic oldies in earnest. Along with the song selection, character names and personalities began to emerge. Pete Shackett, whose hobby in real life was motorcycles, became Motorhead Red. Pete already had the leather jacket and acknowledged that he had escaped the path of his alter ego perhaps only due to a twist of fate. Rather than judging his fellow man, he was fond of saying "There, but for the grace of Rock 'n' Roll, go I." That phrase might be uttered as we passed a bum on the street or some uptight insurance salesman drowning his quiet desperation at a smoky lounge in a Holiday Inn. And it could have been said of Motorhead, who cussed like a sailor and swilled beer from quart bottles, but kept the boys' choppers and rods purring like kittens and played the skins like nobody's business.

John Maxfield became Eugene. His fine blond hair was easy to slick back and since it normally fell down into his face, the slicked back style revealed a visage that most had rarely seen complete. Alan MacIntosh morphed into the glowering, macho Spike; Dan Sibley became silent, strongman Herc.

Mario Casella's moniker soon became "The Duke," a natural for him after the first time we heard him belt out "Duke of Earl" with the gut and soul of a street singer in his clarion tenor. It should have come as no surprise that the female fans would melt when "The Duke" hit those high notes. They screamed like Beatles' fans—something we'd never encountered before and which was at once amusing and downright scary.

As the group's spokesman and front man, Rodney Diamond was full of all the brazen bravado and bluster that a little kid has when he's on the playground surrounded by four or five macho big brothers. I was the king of the world with these guys behind me. I knew my band could beat up your band any day of the week, on any stage in the world. With a Bud in one hand and the mic in the other I grabbed the audience by the throat and bellowed, "I'm Rodney Diamond, and these are the Studs! We're gonna rock you all night long!"

Rodney Diamond and the Studs, Sketch by Rick Hunt

We did songs like "Get a Job," "Teen Angel," "16 Candles" (another one in which "The Duke" made the young girls swoon), "Blue Suede Shoes," and "Blue Moon."

I don't remember much about that first Rodney Diamond and the Studs show, but I know that it went over better than any of us dared dream it would. I think the most amazing thing is that we all thought some of the fans, or surely the bartenders or waitresses, would recognize us. But they didn't. Not one person we saw put two and two together to realize that Rodney Diamond and the Studs were really Gunnison Brook in grease.

The most telling proof we heard, and we heard it more than once, was people wondering where we—Gunnison Brook— were! Why were we not joining our friends and the staff in welcoming and cheering on this fabulous group we'd been promoting all week? It was like Jimmy Olsen asking Lois Lane why Clark Kent wasn't here watching Superman save the day! At that point we knew the deception was total. Complete. This was fabulous. This was theater. An honest-to-God transformation into a whole other world. We were buzzing. The music was working, the disguises were working, and a whole new sub-chapter in our career began.

The change in our appearance was radical. As Gunnison Brook's hippie lead singer, I had a huge Afro, wore colorful, tight, bell bottom pants and wild silk shirts with ornate prints, frilly collars and cuffs. As Rodney Diamond, I had my hair completely greased back (with Vaseline that would take days to get out!), sunglasses, a "guinea tee" and jeans. Motorhead had a pack of cigs rolled up in his white t-shirt sleeve, James Dean style butt hanging from his lip, shades and motorcycle boots.

Naturally, the Wobbly Barn wanted us back. The damn group was more popular than Gunnison Brook! So, every Sunday, we would do the show, letting a few more of the staff members in on the ruse as we went along. But still, the crowd as a whole was clueless. They saw what they wanted to see: a bunch of tough-talking, motorcycle-riding (even in the snow, which made their biker prowess of mythic scale…no one ever bothered to ask where the bikes were!) rock 'n' roll thugs from Hackensack, NJ, who commanded the stage with a take-no-prisoners attitude and had the chops to back it all up.

Through the Vermont ski circuit hotline, the Chopping Block, near Okemo, Stowe's Rusty Nail, and Manchester's

Round House all heard about the act and wanted some of that Rodney Diamond action.

Soon, the Chopping Block welcomed Rodney Diamond and the Studs in fine fashion. The "Block," as it was called, was not quite as trendy and upscale as the Wobbly Barn. There was a little harder edge to it. It hosted a decidedly more working class clientele with a cheaper class of booze, and perhaps a little more of it, being consumed. Gunnison Brook did the obligatory opening set, then retired to the trailer next to the club to effect the metamorphosis.

The Rodney Diamond and the Studs show was considerably more raucous and the crowd seemed even more turned on by the attitude than by the music. I couldn't be sure to what degree, but I felt that unmistakable tinge of violence in the air. A heckler moved from the back of the room ever closer to the stage, taunting Rodney and, it seemed, "itchin' for a fight." As the rest of the band grew tense and looked around for a nearby bouncer, I suddenly recognized the heckler.

It was Tex, an old school mate. As we locked eyes, I knew and he knew that this could be good theater. Before I knew what had happened, we were tumbling across the dance floor putting on an impromptu show that had even the Studs fooled. We let the bouncers pull us apart. As they did, I let the one holding me know Tex was a friend of mine, to take it easy on him—not smash his face in as they were wont to do in those days—and to let him back in after they pretended to evict him from the club. Rodney took the stage once again, dusting himself off, and continued the show. (1)

* * * * *

Once the boys made their debut, the ladies quickly succumbed to the charms of these six greasers from Joisey, under whose tough exteriors beat hearts of gold. The most stunning of the young lovelies was Betty Lou, Rodney's main squeeze. It all began one evening in February 1971.

Betty Lou, aka Joy Moffat, had just arrived at the Wobbly Barn from her day job in Providence, RI, where she was feeling a bit wobbly herself and on the verge of becoming a lost soul. Her friends, who were ski enthusiasts, had decided that the perfect antidote was a ski trip to Vermont. So there was Joy, leaning on the railing of the balcony at the Wobbly, mesmerized by Gunnison Brook, a band she'd never seen. Now here was a reason to come to Killington! Second night, despite a tequila hangover, there was Joy in the balcony, with Gunnison Brook again on stage.

But during the second set, the lead singer said something about some other band coming on later in the evening. Joy thought, "I don't care about this other band, why can't they just let Gunnison Brook do the whole night?" By the time Rodney Diamond and the Studs attacked the stage at the end of the evening, Joy was leaning further out from the balcony, suspicious, indignant, and eyeballing each Stud in detail. "Who are these idiots?" Finally, she noticed a stray lock of hair peeking out from under Spike's baseball cap, and realized that Da Guys were in Dasguise!

Fast forward to The Back Room in Ogunquit, Maine, later that year. The Studs were scheduled to perform and Joy was in the audience. Gunnison Brook played a set and retreated to the cabin that served as the dressing room, where Joy helped Da Guys with their makeup. When the boys stormed the stage, makeup, duds, and Lucky Strikes in place, Joy hung back and broke open her Betty Lou transformation kit. A few minutes later, with teased hair, satin gym shorts, and white lipstick, Betty Lou emerged.

Inside The Back Room, Betty Lou squeezed through the packed crowd toward the stage. Choosing just the right moment, she leapt onstage and boogied with the boys, flashing her Betty Lou moves, sidling up to Rodney, making eyes, squealing, and creating a seismic disturbance. It took Pete a few minutes to realize Joy had earned her sweet revenge, but when the set ended he told her, "Every time we do Rodney Diamond, you can be Betty Lou, my girlfriend!"

The Studs' fame continued to grow, and in February 1972, The Rusty Nail in Stowe booked RD&S. Solo. It was the first and only time the band was hired without Gunnison Brook. Pete Shackett recalls the band couldn't stop laughing about that one for a long time: "Our alter egos had won out over reality!" Gar Anderson, The Nail's owner, remembers that legendary night and a show that was "amazing."

Being Rodney Diamond and the Studs had its perks. On the eve of that fabled performance at The Nail, Shackett remembers "pulling up to The Rusty Nail in costume and already in character. Pete and Mario and I were walking in when I saw this cherry '56 Ford parked right in front of the door. Bein' Motorhead, I popped open the hood to have a look-see at the block. We were all doin' the Joisey accents and commenting on the cool rod when out comes the owner. 'Hey! Who are you guys and what are you doing with my car?' So's we explain to him that we *are* Rodney Diamond and the Studs an' we like his wheels. We all start laughing and the guy says, 'Ya wanna ride?' Oh, yeah! So off we went with us and some women he knew all in the back seat, drinking beer, laughing, cursing, flying at a hundred miles an hour up the road. Crazy! We got back just in time to get up on stage and sing some little ditties, ya know what I mean!"

Rodney Diamond and the Studs played only a handful of gigs over a relatively short period of time. Nevertheless, like a shooting star on a clear summer evening, their presence was so transfixing that they are firmly ensconced in the rock and roll lore of that era.

Then The Muse Tapped Me
on the Shoulder

One of the most well-known and beloved of American poems is Robert Frost's "Stopping by Woods on a Snowy Evening." Some would say the manner in which the poem came to be written one early morning in 1922 in Sugar Hill, New Hampshire, was accidental. Others would say the adjective "accidental" belies one of the mysteries of life, at least the life of the writer, namely that the poem was there all the time, waiting for the right moment to reveal itself.

The story goes that on that long ago spring morning Frost had written all night, completing a long, satiric poem titled "New Hampshire," one of those rare instances where text seems to write itself. Frost pressed on page after page, until the poem had finished speaking to him. As the poem fell silent he looked up, to notice the first light of dawn outside his window.

Exhausted, he got up to make coffee, and opened the door to watch the dawn arrive. As he heard the birds awakening, Frost sensed a new companion. Images from the past and a new stream of words played in his head. Feverishly writing and revising, struggling with rhyme and meter, eventually he found the final promise of the poem and completed the collaboration, tired beyond measure but elated, the sun just coming up. (1)

Quite often it is so with the best writing. Our most powerful stuff announces itself when we least expect it.

In the fall of 1969, in the Tracks band house, Russell Pinkston slumped on his bedroom couch, smoking away at 2:00 in the morning, struggling with an idea.

"I remember being pretty blue, obviously. 'Lethargy' is a pretty bleak song. You just read the lyrics and you can tell where I was in my mind. I was frustrated, I wasn't happy with the music I was trying to write, so I wrote about that.

Russell Pinkston, 1969

"The song starts out like kind of a blue-ish thing, the guitar could be a blues riff. Then it really takes off and becomes this long instrumental. I always thought that was the best part of 'Lethargy,' how it evolves, from this very simple song, and becomes one of the more complicated arrangements we ever did."

Ken Aldrich's vocals masterfully portray the mood Russell means to convey. Ned Berndt's rim shot, like a clock ticking off the seconds, evokes dark despair. Then the song accelerates through time changes, 3/4 to 5/4 to 4/4, ending in a soaring, joyous organ solo. Russell remembers "writing that thing and thinking it was very Bach-like and wanting it to be very Bach-like.

"I think 'Pawnbroker' and 'Marnie' are the best tunes I ever wrote, and I remember vividly both the process of writing them and the circumstances. Tracks was living in the Hartland farm house, where we had a wonderful Steinway grand piano in the living room. From the time we got that piano, which we rented from a local music store for $25 a month, I wrote most of my songs on it, rather than on the guitar. I wrote both 'Marnie' and 'Pawnbroker' on that piano, and both about Margot Booth, then my girlfriend and now my wife of thirty-five years. I wrote 'Marnie' during a time when our relationship was getting pretty shaky, and 'Pawnbroker' shortly after she broke up with me and went home to New York. We got back together a few months later, but I still remember how awful I felt during that time. One of the things that helped me deal with how I felt was writing songs. Those two or three months were by far the most productive and creative period I had ever experienced."

While composing and arranging songs like "Lethargy," "Pawnbroker," and "Marnie" required effort commensurate with the gravity and complexity of the songs, the birth of other Pinkston originals required substantially less work.

A Mexican Bird is a mixed drink created, perhaps apocryphally, by Joel Baden, the owner of The Silver Keg in Burlington, VT. According to the Tracks CD liner notes, the drink is "equal parts tequila and Wild Turkey, best chugged while holding nose." Jeez, just give me a cold beer!

"I wrote 'Mexican Bird' in about 45 minutes," Russell estimates. "We were at the Silver Keg and I used to like the bartenders and waitresses there, we all got along really well, and we played there a lot. They would sometimes make new drinks that I hadn't heard of, and one night they gave me this thing called a Mexican Bird and I liked it. I think I wrote the song the next morning. I just whipped it together and we put it on the very next night, sort of jammed to it and then refined it as we went along."

"Mexican Bird" is a fun song, with a funky Hammond solo by Ken Aldrich, and clever lyrics. At the same time, as the first song Tracks played each night, the tune served notice to an audience that while Tracks hoped to please the audience, the band also intended to play songs it wanted to play. Russell wrote, "I'll try to sing your songs, if you let me sing mine. 'Cause I dig our music, on it I stand, with a Mexican Bird in my hand!"

Alan MacIntosh, the primary songwriter for Gunnison Brook, waxes lyrical about the inspirations for a number of his original compositions. "I didn't bring any songs with me when I came to Gunnison Manor in 1970. I'd created a few meaningless tunes prior to that when I buddied up with Glenn Jordan, who infected me with the songwriting virus. But I had no reason to believe that Gunnison Brook would incubate a number of tunes that would be requested, and yearned for, and applauded over thirty-five years later at a band reunion.

"The first one came from a fall image outside Pete Merrigan's house, one sunny afternoon when the maple leaves swirled and eddied around the house. I imagined an old woman, nearly deaf, and nearly blind, rocking on a rocker on an imaginary porch, with her hand on the cat on her lap. And when the wind blew, and the leaves rustled, the cat lifted its head, and tensed its back muscles, and the old woman would feel it and know there was an autumn sound.

"I remember an old upright in the Manor where I sat and rocked the piano and fabricated the chords and melody and verses to 'Old Cat Lady.' I was surprised, and excited.

Mostly I was surprised, and not one bit sure that this was a song worth showing the guys. But I was curious. Was this excitement just my own vanity, or was there really something powerful hiding in 'Old Cat Lady?' So I timidly auditioned it.

"Some of the songs came from the psyche. I appealed for help to a passerby for insight into utter abandonment in 'Hey Mister.' And I decided that one of those darned girls was just using me in 'Steppingstone.'

"Each band member came up with his own part. I don't recall having any sense of what they should play, except at times the bass line. But I did have a sense of arrangement, again from an image. You get the groove going, you tell the story, let the audience think about it while the guitar player makes his comments, then get back to the story and explain it from a different angle, or add a chapter, then repeat yourself so that everyone knows that The End Is Near, then you stop.

"It never occurred to me when I wrote 'Ninety Nine Percent' that our dance-crazy crowd of fans might not warm to a song about death. The corpse, facing skyward, sings the song to earthward-looking mourners as the casket descends into the grave. It also never occurred to me that perhaps the other guys had better things to do than breathe life into my innermost thoughts. But they did breathe life into them, and they breathed life into me.

"I wrote about the girls in my life—that long lonely feeling after you break up is 'Late Late Show.' And consideration for her feelings is 'Only At Your Convenience.' 'Long Term Wrong Turn Blues' sprang from a bartender friend of ours who was just discovering who he really was at forty-five. 'Marmalady' had to be about my ideal waitress. But always, the songs I wrote were part of the fabric of life that six young men lived in Gunnison Brook. That band surrounded me with a vehicle for songwriting."

Every band worked out unique arrangements for certain tunes. Two of the bands best known for innovative jams and extended solos were Ragweed and Anvil. Dave Cross of Dream Engine and Ragweed, and Brad French of Anvil explain how the process worked.

"One of the most exciting things to me about Dream Engine was that we would have these completely unscripted jams, where someone would just start playing something. I would do a beat or John Maxfield a chord progression or Andy Raymond a bass line and we would just play. More often than not it ended up sounding like it had all been orchestrated. It was very jazz-like—infrequently it became a complete train wreck, but not usually.

"When we became Ragweed, Peter Christensen was our primary songwriter, and our songwriting process was, I think, fairly typical for most bands. Peter would play us a skeletal arrangement of a song on a guitar, and then we'd all contribute ideas over the course of several days until something emerged that was acceptable to all of us."

"In Anvil," Brad notes, "what we did was different from cover bands. We would take a song and we would put our own musical thumbprint on it. When we did the song it was with our arranging and it would certainly be recognizable to an audience, but unlike other bands that tried to sound exactly like the record we would do things our own way. We would start with the core of the song, but after getting a pretty good general idea of the song we took off down our own road, and the song ended up with our own stamp on it."

Tracks was also known for its sometimes unusual arrangements of other bands' material. We spent long hours on "All Along the Watchtower," "Medicated Goo," and other songs. Still, at times all that hard work backfired, as was the case one night in Burlington, VT, with "Street Fighting Man." The Rolling Stones tune off the *Beggars Banquet* album had drawn rave reviews, notably from other musicians, as one of Tracks' most popular covers. We put a lot of work into it, we were damn proud of it, and the organ and guitar solos by Ken and Russell were killer! Our version didn't sound much like the original, except for the lyrics and chord structure. And at eight minutes it was considerably longer than The Stones' 3:09 album version.

Sometime after I left the band, in 1973 or 1974, Tracks was playing a week-long gig at the Silver Keg. One evening, Angelo Mullen from Davis Brothers Garage and Steve Hirsch from Better Days and Company were in the audience. (Interestingly, neither gent was aware of the other's presence until a Facebook conversation in 2010.)

Angelo: "I remember some English guy took offense and starting bitching out the band 'cause they didn't play it like the record! Ha!" Steve: "Wow, man! I cannot believe you were there that night! It was this weird guy 'Abod' (Jordanian, I believe) that played guitar with a band called 'Razz.' They had done a gig the night before with us at Norwich University and blew up a bass amp. I offered to fix it, so they came to Burlington the next day. After I got the amp going, we went out to the Keg for brewskis. The bass player and I tackled him and dragged him out immediately following that incident."

Who would have thought that a genuine effort to be creative and unique would meet with such serious disapproval from a fellow musician. Kinda makes you think of the George Romero "*Dead*" movies.

An Italian Opera Singer

I could tell you about the time John and Paul came knocking at his row house on Boston's Commonwealth Avenue, asking to be his pupils for the day. I could tell you about Mick Jagger, Aretha Franklin, Grace Slick, James Taylor, and other superstars who flocked to Dante Pavone.

Instead, I will tell you about an extraordinary teacher who did what all great teachers do. He made his pupils, both famous and unknown, much better at their craft.

Dante Pavone was born just north of Torino, Italy, in 1910. When he was a little boy his mother took him to the opera in his home town, and he was "completely transported by the experience, deciding there and then music was to be his life." (1) He earned a doctorate in vocal therapy and vocal pathology from the Milan Conservatory, and began singing opera in his native country. After switching to pop and jazz, he toured South America and Cuba, singing Latin jazz. (2) Dante told me one day during a lesson that he had left his homeland to escape the oppression of the Mussolini regime.

Dante settled in New York City in the 1940s, singing pop and jazz in clubs with the likes of legendary blues chanteuse Billie Holiday. He once wistfully recalled, "She loved the way I sang her songs," but seemed puzzled as to why. It was in New York in the 1940s that Dante first began teaching voice. After he moved to Boston in the late 1950s he taught for almost 40 years, until his death in 1997. (3)

How we learned of Dante no one seems to remember. The boys in Tracks can't recollect. Pete Merrigan from Gunnison Brook says, "We heard about him from our piano player, Al MacIntosh. I'm not sure where Al heard about him; perhaps from one of the other bands on the circuit or a Dartmouth connection." One thing is certain. The grapevine was thick regarding his teaching genius. Dante never advertised, because word of mouth among aspiring singers provided him a constant stream of students.

Dante's typical response when celebrities showed up, asking for lessons on the spot, was not to see them. His reasoning was that we, his regular students, came first, and he would not miss a scheduled lesson regardless of who the unannounced visitor was. This philosophy was one of the things that endeared him to us.

Another compelling facet of this master teacher that hooked Tracks from our earliest lessons was his complete control of an astounding voice as he demonstrated what he wanted you to do. Once you heard him sing you said to yourself, "Man, I have to learn everything this guy has to teach me." Dante once said that "If a fire hydrant had a brain cell, I could teach it to sing." (4) Well, we in Tracks may have had only a few more brain cells than a fire hydrant, but it very quickly became obvious that the man was a magician. When he said, "If you do 'A' then 'B' will happen, trust me, you will see," we trusted him, and the results came quickly.

So, we made our weekly pilgrimages from New Hampshire to Boston, or in the summers to Old Orchard Beach, Maine, to sit individually at the foot of the master. Each destination was a trip in itself. Dante's brownstone on Comm. Ave., filled with objets d'art, curios and other treasures, and with its heavy, dark wood paneling, reminded Gunnison Brook's Pete Shackett of the apartment in *Rosemary's Baby*. Weather permitting, Dante's summer home afforded a quick taste of salt air and sand at the beach.

Tracks studied with Dante for several years, as did other bands, including Stone Cross. After accepting the wisdom of

Alan MacIntosh's recommendation, most of the Gunnison Brook lads as well trekked weekly from New Hampshire to Dante's doorstep. One of the side benefits of our regular trips was that we got to check out the "big city" and see how urban cats lived.

That Dante was gay was openly acknowledged by the man himself and his students. But it was never an issue, even when he suggested to his male students, as he once did to me with a twinkle in his eye, that maybe our fences should swing the other way. I know that most of his male pupils, at one time or another, heard this signature line: "Everyone is bi-sexual, Bebe!"

It was never an issue because Dante's results were clear. He saved my life as a rock and roll singer. I was a natural baritone, not quite the register for rock singing, and I always lost my voice after a night or two; not to mention the terrible strain I put on my throat and vocal cords. Dante fixed me up so that I could go six or seven nights in a row. Pete Shackett notes that, "Regardless of his orientation, the method simply worked. My voice was five octaves for a while." And Pete Merrigan says, "He saved, and continues to save, my voice. People are amazed that I can sing seven, eight shows a week and not get hoarse. When I was working The [British Virgin] Islands, circa 2000, I did one stint of twenty-seven nights in a row and wasn't hoarse in the least."

Dante's method revolved around developing one's chest and rib muscles, singing from the diaphragm, breath control, and posture. He used to say that anyone could learn to sing, if they built their muscles, paid attention to posture, and understood the breathing process. We learned to sing from our diaphragms, not from our throats, but it wasn't easy. There was no magic bullet to the Pavone method, no slick "Eat anything you want and still lose weight" hype. I remember spending over an hour a day doing the physical exercises Dante assigned us, and another hour doing the assigned scales and vocal exercises.

Pete Shackett offers this clinical dissection of the Pavone method. "Dante's objective was to double the amount of usable air in your lungs by getting the muscles in the ribs stronger at pulling out and the diaphragm stronger to pull down. This created a larger space in the chest cavity for the lungs to expand, thus giving the singer more air. Plus, improved muscle strength around the lungs allowed for better control of the intake and release of air through the windpipe. With strong chest wall muscles and diaphragm, you could relax the vocal cords and allow the muscles to control release. A simple concept, really, and it succeeded if you worked hard enough to strengthen the rib cage muscle tissue and diaphragm. The idea was to take all the pressure off the vocal cords and pass air through as you saw fit."

Shackett had a colorful name for one of the most demanding of the Dante exercises. He called it "the grueling -------." After the adjective "grueling," Pete inserted the plural noun that Rahm Emmanuel typically inserts after the word "mother," and we are not talking about Mother's Day.

As I write this paragraph I stand up from my desk and do ten repetitions of one of those physical exercises. Was it this much work back when I was twenty-four? Yeah, it was!

Earlier, I referred to Dante as a magician. Never was that characteristic more apparent than in his teaching demonstration with an upright piano and a couch. Dante would seat you at his piano, then cross the room behind you to the couch on the opposite wall. He would say, "I am going to lie across the back of the couch. I want you to play an A above middle C, and I will sing the note. Keeping your back turned to me, tell me when I have rolled off the back of the couch."

You struck the note, and he sang it—pitch perfect, crystal clear. Your senses were fully engaged as you listened with all your might. You could hear vestiges of the piano in the note he was singing. You strained to hear the sound of him rolling onto the seat cushion, or the slightest tremolo in his voice caused by the impact of body meeting leather.

Then you were jumping out of your skin, because he had just tapped you on the shoulder! Dante had rolled off the couch without the slightest sound, his note never faltering. He had sat up, then stood, then walked stealthily across the room, his voice wavering not one iota. He had modulated his voice so that his volume was the same when he was two feet behind you as it had been when he was across the room. Holy shit, how did the man do that!

This is the best example of Dante's Merlinesque qualities, of why we entrusted our voices to him. If he said it, we believed it, believed it would work. And it did.

Yet even the greatest teacher occasionally misses the mark. So it was with Dante and Steven Tyler.

Pete Merrigan and Mario Casella brought Steven to see Dante, and thus were present for his one and only lesson with the Italian master. The lesson ended prematurely as the two of them began yelling at each other—loudly enough that things got uncomfortable for Pete and Mario in the adjacent waiting room.

Steven burst from behind the closed door of the music room, stormed out of the building, and down the entry stairs. Dante followed, shaking his finger. He said to the stunned boys from Gunnison Brook, "Mark my words, Bebies, in three years that boy will have no voice left at all!"

Let's see, Aerosmith has released thirty-four albums since 1973, with total sales of how many million copies?

Hard Times on the Road

Well you walk into a restaurant,
strung out from the road.
And you feel the eyes upon you
as you're shaking off the cold.
You pretend it doesn't bother you,
but you just want to explode.
Most times you can't hear 'em talk,
other times you can.
All the same old clichés,
"Is that a woman or a man?"
And you always seem outnumbered,
you don't dare make a stand. (1)

— "Turn the Page," Bob Seger

In my judgment there is no other song that conveys the downside of the rock musician's life on the road as perfectly as this Bob Seger classic from 1973. Anyone who played in a rock band in the late '60s or early '70s can certainly recall his or her own moments that parallel the sentiments expressed in the second verse of "Turn the Page." When you arrived back home in the early morning hours after a long road trip you could count your blessings if some school of sharks in lumberjack shirts hadn't harassed you for your hair, or your clothes, or what you stood for...or for just existing on the planet.

The threat of danger, of physical violence, lurked everywhere, around every corner. We wanted to dismiss it, so we intellectualized it, or tried to. "These guys don't really

161

hate us. They don't really want to do us harm just because of how we look." But, oh yeah, the threat was real, it was palpable, so instead of dismissing it we usually were wary. Sometimes, however, even our circumspection didn't suffice.

One evening Tracks was returning from a gig and stopped in White River Junction for a bite to eat at The William Talley House restaurant, one of our favorite spots for an early breakfast. We knew that any late night stop was risky, but at 3:30 in the morning hunger often trumps reason. And the Talley House scrambled eggs, bacon, and toast went down easily and inexpensively. That night, however, a bunch of locals were at the restaurant, and they had been drinking.

As we walked in it started: the guffaws about long hair, and multiple remarks concerning whether we were "girls or boys?" We were standing in line near the counter, waiting to place our order, when one of the guys at the counter said, "Let's check." He got up, stood behind Russell Pinkston, reached through his legs and latched onto him.

That attempted heist of the family jewels touched off a bit of a fracas, as one might imagine. The exact extent of the fracas is a tad hazy after forty years. One of the fellas remembers a police officer who happened to be in the restaurant and stepped in to cool things off when they turned physical. Another band member recalls something about a body hurtling through the plate glass window that separated the Talley House from the Vermont Transit Line ticket office that was in the same building. Regardless of how things finally went down, I still categorize that incident as just another night at the office.

Ragweed played a gig at the Crescent Beach Motor Inn in Mascoma Lake, NH, during the summer of 1970. At that performance, says Dave Cross, "A very large man with a very large beard in classic woodsman attire—red and black checked woolen shirt, heavy denim pants, hunting boots, the whole nine yards—requested, in a very large voice, that we play 'Wipe Out.' I responded that I, the effete artiste percussionist, no longer played such pedestrian drivel, or something to that effect. Mr. Bunyan then shoved a substantial amount of cash, either a twenty- or fifty-dollar bill, into my puny hand and snarled, in an *extremely* large voice, 'You do now, you little shit!' I've never turned down a request for 'Wipe Out' since, but neither have I had cash shoved at me to do it. I should start refusing again!"

Pete Shackett recalls a gig in Plattsburgh, NY, when he was drumming for Better Days and Company. The band was at "some grimy little dive" near the Air Force base.

"I was on break, sitting by myself way in the back, and there weren't many people in the club at that point. Three rednecks started yelling at me from the bar about my stage 'get-up' and hair. These guys were obviously military, close cropped haircuts, starved for entertainment, and drunk. I didn't respond when they hooted at me, but finally one of them said, 'Come up here and tell this guy you ain't a faggot!' That one got the best of me so I stood up, walked up to the bar right next to them and ordered a longneck Bud. I grabbed the neck with my hand flipped upside down so that I could slam the bottle into the guy's face if needed. I took a very long pull from it with my eyes turned sideways toward these drunken idiots. The bottle was still ready to be used.

"Then one guy holding on to his drunken buddy said, 'Hey man, he's going into the service tomorrow...he didn't mean nothin' by it.' I nodded, turned the bottle back around in my hand and walked back up to the stage not saying a word.

"Those young guys could have kicked the living crap out of me, but somehow I called their bluff. Afterwards the whole scene scared the hell out of me! But they left, we played and finished out that week. What a nasty gig, but we got paid...good enough."

Steve Hirsch has another bad memory from his days playing guitar for Better Days and Company. "I had a car full of rednecks chase me all the way from Rutland, VT, to the Chopping Block in Proctorsville. I used to drive down Route 7 to Rutland from Burlington and then go a little south of Rutland to turn east on Route 103. That night a bunch of yahoos started tailgating me right about where 7 and 103 meet. I had really long hair at that time, which no doubt triggered their behavior. Don't forget that Route 103 is this narrow little two-lane road. Anyway, they kept sidling up beside me, trying to pass me, that sort of thing. My life really flashed before my eyes, but fortunately I had an Opal Manta with heavy shocks and suspension on it that could really handle. So I just put my foot down the whole way to Proctorsville and they peeled off when we got to the Block and they saw I had reinforcements in the parking lot."

During the summer of 1969 Tracks had a summer-long gig at The Purple Hat, a nightclub on Cape Cod in West Harwich, MA. For the duration of the summer we lived adjacent to the club in a two-story house that, putting it politely, should have been condemned. We shared the house with members of Ultimate Spinach, a Boston-based band of some renown. We slept on the second floor, they on the first, and we shared the first floor kitchen, a dreadful bathroom on the second floor, and an outside shower on the back porch. Kinda gives me the "willies" thinking back on it, but what did we know. We were young and living the dream.

That nasty brown house was where we first met Jeff "Skunk" Baxter, who played guitar for the Spinach, later was the founding guitarist for Steely Dan, and then wielded his axe for the Doobie Brothers. Skunk would show up at a Tracks recording session in Boston about a year later with, ah, interesting results, but that's another story.

One day Nigel Earthworm II, the Ultimate Spinach's bassist, was mowing the yard in front of that sorry house—for what reason I have no earthly idea. Nigel was spindly, freaky looking, and had very long hair. A couple of Cape rednecks pulled over in their car and began harassing Nigel. All at once Spinach leader Ian Bruce-Douglas burst out of the front door of the house screaming like a madman, and went raging across the front lawn brandishing a table leg over his head like a war club, bent on confronting "the enemy."

As I watched the scene unfold I wasn't at all surprised to see the two strangers hop in their car and haul ass down Route 28. Think back to Bob Seger's lyrics. Ian took a stand that afternoon. And I thought, "For once, the good guys win."

In February 1970 Tracks was in Boston for a two-week gig at The Improper Bostonian. We were staying in Newton, MA, west of the city, at the very nice suburban home of Daddy Warbux, a group that had made some national noise. Warbux had rented the house to us for the two weeks while they were on the road.

At the end of our initial Saturday night show, 2:00 a.m., we asked the manager of the club where we might go to get some late night chow and not get hassled, our instinct for self-preservation having been finely honed. He suggested a restaurant out in Cleveland Circle, to which he had directed bands in the past.

Sometime around 2:45 a.m. that night we walked into the restaurant, which was virtually deserted. We were greeted by two businessmen in suits who were sitting on the front door side of a horseshoe-shaped counter. One squinted at us over his shoulder and said to the other, "Hey, look what just walked in. The scum of the earth." Our vast experience in such situations had conditioned us not to respond, so we continued on to the other side of the counter. For the next twenty minutes the two "gentlemen," who were clearly skunk as drunks, kept up a running commentary about our various defects and those of our ancestors.

F-i-n-a-l-l-y they left, at which point the counterman apologized to us. We assured him we appreciated his position, but it clearly wasn't his fault. About ten minutes later we paid our bill, said goodnight, and walked out.

Outside the restaurant, we crossed the sidewalk to the street. Stepping off the curb, we heard a roar from down the street to our left. A Cadillac squealed out of the darkness, its occupants literally trying to run us down. We had to jump back up on the sidewalk to avoid being roadkill. The suits had been waiting in their car, the lights off and the motor running, since they had left the restaurant ten minutes earlier.

There was one humorous upside to what was a frightening incident. For a long time afterwards, we frequently referred to each other using the suits' derisive epithet, as in: "Hey, scum of the earth, it's time to rehearse."

Being in a rock band was a lot of fun, but it wasn't all fun and games. Sometimes people could be downright stupid, and scary as well. I hope this chapter might prompt the reader to consider that, four decades later, we still have not divested ourselves of our prejudices. And many of those prejudices are rooted in issues much more significant than long hair or funky clothes. Skin color, ethnicity, religion, sexual orientation...people still can be stupid, as well as downright scary.

"Hey Leadah..."

On Saturday, February 27, 1971, Tracks was playing DU fraternity at Middlebury College in Vermont. It was a cold, very snowy evening as we hauled our equipment through the front door and set up in the living room.

Near the end of the first set, a young lady sitting on a heat register at the back of the room piped up in a Joisey or Lawnguyland accent. In a voice that rang out over the hum between songs, she demanded, "Hey Leadah, do youse play Magic Cawpet Roide?"

Big smiles all around. Yep, we played the Steppenwolf hit. It wasn't on our first set list, but we "changed on the fly" and launched into it. The young lady had given us a gift.

In the days that followed, the boys in the band took to calling me "Leadah" at every turn. The first few efforts by sound man Jeff Wilkes, with an impish grin on his face, set the tone. The moniker took, and that moment in Middlebury became a durable part of Tracks lore. To this day, if I get an email or a phone call from one of the band members, I often read or hear the salutation, "Hey, Leadah."

1968 was a momentous year in many ways: the Tet Offensive, the assassinations of Martin Luther King and Bobby Kennedy, the Democratic Convention in Chicago ("The whole world is watching!"). 1968 was also a big year for me. I joined my first rock band in January. In June I graduated from college—in the bottom quarter of my class. I hitchhiked home to Minnesota in July and flunked my draft physical, thus avoiding the jungles of Southeast Asia. In the fall I returned to Hanover, and Tracks formed.

Tracks began as a cover band, like most others, but it quickly became apparent that our progression as a band was not going to be 1-4-5 for long. Early on it was evident in arrangements of songs like Traffic's "Medicated Goo" and Dylan's "All Along the Watchtower" that this was a band destined to soar musically. We continued to demonstrate our creative chops in other unique arrangements, such as "Street Fighting Man" by The Stones, a medley of seven tunes by Sly and the Family Stone, and a Santana-esque turn on the John Lee Hooker classic, "Daddy Was a Jockey."

Most Tracks fans will be surprised by a list of the band's original personnel from September 1968. Of the stalwart "big three" who were the heart of Tracks for six years, only guitarist Russell Pinkston was a founding member. Steve Calvert (keyboard, guitar) and Peter Logan (drums) from the Night Watchmen, and Dom "Pooch" Puccio (bass) and yours truly (lead vocal) from Ham Sandwich, filled out the lineup.

Steve headed off to Naval OCS in October, replaced on keyboards by stalwart #2, Ken Aldrich. In November, Jeff Wilkes replaced Pooch on bass, though Pooch would return for a second stint in 1970-71. By December 1968, Ned Berndt (stalwart #3) had signed on as drummer, and the core of the band had formed. Skip Truman joined up as co-front man for about eight months, but then was drafted and inducted in December 1969. Skip would return to Tracks in 1972, the third in the band's string of four bass players.

From its inception, Tracks focused on vocals, because every iteration of the band featured at least three talented singers. Thus, the heavy emphasis on harmonies in many of the group's popular songs, notably "Eli's Comin';" "Suite: Judy Blue Eyes;" "Medicated Goo," with its barbershop quartet beginning and ending; and our version of "All Along the Watchtower" with its four-part vocal arrangement. A number of Russell's originals also featured three- and four-part harmonies. Like many other observers, the thing that Pamela Brandt of Ariel remembers most about the band is that "The harmonies were so good."

Tracks gained a strong following by covering the popular acts of the day: Cream, Hendrix, Jeff Beck, Spencer Davis, The Stones, Steve Miller, Traffic, and The Band. But from the very beginning Russell and Ken were writing original songs. Eighteen months after the band formed, armed with six Pinkston and two Aldrich originals that we had been performing live for more than six months, Tracks headed into the studio with Wayne Wadhams. Those February 4 and 5, 1970, sessions at Petrucci and Atwell on Newbury Street in Boston yielded a demo tape that included three originals and "Watchtower." On March 10th Russell and I flew to New York for an appointment with a CBS producer. Sad to say, the most memorable part of that meeting was that he broke our tape in his player after listening for only a few minutes. We were horrified, but by then he seemed uninterested. He gave the tape a very perfunctory listen, as if he couldn't wait to get us out of the office.

The February 1970 recording sessions were also when Jeff "Skunk" Baxter paid us a visit. I must confess that for decades, every time I listened to the studio version of "Watchtower," I couldn't understand why the cut was so sloppy, especially Kenny's organ playing. Ken has since reminded me why. "For one thing, I was using the organ that was in the studio and its Leslie switch was severely delayed. Also, that was the session at which Jeff Baxter showed up with some dope and we got stoned. I lost my musical discipline and was worried that I wouldn't play well, but I didn't get high enough not to worry." Mystery solved!

Between 1970 and 1974, over the course of eight different studio sessions, Tracks recorded more than two dozen original songs, a pretty decent catalog for a band that never signed a recording contract with a major label.

They say you should never read or believe your press clippings. Peer reviews, on the other hand, seem safe.

Pete Shackett says, "Who do you think most every band member in the circuit that I knew revered and would go out of their way to see when they wanted to listen to a musically excellent band? Tracks, of course, the eclectic and quintessential group of talented, dedicated musicians whose music was always a cut above. Everyone had a great respect for what your band was doing."

Alan MacIntosh: "We looked at Tracks as the 'Advanced State of the Art.' I remember the times we took in Tracks, talking with the guys. They were outside my musical comprehension; all I knew was, they were talking a musical language that stood apart. Their music was stimulating."

Eric Van Leuven offers that "I was a music major and played in rock bands my whole life. It was so great to hear a band that was serious about its music. Tracks had a dilemma because they had to play all the clubs and frats, but they also got into some really progressive music, 'Isengard' [a Pinkston original] for example. They did a great job of mixing dance stuff with what they really liked. Tracks did 'Roundabout' better than any group I have ever heard, and not just anybody could do songs by Yes. They were musicians' musicians."

Tracks had many musical influences, including a group out of Burlington, VT, named Lime Cirrus. The band offered a superlative combination of musical tightness, personified by stone-faced Brian Bull behind his Hammond, Jim Lawler, the master of steady on the drums, and John Boncaddo on bass; and joyous showmanship, in the persons of dual lead singers Lee Diamond and Brad Sumner, and guitarist Ralph

Loconto from "Woostahmass." Ralph's trademark comment, applied universally, was "Wicked cool!"

Ken recalls that "They were careful to keep the sound level moderated and they were unbelievably tight." Lime Cirrus sported great musicians and great showmanship, they were professional to the nines, and they were the only band I ever heard that did live fades and made them work. They tended to kick-start their sets with rollicking numbers like "Can't Get Enough of It" by Spencer Davis or catchy tunes like "It's Alright" by JJ Jackson. Lee and Brad sent sparks flying with duets such as "Ain't No Mountain High Enough." In addition to lifting "Can't Get Enough" from them, Tracks' elders believe that Lime Cirrus is where we picked up our slowed-down version of "Gimme Some Lovin'."

Beginning in June 1969, Tracks had a summer-long gig on Cape Cod, at a West Harwich, MA, club, The Purple Hat. It was a splendid opportunity for a band only eight months old to hone its act and its skills. We played six nights a week, and had the club to ourselves to practice every day…when we weren't sitting on the amazing beach facing the Atlantic Ocean. On that beach one afternoon, Russell recalls, Skip got a nasty sunburn.

Skip's memories of that summer gig include "Playing on the stage, and the show that we had fallen into. Russell was a bit frustrated because he was really into writing originals and he was trying to push the show back, but I really enjoyed being an entertainer. The Purple Hat is where we developed the Sly Medley, which worked so well with us as co-front men."

Another image from that summer is Ken's broken nose. One night in The Purple Hat's parking lot he tried to play peacemaker and prevent a fight between two patrons. When he stepped between the two he got sucker-punched by the brother of one of the pugilists. I remember the visit to the emergency room, the wince-inducing pair of stainless steel cylinders the doc forced up into Kenny's nostrils to straighten his twisted proboscis, and my thinking, "Jeez, Ken's a lot tougher than I am!" (1)

I also have a crystal clear picture in my mind of afternoons practicing on the club's stage, trying to perfect "Wooden Ships" by Crosby, Stills and Nash. After many long hours we finally decided we couldn't duplicate the studio sound of that tune live. Besides, it wasn't much of a dance song (duh!). We never did perform "Wooden Ships" live.

Tracks in the Spring of 1969. Clockwise from bottom right: Jeff Wilkes, Ned Berndt, Ken Aldrich, Skip Truman, Peter Wonson, Russell Pinkston

And then there was this little music festival in August. We had talked the club owner into giving us that weekend off to travel to Woodstock. He booked a replacement band for Friday and Saturday nights (the club was closed on Sundays), but he sternly stipulated that we *had* to be back by Monday. We thought about that part, and after some earnest conversation decided we really needed the gig for the rest of the summer and didn't want to chance returning late. Grudgingly, we opted out of the trip to Max Yasgur's farm. If you're wondering about the iconic photo of Skip dancing on stage with Sly Stone during "Higher," I had that photoshopped in 1999.

In retrospect it was fortunate that we made the decision to skip Woodstock, because sometime after 1:00 a.m. on Monday, August 11, thieves broke into the club and lifted about $3,000 of our equipment, including, as Jeff recalls, "Russell's irreplaceable Gibson ES-335, my Jazz Bass, and some nice amps." In a letter home dated the day before Sly took the stage at Woodstock I wrote, "Fortunately it was all insured. A band from Lake George, NY, called Oz and Ends was playing at a club in Sandwich that folded, and they are subbing for us tonight at the club. So Russ and Kenny took off for New York late last night to try to find new equipment." That trip to Sam Ash Music in Brooklyn resulted in Ken bringing home his first Hammond, an A-100 with two Leslies, and Russell purchasing the Les Paul SG that he still owns.

When we returned from the Cape after Labor Day we moved into our first band house at 4 South College Street in Hanover. Located in town just off a main drag, the house ledger featured mostly debits, including practice space. Ken remembers, "We put up 'sound stop' in the very small living room so we could practice. The Leslies and the Hammond took up about a third of the room. The drums took up another third. Russ, Jeff and Peter had to cram into the remaining area."

After a year on South College Street, the band moved to the house where it lived during the rest of its time together, out in the country on Watkins Road in North Hartland, VT. All of us loved it out at Hartland. My memories include the Pro Quarterback (a board game) league we formed among the band members; working out the harmonies to Stephen Stills' "Love the One You're With" a cappella in the dining room; climbing to the top of the high hill/small mountain in back of the house; and the overall beauty and serenity of the location. It just seemed right that a rock band should have a farm like that, or like Gunnison Manor. Bob Neale says that, when he joined the band, "I had a great room at the farm in Hartland. It was cold, having been added on to the original house, but it had this large window with a beautiful view that overlooked the valley behind the house."

The lone Battle of the Bands in which Tracks participated, referenced earlier in The Sprites chapter, deserves elaboration. Most of the other bands in Greenfield, MA, the evening of May 1, 1970, were relatively young and inexperienced, but one of our competitors gave us pause. Wrought was a local band with a strong following. Ken recalls, "We thought, because Wrought had a following of locals who showed up, that we wouldn't get enough votes. After the show a Wrought fan came up to me and told me she loved Wrought, but thought we were fantastic. They were quite good, but they were a jam band and we had really practiced our show. The amount of equipment we used was huge, and the audience was dazzled. Wrought was packing their stuff before we finished." Our set included "Watchtower," of course, and Hendrix' "Fire," with the flash guitar segment from Led Zeppelin's "Whole Lotta Love" inserted. After being named the winner of the $1,000 first prize, we played "Feelin' Alright" as our encore, at an up-tempo pace accompanied by broad SEGs.

On June 19, 1971, I played my last gig with Tracks at a Dartmouth class reunion tent. Perhaps it is symbolic that, after so many performances at Dartmouth fraternities, my last show was for drunken Dartmouth alums. I shared the lead singing that night with my successor, Wiley Crawford from Boston, whom the band had found via Dante Pavone.

The Wiley Crawford era was short-lived. Within three months Tracks had splintered. Pooch and Ken left, the latter joining former Tracks member Skip Truman and future Tracks member Bob Neale, as well as guitarists Dave Nye and John Chickering, in a band called Hokum. Russell and Ned stayed on with Wiley and formed a group named Anansi, adding previous bass player Jeff Wilkes and former Ham Sandwich guitarist Dan Morgenroth.

By the beginning of 1972, Tracks was back under its original name. Dan Morgenroth moved on, Jeffrey rotated out of the band for a second time, and Ken came back in, reuniting the core trio of Aldrich/Berndt/Pinkston. Skip rejoined the group, this time as its bass player, and Eddie Kistler replaced Wiley as a lead singer and piano player. Russell says the addition of Eddie came thanks to some assistance from Ed Malhoit. Don Solomon, who had played with Eddie and Steven Tallarico in Fox Chase, and had been in several bands with Steven, also played briefly with Tracks. Very briefly; as Ken recalls, "Four practices and two gigs, or thereabouts."

Back together again, with this lineup, Tracks reached the pinnacle of its success. Some of that success was due to the fine songs Russell was writing. Some of it pivoted on the old adage "practice makes perfect;" the longer the guys played together the better they became. And some of the improvement was Eddie. He could play something other than tambourine and cowbell, and gave the group more musical flexibility and a richer sound. Eddie was an exceptional showman, and he had an incredible voice. He could sing those rock song tenor notes I couldn't get to even by squeezing the old cojones. (2) In the summer of 1973, when I was in grad school at Dartmouth, I went to hear Tracks play one night at a high school gym. One of the songs they performed was The Stones' "Gimme Shelter," with Russell singing the Mick Jagger lead and Eddie taking the Merry Clayton part. Dear God, Eddie was otherworldly.

The band played numerous concerts, opening for major acts such as the Chambers Brothers, Tom Rush, and Canned Heat, and earning a rabid, far-flung following throughout New England. At the same time, Tracks dug down deep and worked even harder on its skill level and its original music.

Skip says about those years, "That was when the band had a very focused direction in terms of original material, and with the lifestyle of everyone living in the house, we practiced every day in the barn practice room. It was just go, go, go, which was wonderful. Russell taught me so much on technique, and how to listen to the other instruments and intertwine while keeping the root and staying tight. Ned and Russell were instrumental in terms of the band's focus."

R.F.D. Watkins Rd.
Hartland, Vt. 05048
802-436-2309

Tracks circa Fall 1973. L – R: Ken Aldrich, Ned Berndt, Eddie Kistler, Bob Neale, Russell Pinkston

Bob Neale, who replaced Skip as bassist in 1973, recalls that "We practiced all the time, and there was not a lot of down time. It was a great experience for me, because as a student at Hanover High School one of my regular things to do after school was to swing by Webster Hall to see who was practicing. I used to dream of playing with Tracks, and Jeff Wilkes was my hero."

Other musicians had the same take on the band's focus. Steve Hirsch of Better Days can call up "this powerful memory of the Tracks farm in Hartland, Russell walking around all day, talking to people, talking on the phone, with a guitar strapped around his neck. He, like, played all day. Russell was a major influence on my guitar playing."

By early 1974 Eddie had left the band, and Ned says that "When we got down to the four-piece band we became almost a jam band in the sense that we did these long arrangements like 'Isengard' and 'Lethargy,' just kinda going with the musicality. Russell and Kenny were doing the lead singing and we weren't able to sing like when Peter and Skip were in the band. We weren't gonna be doing the CSNY thing. So we started doing more original material, and the whole game plan was get enough money to go back in the studio. We rehearsed all the time; we were trying to make something happen."

At the same time, Tracks' continuing unsuccessful efforts to secure a recording contract were wearing down the band. Russell admits, "Let's face it, there were so many crushing disappointments about writing these tunes, thinking they're great, Wayne's gonna take 'em all around, and only hearing, 'No, No, No.' Every single time, everybody passed on them. None other than Ahmet Ertegun passed on them. I remember thinking, 'What the heck are we doing wrong here, these are good songs.' And then in the end we had simultaneous offers from two producers, one of whom was Tommy Mottola.

They both wanted to sign us to a contract in which they would own and publish the music, therefore they'd have the royalties forever, but the contracts guaranteed nothing."

"We ended up going to Jon Appleton's lawyer, Chuck Seton, who had also been the Jefferson Airplane's lawyer. [Appleton, a developer of the Synclavier keyboard synthesizer, was Russell's mentor in Dartmouth College's electronic music laboratory.] It was fall of 1974, we had done the Suntreader recording sessions, finished the spring and summer gigs we were contracted for, and I was back at school. I must have mentioned the contracts to Jon, and he said, 'Let me have my lawyer look at it.' I remember going over to his house, sitting around and having a drink, and Chuck saying to me, 'Look, if you're telling me that you're either going to accept this contract or you're going to go back to school, I'm gonna tell you to go back to school. They are taking everything that they are allowed to take by law, and they are promising you nothing.'"

Russell took Chuck Seton's advice and stayed in school. After six years the rock band Tracks was history.

Earlier, I mentioned Tracks' highly regarded vocals. While our vocals and harmonies did set us apart from other bands, to me the most impressive part of Tracks was the incredible musicianship of Ken, Ned, Russell, and our bassists.

To really tell you the tale, I would have to play you our old live tapes, and have you listen to those songs, on which there were no retakes or overdubs on expensive equipment. Just one Shure microphone hung out in the back of the room, and a good quality TEAC reel-to-reel. Know what? The playing is amazing: Ned's drum work on "Daddy Was A Jockey," Pooch's bass line on "Medicated Goo," Ken's Hammond solos on the "Blues Medley" and "Street Fighting Man," and Russell's solos on "Street Fighting Man" and "Now What."

In a live performance you can't hide talent, or the lack of it, and my mates were flat-out phenomenal.

Tracks' legacy lives on in the memories of its many fans, and in the album and CD that Wayne Wadhams and the band produced. But the band's legacy was manifested in another, very special manner.

In 2010 I received an email from Paul Hayward, a keyboard player from Littleton, NH, who began playing in rock bands in the late 1960s. Paul wrote that in the 1970s, in his bands Sly Dog and Lazy Livin' (named after an Alan MacIntosh song), he and his mates covered "Scapegoat," "Everyday Dreamer," "Mexican Bird," and also the Tracks' versions of "Watchtower" and "Street Fighting Man." Paul told me, "You guys were musically 'back on the road again' with us, on our song list. We all admired Tracks' precision, crisp vocals and lead lines, and imaginative arrangements. Your band was one of the few that inspired us to take songs and arrangements one step further. That has always stayed with me and I thank you *all*. Sly Dog played at many Tracks haunts, and people would recognize Russell's songs, often with pure admiration."

Davis Brothers Garage covered Pinkston originals "Marnie" and "Pawnbroker," and Better Days covered "Mexican Bird." When your songs are covered by other fine bands that are your contemporaries, it says a lot.

In July 2009 I called Ed Malhoit at his place of business in Claremont. I hadn't seen or spoken with Ed since 1971. When he answered the phone I said, "Ed Malhoit, this is a voice from your past. You probably won't remember me, my name is Peter Wonson." Mind you, I hadn't given the lady on the switchboard my name. Without a second's hesitation Ed responded, "Peter Wonson, lead singer for Tracks. We always thought you guys were the ones who were going to make it."

The late Dan Morgenroth, guitarist for Ham Sandwich and Anansi, 1973

The late Bob Hathaway, lead singer for Anvil

The late Dom "Pooch" Puccio, bassist for
Ham Sandwich and Tracks

Steve Calvert and Mitch Wonson, June 2010

Gar Anderson

The Gar Anderson I have known more than forty years is bright and talented enough to have chosen almost any college in the country coming out of high school. His college counselor at Monson Academy in south-central Massachusetts surely would claim Gar selected Johnson State College in northern Vermont for the most frivolous of reasons. Those of us in rock bands who played at The Rusty Nail in Stowe, VT, and have the privilege of knowing the man, can count our blessings and say, "Thank God Gar loved to ski!"

Gar Anderson was born in 1943 in Bridgeport, CT, raised in Trumbull, CT, within a couple miles of where his friend, Vinnie Buonanno, grew up, and went to boarding school at Monson. (1) Upon graduation Gar matriculated at Johnson State College, "just over the hill" (Mount Mansfield) north of Stowe. When I asked Gar why he chose Johnson State, his one word answer was: "Skiing."

Gar graduated from Johnson State in 1967. By that time his pal Vin was serving a tour of duty as a G.I. in Viet Nam. It was a simple fact of life in the late 1960s that unless a healthy young man had made other plans coming out of high school Uncle Sam was going to want him as a grunt. Gar recalls, "I had been deferred initially because I was going to college, but when I graduated I knew they were gonna want me, so I enlisted in the Air Force."

At Johnson State, Gar chaired winter carnival, and was responsible for booking the featured band. Gar says, "I went with a folk group out of New York City who had just released their first album before they came to play at Johnson. They showed up on a snowy night and played the most incredible concert with everyone sitting on the floor of the gymnasium. The band was called Simon and Garfunkel and the album was *Sounds of Silence*. That was the first band I ever booked."

That's a pretty good first experience as preparation for booking bands as a nightclub owner, but maybe Gar misremembers just a tad regarding its being his first time. Vinnie says that "Even though I went to public school and Gar's parents sent him off to private school, we had a mutual friend, Topper Mogenson. Topper, Gar, and I used to hang out on weekends at the Cozy Cabin in Cross River, NY, where the drinking age was 18. Gar's parents had a place with this kind of deck on the top of the garage, and he would get the band from the Cozy Cabin to come play there when his parents were out of town. The neighbors would go crazy because it was so loud, and it was the kind of neighborhood where the houses were right next to each other. Gar's mom was Clerk of Probate at the town hall and a good friend of the chief of police. Another friend of ours used to call her 'City Hall,' as in 'Okay, City Hall, take care of this neighbor problem for us!'"

How did a young man who was supposed to become an Air Force pilot after college end up in Stowe as a nightclub owner? Gar claims that "I just fell into it." Literally, pun intended. "When I enlisted I got put into a deferred program, and was told to report for duty on December 30, 1967, at Lackland Air Force Base in Texas. So I came to Stowe to try to find work for a few months, and I got a job painting the ski towers on the new gondola. They were looking for someone who wasn't afraid of heights and was willing to climb the towers.

"There was an early snow that year, and by early November there was three to four feet on the ground. I joined the ski patrol and told them I'd work until the holidays and then I'd have to go. The week before I was supposed to report to Lackland, I was skiing down with a toboggan, fell and dislocated my cervical spine. It was actually a fairly minor injury, but the x-rays showed a dislocation. I went to Texas and took my x-rays and they said, 'Sorry, no, you can't fly, go home.' I came back to Stowe and worked ski patrol the rest of the winter, but I was still eligible for the Army. I was drafted in 1968, went home to Connecticut for my physical, and took the same x-rays. I showed them to the captain in charge, he took one look, and wrote 4-F on my application. He said, 'We can't take you with that kind of risk.'"

What's a young man to do? Turned down by the Air Force and the Army, missing out on a chance to make friends with the jungle rats and the two steppers? Gar went back up to Stowe in the summer of 1968, and like most summers back then there was nothing much going on. He stumbled across a property for sale on the Mountain Road and talked his mom and dad into buying it. They bought the Gale Farm for $35,000—two acres of land, a farmhouse, barn and connecting shed. In June 2010, when asked how much the land alone would be worth today, Gar replied, "Two acres on this road? A million dollars, easy.

"I knew that all the ski patrollers, instructors, and locals who worked in Stowe, affectionately known at the time as 'Ski Bums,' were always looking for a place to stay, so in the fall of 1968 I opened a boarding house in the old farmhouse. The boarding house was successful and the next year I said to myself, 'Well, I've got this big barn, what am I gonna do with it?' I got to talking with a couple of guys in town and one said he'd like to open a record store, and the other said he'd like to open a leather shop, so I opened the first shopping center in Stowe with six shops in the lower level of the barn.

"Then I said, 'Well I've got the whole upstairs (this loft which was full of hay at the time), and I've got the front section of the barn which is a wreck...' and I got to thinking." Stowe was a hip town in 1969 but there were only two options for entertainment: Sister Kate's, featuring Rock King, the comedian and singer who played every night in the winter for more than twenty years; and the Baggy Knees, featuring the Gene Cipriano Trio each night throughout the winter. Gar asked himself, "Why not rock and roll, with a new band every week? After all, what else could one do with a huge old barn located right on Mountain Road across from one of the best local restaurants and bars, The Shed?"

So Gar got to work cleaning out the barn with a goal of having it ready for ski season. But it was not an easy task—the barn had been a riding stable and never got mucked out. The manure was so deep the horsehair was stuck to the ceiling, and "We had to shovel all that shit out to get down to the floor." Plus, it was August 1969 and everyone was talking about some outdoor concert in Woodstock, NY. Gar told me, "I really wanted to go and see those bands, but I couldn't do both and be open in time for Christmas week. So I stayed to work on The Nail and just barely made it on time. The liquor license didn't arrive until the day before the opening. We debuted on Friday, December 19, 1969, with a band named 'Tracks.' Talk about instant success! Tracks packed The Nail on opening night and continued to do so for almost three years until I sold the property in 1972."

Ken Strong opened The Shed, the restaurant and bar across Mountain Road from The Nail, in 1965. Forty-six years later, Kenny and The Shed are still going strong! The Shed was originally a blacksmith shed in the late 1800s, then a cider mill. Just up the road next to the Gale Farm barn was the Baptist church in town. Ken chuckles when he tells the story of Stowe farmers who would drop their families off at the church on Sundays, then head across the street to the cider mill to bring their fall apple harvest to the mill for processing. The farmers would sit around and drink hard cider, shoot the breeze, and then head back to the church to pick up their families after the service.

Regarding Gar Anderson's decision to open a nightclub across the street from his own establishment, Ken says, "Gar's transformation across the street was amazing. The Baggy Knees was getting softer and softer and there was really no place for top entertainment, and Gar's place was in the right place at the right time."

Gar's Connecticut buddy, Vinnie Buonanno, ended up in Stowe too, with a little help from his friend. When Vinnie returned from the army, he headed to Stratton Mountain in southern Vermont to see old pal Topper Mogenson. Topper and Vin had talked about doing a Bed and Breakfast together, and Topper had opened one at Stratton called TopsHaus. Vinnie remembers, "I went up there from Connecticut to see his operation and I realized very quickly there was only room for one person. But, I said, 'Let me just work for you for one winter' and I did. I got $25 a week and a season's pass, and I had money in my pocket at the end of the week because Topper bought all the beer. Free skiing, the best time I ever had, and it was just what I needed to get over having been overseas and everything.

"Then the next season Gar mentioned that he had a place in Stowe and he said, 'Why don't you come up?' I started out at The Nail as a waiter, and then one of the guys who was originally a partner, John Miller, went back to the Cape. He was one of the bartenders, so they pushed me into bartending and a guy would stand behind me and tell me how to make drinks and I just did 'em. We had a great time, we filled the place every night, the Baggy Knees was full every night, I really don't know how we did it. These days you can't get a full house.

"I came up for a year and never left. Yeah, that's what happened. I met my wife and after a couple years Gar sold

The Nail, and he sort of packaged me in for the guy who bought it, you know, 'My manager will come with it.' So I stayed for a while, but then Gar and I decided to buy the existing movie theater in Stowe. We had talked about it earlier, and Gar called me one day and said, 'Are you still interested in the theater, because I just ripped 100 seats out of it. Come down and take a look.' To increase revenue we came up with another first in the movie business; we put a bar called the 'Projection Room Lounge' right in the movie theater. But after about a year Gar had too much energy to sit in something like that and he said, 'You and Nancy ought to do it anyway, but there's not enough for all of us.' He had put in $5,000 and I had put in $5,000, so I paid him his $5,000 and forty years later we're still running the theater."

Vinnie also tells this story. In the summer of 2010 Vic Harris, an old friend who had tended bar at The Nail, passed away, and Vin spoke at his wake. "I wrapped up my remarks with, 'I'd like to think that Heaven is a lot like Stowe was in the late '60s and early '70s. It was just a beautiful place with lots of really good people having a good time.' And I really feel that way. I think we were so blessed to have a place and time like that in our lives."

In 1972 Gar sold The Nail for the first time. "I took the second mortgage back, the guy I sold it to got into cocaine, his wife, whose family had the money, left him and took the checkbook, and he drove the club into the ground within months. He sold it to some guys who owned a big rock club in Fort Lauderdale, FL. They came up here with all their Florida policies, but those ideas didn't work in Vermont, and they drove it further into the ground. After a while, when they hadn't paid their mortgage in six months, I started foreclosure. One night they packed up everything that wasn't nailed down, all the electronics, all the booze, loaded it into a couple of U-Haul trailers and left town.

"So I took over managing The Nail for a second time, and it was a success for several years until someone else came along and bought it again. In the meantime I got involved in lobbying. We used to have blue laws in Vermont that required us to close on Sunday nights at 11:00 p.m. That didn't work for anyone up here on long weekends, because people wanted to keep partying late on Sunday nights. I got a group of the nightclub owners together, and we went down and lobbied the legislature in Montpelier to try to get the Sunday closing time extended to midnight. Well, I got it extended to 2:00 a.m. and everybody said, 'Unbelievable, you have to do more of this.'

"At the time we had a Vermont Nightclub Owners Association, and I got a call saying we want to have a Vermont Hotel and Restaurant Association and we want you to run it. I got into association management that way. I was a lobbyist for three or four years, then got hooked up with the Vermont Realtors Association for thirteen years, and for the past ten years I have been with the National Association. I'm the vice-president of the NAR outreach program. I travel all over the country, cover all fifty states. My office is in Chicago, but I'm rarely there. It looks like I'll work a couple more years, and then hopefully retire."

Gar met his wife, Moira, "right here in Stowe." Moira was from Scotland, she liked to travel, and she had gone to school in France and Germany. Moira was also a terrific athlete, a swimmer who held two national titles. She came to the United States, visited Stowe, and stayed in town to work.

Moira and Gar met at Stowe's Winter Carnival in 1984. The town sponsored a race called the Wintermeister, a sort of triathlon that included downhill and cross-country ski races, and speed skating. Gar remembers that "None of us had skated before, so they randomly matched people up and I was paired with Moira. In the speed skating we took off, and

I was about half a lap ahead of her until the final lap. She was in much better shape than I was, and she caught up and was right on my heels. As we were coming to the finish line she caught her skate in a crack of the ice, fell and cut her head. You know how in speed skating your arms wave out behind you? Well, it must have looked like I had hit her, because when I came to the finish line everyone was going 'Boo, boo!' and I looked back and there was Moira with blood streaming down her face. That night I brought her some roses, we started dating, and one thing led to another. We just celebrated our twenty-sixth anniversary."

The Andersons have two daughters: Metzi, a Mount Holyoke grad, and Robyn, a Middlebury alum. Gar insists that "The girls take after their mom—they're both great athletes. Metzi went to the U.S. Collegiate Nationals in cycling, and Robyn participated in the NCAA finals in cross-country skiing two years in a row, and went to the Junior Olympics and won four medals."

Gar Anderson, June 2010, at the Gale Farm Shopping Center on the former site of The Rusty Nail. Across the road in the background is The Shed.

Today, the Gale Farm Shopping Center sits on the former site of The Rusty Nail (also the site of the first shopping center in Stowe), and it is a classy looking place. But for me, when I visited in 2010, seeing a bunch of shops where The Nail used to be was a dagger to the heart.

Like every successful business owner Gar was very hands-on, constantly working. As he noted in a 2010 interview, "there was no down time at The Nail." His work ethic and life experience as a young club owner no doubt inform his current work for the NAR. Still, I had to smile when he told me that he "hopefully" might retire in a couple of years. I mean, c'mon Gar, you're sixty-seven years old! But that's Gar, always the go-getter.

The Rusty Nail

Close your eyes and imagine a favorite destination. For my wife and me it would be the isolated northern beaches of North Carolina's Outer Banks. Whenever I think of traveling there, my anticipation is Kodachrome vivid. I see and feel the broad beaches and the dunes that shelter the wild ponies; the relentless rows of waves advancing into the rumbling surf; the fierce winds snapping red warning flags stationed like sentries at quarter-mile intervals along the tops of the sand dunes.

So it was for me every time Tracks was scheduled to play at The Rusty Nail. I could close my eyes on the trip up from Hanover and visualize our week-long gigs at one of my favorite destinations. (1) The Nail was memorable for me in part because Gar Anderson and his employees treated bands like royalty. A second, perhaps somewhat unusual, reason was that every time we arrived at The Nail the interior was different. Gar was constantly renovating, and I couldn't wait to see what new look awaited us, including where in the building we would sleep for that week. (2)

On a surprisingly flat, straight stretch of the Mountain Road, Vermont Route 108, sat the Gale Farm, on the right side of the road as you headed north toward Smugglers' Notch and Mount Mansfield. It was a beautiful, Vermont-picturesque location, serene fields framed by the mountain rising in the background. I am told that the first air show ever held in Vermont took place there.

You will recall from the previous chapter that when a skiing injury derailed Gar Anderson's military service, he bought the Gale Farm and set about repurposing it. First there was the boarding house he opened in 1968, and then the refurbishing of the farm's barn so he could open the premiere night spot in Stowe. The Rusty Nail was just a traditional, old Vermont barn on the outside, as you can see in the wintry photo below. On the inside, it was an ever-changing construction project. If building permits had been required in 1969, I suspect Gar would have run a tab at the town office.

Gar Anderson in front of The Rusty Nail, February 1971

The club got its name, as many readers may divine, from the drink of the same name, a mix of Scotch and Drambuie. Gar says "We named the club The Rusty Nail after the drink, and also for the fact that the building was a barn with a lot of old rusty nails in it. There was never any doubt about what the name would be, and we sold a lot of those drinks. They were very popular."

The locus of The Nail for bands was the front section of the building. You entered from the side parking lot on the lower level onto the dance floor. The stage was to the left, against the front wall of the barn, but getting to the stage wasn't as simple as just turning left. The stage was elevated ten feet off the dance floor, and the only access was up a narrow, spiral staircase without any railing. A band's large equipment was generally loaded straight up onto the stage in the following manner: a crew on the dance floor hefted the equipment up to be received by another crew of several people standing on the stage. Gar and his staff generously pitched in on load-in day. We were all young and strong back then! (3)

Another thing about the stage was its small size. We could barely squeeze our equipment onto it, and surely other bands had the same issue. Sometime after I left Tracks, an extension was built out to the right of the original stage along the barn's front wall, which gave bands space we didn't have in the early years of The Nail.

An additional drawback of Gar's stage was that it was hard to see and interact with the crowd on the dance floor, unless you were willing to risk life and limb by dangling out from the stage and looking straight down.

In contrast, probably the best part of the stage setup was that directly across a thirty foot gulf of thin air above the dance floor was the upper bar with a railing and a space to stand facing the stage. While the dancers filled the chasm below the band, the railing was always packed with customers who watched and cheered on the band at eye level. I loved that arrangement; it made me feel I could fly across that chasm like Peter Pan. No drugs required.

Across the Mountain Road sat The Shed restaurant and bar. Ken Strong had opened The Shed in 1965, and by all accounts he had the best food in Stowe. His Danish chef, Steen Neilson, trained in Copenhagen, was a culinary marvel. When The Nail opened, Gar and Ken developed a unique business relationship that was mutually beneficial, as Gar describes.

"Vermont had a state law that you could not have a liquor license unless you had a restaurant. It was never enforced, but something like 60% percent of your revenues were supposed to come from food. Now The Nail didn't have a kitchen, none of us knew how to cook, nor did we have the desire to cook. So Kenny and I worked out a deal that any time a customer wanted food, we would call over, Steen would cook it up and run it over. We had a door specifically for this purpose, a direct line to The Shed. We also had a dummy kitchen and a dummy menu with "Rusty Nail" on it, even though it was The Shed's menu. Kenny had no objection, because he was making money too. We had such a great relationship, the two places worked so well together."

Anyone who has ever spent time around a rock venue knows that things can get a little loud, and not just on the inside. Early on Gar found himself with two major challenges regarding the sound emanating from The Nail.

Directly across the two-lane Mountain Road from The Nail lived two gay gentlemen from New Orleans. Ray Roberts and Lonny Dean had come to what they believed was a quaint New England town to open an antique crafts shop. Gar recalls that "They were very creative, but very much out of their element. Stowe was totally foreign to them, and they only stayed a couple years. They had come up here for what they thought would be a nice, quiet little town experience!

"They were good guys, and they didn't want to put me out of business, but they said the music from the club was so loud that it would shake their house. Their bedroom was on the street side of the house, only about forty feet from the stage. When they would get stressed out I would go over, take them a little gift sometimes, we'd have tea, and I'd smooth things over. I knew they just wanted to sleep at night."

The other sticky wicket was the Stoweflake motel that ran parallel to The Nail on the far side of the parking lot. The owners became concerned because they were starting to receive complaints from their guests about the noise, and they threatened to go to the town selectmen and have the club's liquor license revoked. Gar addressed that potential stumbling block with an ingenious solution.

"Because it was an old barn and had no insulation, the sound would travel. We insulated the walls, and I went over to the motel to meet the owners and see if we could work things out. We brought in engineers who did a sound engineering survey, measuring the decibels and everything. Then they installed a house sound system, and if a band exceeded a certain decibel level a red light right above the stage came on. The motel owners, Chuck and Stu Baraw, even allowed us to use a room at the motel to do the test measurements."

Gar reminded me, because I had forgotten after forty-two years, that Tracks was the band that helped test that sound system by cranking it up for the cause one afternoon from the elevated stage at The Nail. "Tracks would play, the engineers would do a measurement, then they'd say, 'A little louder,' they'd do another measurement, and so on, until we finally determined the level at which the red light had to go on. The system worked like a charm, and bands were really good about respecting the red light."

That house sound system and related costs came to $10,000 in 1969. I can't imagine a club owner spending that kind of money today, but back then that sort of thing was simply an accepted part of the cost of doing business.

There were so many fine bands that played at The Rusty Nail it would be impossible to mention them all. Gar's list of the outstanding bands that played The Nail includes: The Fat Band from Rochester, VT; Benefit Street, Jonathan Edwards' early band; New Heavenly Blue; Uncle Sam from Burlington, featuring Kip Meeker on guitar; Bull (formerly Lime Cirrus), another fabulous band from Burlington; Ariel, an all-female band; Daddy Warbux; and Gunnison Brook.

Gar maintains that "Without a doubt our most famous bands were Tracks, Swallow, and the Beaver Brown Band." Tracks opened The Nail with a week-long gig, December 19 through December 25, 1969. According to the original advertisement for the club's opening, its hours were 4:00 p.m. to 2:00 a.m., and we played four sets from 9:00 until 1:00. The first Sunday, December 21, the Fat Band took our place on stage for a matinee show from 4:00 to 6:00 p.m.

Tracks performing Suite: Judy Blue Eyes on the elevated stage at The Nail.
(Yes, I'm sure! Kenny is playing guitar, and I have the maracas.)

Swallow was a horn band out of Boston, led by bass player Vern Miller, which recorded two albums during its time together. Horn bands, notes Gar, "were really popular at the time." Miller was the former bassist of The Remains, also from Boston, who are best known for being one of the opening acts on The Beatles' final U.S. tour. Gar had such a good relationship with Swallow that they asked him to come on the road with them as their manager.

The Beaver Brown Band, from Narragansett, RI, had a huge following in Rhode Island, Connecticut, and Massachusetts, and at the Stone Pony in Asbury Park, New Jersey. They achieved their greatest fame when they performed the soundtrack music for the 1983 movie, *Eddie and the Cruisers*. Their single from that movie, "On The Dark Side," reached #7 on the *Billboard* Top 100.

The story of New Heavenly Blue at The Nail is one Gar loves to tell. "A local girl from a very well-known family, the Hewitts, came up to me and said, 'I have a boyfriend in college in Michigan. He's in a band and I've invited them to come to Stowe for a week or two next summer. Is there any way you could put them up at The Nail and let them practice, and if you do they'll play for you free of charge on the weekend.' Well, that was fine with me, because summer business in Stowe is pretty slow. I said 'Okay,' I'm not taking any risk there. I think they were the first band we ever had in the summer.

"Lo and behold, the week they showed up from Michigan they were on the front page of *Life* magazine because the week before they'd played the first-ever performance of *Jesus Christ Superstar* in the United States. Chris Brubeck, Dave Brubeck's son, was in the band, and they were absolutely phenomenal.

"Earlier that summer we had gotten a bunch of night club owners together and decided we would have a multi-band concert at The Nail. They asked me to invite eight bands, and invite all the nightclub owners from New Hampshire and Vermont. We'd listen to the bands and approve them for the coming winter.

"The second week New Heavenly Blue was at The Nail we staged the concert. Because they were unknown in New England they said they would start it off. So they got up on stage, and in the meantime everyone was messing around with their guitars, tuning up, getting ready, you know, and they weren't paying attention until New Heavenly Blue struck the first note. Within five seconds every single band member in the place was transfixed. They couldn't believe what they were hearing, those guys were so good. They played the entire rock opera of *Jesus Christ Superstar* from start to finish without a break.

"We had 1024 people at that event. There was a waitress who was working that day, Georgia Lesnevich, and she always had trouble with her numbers. Her dad was Gus Lesnevich, the National Boxing Association World Light Heavyweight Title holder from 1941 to 1948. During this concert she came running up to me and said, 'Gar, Gar I got a hundred dollar tip!' One of the nightclub owners liked her so much he gave her a $100 tip, which made her week."

Another of Gar's favorite stories is about Swallow's lead singer, George Leh. George was blind, and Gar remembers, "He had a voice that was absolutely unbelievable, so powerful. Playing on that elevated stage, you can imagine the potential problems since there were no railings. We would take a piece of 2x4 and nail it down at the front of the stage, and George would put his right foot on top of the 2x4 so he would know where he was. George also had the habit of rocking forward as he sang, and when he would rock he would hang out over the people on the dance floor below."

On Sundays folk singer Peter Isaacson would play a toned-down show in the mezzanine bar. Gar remembers Peter as "One of the nicest people we ever worked with. He is still playing today, he went into country music, and he goes by the name Clay Canfield."

The Rusty Nail was a friendly environment, a place where musicians of just about every stripe could find a receptive audience. Pamela Brandt told me, "Oh, yes, I remember The Rusty Nail and I am intensely grateful to them also, because The Rusty Nail really liked Ariel, which wasn't that usual given the weird kind of music that we played. For example, we played Jefferson Airplane but we didn't do the hits like 'Somebody to Love' or 'White Rabbit.' What we played was one whole side of *After Bathing at Baxter's.* Practically no one knew it, but at The Rusty Nail it went over well."

Pam continues: "Later on after Ariel had broken up in June of 1970, and before The Deadly Nightshade got together, Helen Hooke and I were playing as a duo. We hooked up with Jeffrey Wilkes as our sound guy, and we had two entire van loads of equipment. We were like the loudest duo in the whole world. I played bass and Helen played power guitar and a little bit of power fiddle. We were playing Jimi Hendrix and things like that, and The Nail loved us."

Vin Buonanno recalls the good times employees of The Nail had. "Vic Harris and I both drank Scotch; he drank Johnny Walker Red and I drank Dewar's. I came in one morning, went up to the bar and said, 'I'd like to pay my tab for last night.' Whoever was at the bar at the time goes, 'Here it is, it's $25.' At the time drinks were like a buck apiece and I said 'Let me see that.' And he said, 'It's all right here, it's all Johnny Walker Red,' and I said, 'No, no, that's Victor, he drinks Johnny Walker Red.' He said, 'Well, you better go find Vic, because he paid your tab which was $30.'"

Vinnie also says that "Gar had a great reputation as running a clean place, and he kept people under control. Plus we had a doorman, a big bruiser of a guy named Ron Paquette—no neck, a great guy, I think Gar carried extra insurance on him." Nevertheless, there were still occasional incidents. The Nail had an alarm system behind each of its three bars, and if there was an out-of-control customer the bartender pushed a button that was coded to let everyone know where to converge. Gar says, "I remember one night in particular we had a guy who was about to start a fight and he grabbed Mitchell Phineaus, the bartender, and pulled him half way across the bar. Mitch hit the button and Vinnie and I arrived along with Ron Paquette and two-hundred-fifty-pound Dougie Matteson and had this guy out the back door in a matter of seconds. He took a few hits, and so he went to the police to complain. The police arrested him."

Gar also remembers "the biggest threat we ever had, which occurred at 3:30 in the morning. I had that apartment in the area of The Nail we called Siberia, and I was awakened by a noise in the upstairs bar area. Vinnie was in the next room over in Siberia and I went and knocked on the door and said, 'Vinnie, wake up, there's something going on at The Nail.' Vinnie was a golfer and had his clubs in his room. I took a driver and he had a wicked iron, and we went down in the club, crept upstairs and then threw on the lights. It turned out it was Joanie Rhinehart, who was Doug Matteson's girlfriend. She had gotten drunk, passed out on a bench, and we never saw her when we locked up. She woke up, tried to get out, fell over a table and made that racket."

No tale of The Nail would be complete without mentioning Bruce Arnold, better known as "Humpty," bartender and music lover extraordinaire. Humpty came to Stowe from

Burlington to work on the ski patrol. (He and Gar worked together in 1967, the year the gondola was built up the mountain.) He started tending bar at The Shed, and Gar and Ken agree that, "Humpty had a great personality for bartending. He was a fun guy to be around and he loved working with people."

Humpty also loved Tracks, and in particular the band's version of "All Along the Watchtower." When Tracks was playing The Nail and Humpty was tending bar at The Shed he made the folks at The Nail promise to have Tracks signal the upstairs bar when we were about to play the song. The upstairs bartender would call The Shed and tell Humpty that "Watchtower" was up next. Humpty would take a break from tending the bar, tell the customers to fix their own drinks while he was gone, then run across the street to a place reserved for him along the upstairs railing.

In 2009 Russell Pinkston wrote to Gar, reminiscing about "the good old days of The Rusty Nail. My memories of those days with Tracks are still quite vivid in my mind. They were definitely some of the best days of my life, and our visits to Stowe were some of the best of the best. Here are a few random snapshots, some of which you may remember. The excellent spinach soup from the restaurant just across the road, my naively asking the chef for his recipe, and his smiling response…'Oh, a little of this and a little of that.' My feeling of elation and accomplishment upon successfully backing up the trailer through the snow and ice to the club's back door after numerous failed attempts. Your confronting someone who was very big, drunk, and intimidating, and was abusing his girlfriend in that same parking lot, saying, 'We don't do that around here.' That climb up the spiral staircase to the stage, the sea of dancing heads below, and the row of friendly faces on the balcony across. What a great time it was, and what a great place you had, Gar."

Davis Brothers Garage Band

This is the story of a garage band that got its start by jamming in a living room.

Davis Brothers Garage Band was conceived in the summer of 1965 in Brownsville, Vermont. The band didn't commence playing out, however, until September 1968, and then only in a galaxy far, far away from Brownsville—two-thirds of the way across the North American continent.

Jeff and Rick Davis were Windsor High School students from Brownsville, who played during their high school years in bands like The Links, The Missing Links, and The Watchband. Their cousin from Metuchen, New Jersey, Lane Gibson, also played in high school bands in his home town. During the summers of 1965, 1966, and 1967, Lane visited "upta" Vermont for about two weeks each summer, and the cousins would jam in the Davises' living room. Rick remembers Lane's "beautiful Lake Placid blue Fender Jazzmaster guitar, complete with a Fender Bandmaster amp and a Premier reverb."

It was during the summer of 1965, while noodling in the living room, that the cousins pledged to each other that when they graduated from high school they would all attend the same college and form their own rock band. In the meantime, when Lane visited in Vermont he would on occasion sit in with the various combinations of players who were band mates of Jeff and Rick's: Nate and Chris Thompson, Mike Mulroy, and Bill Barrows. In his bands in New Jersey, Lane was the "swing player" who was so indispensable to mid-'60s bands, the guitarist/keyboard player, so his flexibility made sitting in easier.

Jeff graduated from Windsor High School in June of 1967, and in the fall matriculated at the University of Denver in

Colorado. His college choice centered on one word, the same word that motivated Gar Anderson, the future owner of The Rusty Nail in Stowe, to enroll at Johnson State—skiing. Says Lane, "Jeff and Rick were both exceptional skiers, and Jeff wanted to join the highly regarded ski team at Denver."

The following June, Rick and Lane both graduated from high school, and September 1968 found them honoring the first part of their pledge and enrolling with Jeff in the Mile High City. True to the second half of their pledge, the three cousins soon formed a rock band. Casting about for a name for their group they looked back to the Davises' Brownsville roots. Rick and Jeff's father, Arthur, owned a new car dealership in town called Davis Brothers Garage.

In addition to Rick on guitar, Jeff on bass, and Lane as the second guitarist/keyboard man, the Yankees from Vermont found Craig Miller to play drums, though Craig was soon replaced by yet another cousin, Burt Sisco. The band's first gig, and first big break, was at the student union on campus. In the audience was the son of the mayor of Vail, Colorado's famous ski resort. He approached the band and said, "Hey, I like you guys, do you want to play in Vail?" The band said, "Sure." Back to Vail the young man went to have a talk with Steve Ruder, the owner of the Keg, and soon Davis Brothers Garage wended its way up the slopes west of Denver to start a long run of gigs at the Keg and the Casino Vail. During this initial, busy year of the band's life, second-year student Jeff was still knocking the cover off the academic ball to the tune of a composite 3.7 GPA for his first two years—as an engineering major!

Summer break 1969 found Jeff and Rick back in Vermont, driving Tip Top bread trucks. Rick recalls asking his boss at the Tip Top bakery in White River Junction "if I could take a truck over to the Woodstock Music Festival in New York to feed the needy, and he, staunch Republican that he was, said, 'No, no way.'" Clever try, Rick.

Rick says, "That summer I tried to keep tabs on what was going on around the area musically, although with our work schedule of up at 3:00 in the morning it was kind of tough. My route took me around Sunapee and New London, NH. Driving around the streets of New London, some mornings I would see this kid in sailor jeans and boots, with an angry look on his face, smoking a cig. It was Joe Perry. Next thing I knew he and Tom Hamilton were in the Jam Band, and we saw them at The Barn that summer."

In September Jeff, Rick, and Lane went back to Denver, but after one more school year all three dropped out in June 1970 after discovering that college and full-time rock don't mix well. Rick laments that "The GPAs started to slip. Jeffrey made it three years, and Lane and I made it two years."

The band continued to play full-time, six nights a week, with new drummer Tyler Plotzke. Rick recalls that "We were working all the time, and in those days we were one of the biggest Top 40 bands in Colorado. One of our favorite gigs was Mr. Lucky's in Denver."

Lane describes Mr. Lucky's as "a huge nightclub, with two floors and a stage both upstairs and downstairs. There were separate bands six nights a week on each floor. One band had Sunday off, the other had Monday off. We used to play six months at a time, five sets each night during the week from 9:00 p.m. to 2:00 a.m., and *seven* sets from 9:00 until 4:00 a.m. on Friday and Saturday nights."

In 1971 Bob Miles replaced Tyler Plotzke on drums (four drummers in four years!), and the band's success continued. But in the summer of 1972 Jeff Davis decided to leave the band. According to Rick, "That meant that it was time for the Davis Brothers to come home to Vermont, so that's what we did. In August of 1972 we moved back, we brought our drummer Bob Miles, and we also brought a new bass player, Bill Dworske, who was a Denver boy like Bob."

Davis Brothers Garage in Denver, 1971, L – R: Bill Dworske, Jeff Davis, Lane Gibson, Bob Miles, Rick Davis

Rick continues, "Most of our friends and family had never seen the band, unless they visited Denver, which a few of them did through those years. We began to establish a presence in Vermont, started playing the Chopping Block, the Wobbly, The Rusty Nail, the Silver Keg in Burlington, all of the high schools on the Malhoit Circuit. I think we even played one night at the Savage Beast in Ascutney."

Things were going well, but in 1973 Bill Dworske got homesick and decided he wanted to return to Denver, and homeboy Bob Miles also made the move back to Denver. The band convinced former drummer Tyler Plotzke to come East, but what to do about a bass player? Rick says, "We were big fans of Tracks, and we heard their bass player, Skip Truman, might be leaving. This was spring of 1973, so we went up to a Dartmouth frat party to see Tracks, with Eddie Kistler on keys, both Skip and Bob Neale, sitting in, on bass, and of course Russell Pinkston, Ned Berndt and Kenny Aldrich. We were blown away, what a powerhouse lineup!

"Skip joined Davis Brothers, and Bob took over in Tracks. With Lane on guitar and keyboard, Tyler on drums and me on guitar, from '73 to '76 was probably our most well-liked lineup. Tyler was a showy drummer, and we also had Flash Gordon and his light show during that time. Ed Malhoit booked us, but we also kept up our accounts in Denver."

Fans and a fellow musician comment on Davis Brothers' popularity. Annie Dolan says, "Davis Brothers Garage was one of my favorite bands. They were pretty much like the house band at the Chopping Block, and Lane was just awesome, one of my favorite keyboard players ever."

Gardner Berry of Stone Cross recalls that "Davis Brothers was my favorite band back then. We did a lot of things together, and had a great time."

Joy Moffat observes that "Rick was so solid and Lane was the ultimate ARP player. He got the most out of a synthesizer aside from Emerson, Lake & Palmer, and Davis Brothers did a lot of ELP and Argent."

Between 1969 and 1975, in addition to ELP and Argent, the band performed songs by The Beatles, The Stones, the Steve Miller Band, Little Feat, Steely Dan, the Allman Brothers, the Doobie Brothers, CSNY, Sly and the Family Stone, and Stevie Wonder, as well as several medleys, including a

Cream medley and an Elton John medley. In a nod to Tracks, Davis Brothers also covered two Russell Pinkston originals, "Marnie" and "Pawnbroker."

In the winter of 1974 the band took a six-week trip to Denver and Oklahoma. One night in a club called Dirty John's in Oklahoma City the band got some onstage assistance from several young ladies they had met during their three-week gig at the club. Rick recalls that "Dirty John's held about six hundred people, it was a three-two bar, and these girls we had gotten to know were there. During the show these four cuties went to the Ladies' Room, shed their clothes, wrapped themselves in sheets, and came back out onto the dance floor and up onto the stage. We were playing 'Honky Tonk Women,' they took their sheets off, and they were buck naked on stage.

"Well, the crowd was dancing like crazy, but they finally realized what was going on, six hundred people on a Saturday night, this big dance floor, and the crowd starts to get closer and closer to the stage. The cops were called, but before they arrived the girls ran back into the Ladies' Room and got dressed again. Nothing wrong here, officer! Anyway, the cops showed up, and it was like the Keystone Kops, they're running all over the place. That was one night we will never forget."

Davis Brothers, 1974, L – R Rick Davis, Tyler Plotzke, Skip Truman, Lane Gibson

At that same club, Tyler Plotzke was in the office one day talking to the manager when a rat ran into the office. The manager pulled out a gun and plugged the rat, shot him dead, with Tyler sitting slack-jawed on the couch.

Another Oklahoma City club the band played was named Filthy McNasty's—gotta love the names of those places. Rick remembers that "One night, at closing time, shots were fired in the front parking lot, so the club's manager ran out and started firing his own piece as people were leaving. I mean, it was the Wild West."

Lane has one last story from the Sooner State. "I was playing an ARP 2600 synthesizer, and a guy came up to me on a break and said, 'Hey, I got one of those at my house, you wanna buy it?' They were going for about $1800 and this guy said, 'I'll sell it to you for six or seven hundred.' I ended up buying it from him for $700, even though I already had one and even though I shouldn't have gotten involved in it because it had to have been stolen. When we were making the transaction the guy said, 'You know, I don't mind telling you I got a .38 right here in my boot.' He thought I was gonna pull a fast one on him.

"I figured I could make some money on the deal, so I called an acquaintance up in Denver and I said, 'I've got a 2600 synthesizer, will you buy it when we get back to Denver?' The guy said yes, but he knew it must have been hot, so he ended up giving me about half of what I was asking for. I still made a small profit on it but not what I expected. And I never got to see that .38."

Lane remembers, "Oklahoma City was something else. Everybody carried guns." And Rick adds, "At the time Oklahoma City was either Bible Belt or totally the other way, nothing in the middle."

In 1975 Davis Brothers went back to Denver for the summer, carrying with them Jeff "Flash" Gordon and the Jefferson Light Show, and Jeff Wilkes as their sound man. Jeff Wilkes tells a story about the cross-country trip.

"Flash and I drove the truck out. Well, Flash had an expired driver's license so I literally drove the whole way. We dropped down from New England to my home city of D.C. and then headed out for Denver. After spending the night in Washington we had driven for fifteen or sixteen hours straight, we were somewhere in Kansas, and I was exhausted. We pulled into this truck stop at 4:00 in the morning, and there was a whole line of semis. Flash went in the back, spread out a bunch of packing blankets and slept on the equipment. I laid out in the front seat of the cab and was gone. I was just, like, unconscious.

"Sometime in the night I heard this little tap, tap, tap on the window, and I was trying to wake myself up and I was thinking 'Where am I, how did I get here, what is this?' I looked up and there was this woman standing on the running board saying, 'Are you looking for a good time?' Nothing like this had ever happened to me, and what flashed through my mind was that her guy was probably in the Kenworth sleeper two doors down, keeping an eye on his little woman. I just said to her, 'You better try somebody else.'

"We drove all the way across Kansas and it felt like five hundred miles, like driving across the Gobi Desert. (1) We got to within fifty miles of the border with Colorado and saw a sign that said, 'You must have weighed your truck or you will not be permitted to leave the state of Kansas.' At that point we figured we were screwed, not having weighed the truck, but we couldn't go back. So we went for the border and somehow we made it."

Back in Vermont, the Wobbly Barn in Killington was one of the band's favorite places to play. Rick says that when the band was trying to establish itself in Vermont in the fall of 1972 "We did a sort of paid audition at the Wobbly, and ended up almost being the house band there. We started in November of 1972 and played there one week a month from '72 through about 1980. We played six nights a week from 9:00 p.m. until 2:00 a.m. Our sound man was Doug Phoenix, one of the best sound men around, and during our Wobbly days we also added the Jefferson Light Show. The Wobbly was just a great Vermont restaurant and club, like the Baggy Knees in Stowe."

Another place that Davis Brothers Garage played was the Hampton Manor in Hampton, NY. One Sunday afternoon in the early '70s was especially memorable, as Rick explains. "We were playing the gig and a biker gang came in and they took over the place. They were partying down, literally hanging by their boots from the rafters, which were I-beams, it was total pandemonium. So we went up on stage to start a fresh set and we said to ourselves, 'We're gonna take control of this room.' We decided to play one of our showstopper songs, 'Hoedown' by Emerson, Lake & Palmer. We started the song, the front double doors opened up and a guy roared in on a Harley. He started doing pinwheels on the dance floor and drowned us out completely!"

Like Fox and Company, and Stone Cross, Davis Brothers played on into the 1980s, occasionally adding new members like drummer Brad Gibson, bass players Angelo Mullen and Frank Barnes, and guitarist Nobby Reed.

The band recorded a studio LP in 1981, and the album made the list of *Billboard* magazine's "Recommended LPs" for the week of July 25, 1981. According to *Billboard*, the album's "best cuts" were "Lookin' for the Money" and "Nasty Situation." As a result of the *Billboard* publicity, the band landed a single deal with the Famous Charisma record label in the UK, the label that Genesis and Peter Gabriel were recording for at the time. The single was "Lookin' for the Money," penned by Lane.

Though the group had marked success in the 1980s, we end this chapter with a '70s tale that links the wanderlust of Davis Brothers Garage Band to the keen entrepreneurial spirit that is a hallmark of our great nation. Here is Rick's coup de grace about bringing a taste of the rough and rowdy Wild West back to the home fires of Vermont.

"In the 1970s Coors was a mythical beer here in the Northeast. So at the end of the summer of 1975 I decided to take some of my summer earnings and buy a bunch of Coors to export back to Vermont. On our last day in Denver I went down to the liquor store and bought *seventy* cases of Coors at $4.34 a case. The band had a Chevy C-60 truck for our equipment, but it wasn't completely full, so I used a hand truck to load all the Coors into the back with our gear. Jeff Wilkes, our sound guy for the summer, had driven the equipment truck out to Denver, but he had found a wicked deal on a Chevy Suburban and bought it. So I got to drive the truck, and my beer, back to Vermont.

"When we got back to Vermont those seventy cases went in three days, strictly by word of mouth. People were calling me, stopping me on the street, I tripled my money. Best deal I ever did."

The Wobbly Barn

The answer to the question sounds like the proverbial broken record. Ask band members from the 1960s and 1970s about the clubs they loved to play, and invariably they include the Wobbly Barn in Killington, Vermont.

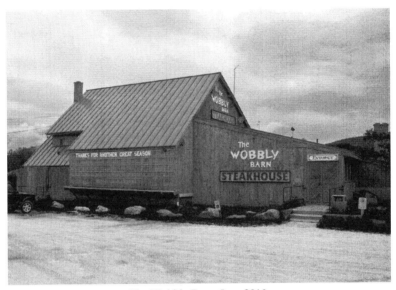

The Wobbly Barn, June 2010

The Wobbly Barn opened for business in December 1963, at the start of ski season that year. Owners Jack Giguere, Tom Standish, and George Stevens built the Wobbly out of wood gathered from derelict New England barns. Unlike some older barns that found new life as rock and roll joints, the Wobbly began life as a night spot. The building today is essentially unchanged from the structure raised in 1963.

In 1971, Jack purchased another club about a mile down the Killington Road. The place was originally called the Sugar Shack, and then the Showcase East. Jack re-named it the

Pickle Barrel, and it became his second rock night club. Many of the bands that played at the Wobbly Barn also played at the Pickle Barrel. Members of Fox and Company and Davis Brothers Garage shared memories with me of both venues. Between his two clubs, Jack Giguere provided the best entertainment at Killington.

Of all the places we played, the Wobbly was, as a rule, the diciest destination between November and March. The club was two and a half miles up the Killington Road, no picnic in the snow. There was never any guarantee a band's truck could snake its way up the mountain to the Wobbly, or avoid sliding off a curve on the way down. Steve Galipeau of Fox and Company remembers how "We got stuck in there a couple of times by black ice. Some times at the end of a gig you just knew you weren't going anywhere. You'd walk out into the parking lot and fall down four times before you got to your car and think, 'I don't believe we should drive down the mountain tonight.'"

Gardner Berry of Stone Cross replays his favorite winter weather story from the Wobbly. "We were scheduled to play at the Wobbly, and there was a blizzard coming. We would always get an early start anyway and set up early, and we certainly did on that trip. The Monday that storm hit we were the only band in town because the weather was so bad. The kid who was driving the truck for Davis Brothers Garage and who had come in ahead of the band showed up to see us that night. I remember getting up the next morning and seeing the truck stuck in the snow. He'd tried to drive it, gotten maybe twenty feet, and got stuck."

In spite of the trek in and out, band guys loved the Wobbly. Lane Gibson of Davis Brothers says, "It was one of our favorite places to play. It seemed like a good fit, and the people who came there really enjoyed the band." Rick Davis is more succinct: "It was my favorite place to play!" Don

Coulombe of Fox and Company chimes in that "The Wobbly was just a really fun place to work, just a great rock and roll club." And Dan Sibley of Gunnison Brook, when asked to name his favorite places to play, responded, "The most memorable for me would be the Wobbly Barn in Killington, VT. It was in a ski resort area, we got room and board, there was a guaranteed packed house and vintage wood for great acoustics. What's not to like?"

The interior of the Wobbly looked exactly as you'd expect a Vermont ski resort club to look: rustic, lots of wood, multiple levels, dripping with atmosphere. The stage was even smaller than the stage at The Rusty Nail, sort of a cubbyhole set back into the front wall of the club. The dance floor, also pretty small, was right in front of the stage, and a second floor balcony with a railing ran above three sides of the dance floor below. There were two bars on the main floor and one bar upstairs, with two staircases connecting those levels. Down a third staircase, in the lower level, was the club's restaurant.

Gardner Berry observes that "there was always a really appreciative crowd, and I loved the setup with the balcony people up there. I thought the sound in the room was great, the Jefferson Light Show always looked spectacular, and with Flash's parachute behind us on that smaller stage it just lit up amazingly and made us look great."

During the late '60s and throughout the '70s the daily and weekly schedule at the club remained pretty constant. Bands played six nights a week and a Sunday matinee. Rick Davis remembers that "In 1973 and 1974 we played the Wobbly with a happy hour band that played downstairs in the restaurant. They were a three-piece bluegrass band called the Pousette-Dart Band, and they were just wonderful. They had great vocals, with Jon Pousette-Dart, John Troy, who was an excellent bassist, and John Curtis, a multi-instrumentalist on mandolin, banjo, fiddle or electric guitar. We'd hang out downstairs and watch them, then they'd come upstairs and watch us.

"It was interesting following their career, because Pousette-Dart was a kickass bluegrass band, but when they got a deal with Capitol Records they tried to make the transition to a country rock band like the Eagles. They tried for five years, but never really made that transition. What I thought they really did the best was from their roots."

The Pousette-Dart Band recorded four albums with Capitol, and toured with such big names as The Byrds, Bonnie Raitt, Little Feat, James Taylor, The J. Geils Band, Charlie Daniels Band, Emmylou Harris, Randy Newman, and Billy Joel.

Joy Moffat, who for a time worked the Jefferson Light Show with Jeff "Flash" Gordon, recalls that "The Wobbly ran movies before the band came on, so if you worked there for a week you would see the same movie each night. The Wobbly

215

is near and dear to my heart, because that's where I first saw Gunnison Brook."

And, you will recall, the Wobbly's Sunday matinee was the kettle in which the Rodney Diamond and the Studs stew was first cooked up, the place where the RD&S stage show with all its audacious theater was born.

Speaking of cooking, Gardner Berry will tell you that "The food was always great at the Wobbly. The chef there was a guy named Bali Sabo, he was Hungarian, and he used to bring his congas up on stage and play with us."

The Hungarian chef was just one of a large cast of interesting characters at the Wobbly. Lane Gibson notes that "We really enjoyed playing there, but at the same time you used to get your share of people getting a little out of control. Some of the guys who worked there were pretty good-sized, like Brent Gifford and Ronnie Truro, and "Mad Dog" Dave Gaucheault, the manager. The Wobbly had these two huge, wooden doors, probably two inches thick, and I remember if somebody got unruly they would take the guy and run him right through the doors, open the doors with his head. They didn't fool around!"

Rick Davis adds a "Mad Dog" tale. "In 1972 when Davis Brothers Garage moved back to Vermont we went looking around for work the way all bands did, and we played a night or two in the fall up at the Wobbly. 'Mad Dog' was a former green beret, and he loved us, maybe because we played 'The Ballad of the Green Berets.'" Another favorite of many of the bands was Dwight Aiken, who also served for a time as manager of the Wobbly.

And then there's this appetizing story told by Rick. "One night 'Mad Dog' shared with me that during the afternoon some guy who'd had too much to drink went over in the corner and took a leak into the back stairwell. The only problem was that the back stairs led right down to the restaurant kitchen, and the pee splashed down the stairs and into the evening's pots of clam chowder that were waiting on the bottom stair to be cooked." You know when you go to Mexico and they tell you not to drink the water? Well, that night at the Wobbly it was, "Don't drink the soup, man."

One of the Wobbly's mixed blessings was the house that it maintained for visiting band members. Located just across the parking lot on the mountain side of the club, the house was, on balance, mostly a positive, since it meant that bands had no housing costs for their week at the Wobbly. At the same time, said lodging was clearly not the Taj Mahal.

The house was a two-story building with two apartments, both upstairs/downstairs affairs. A visiting band got one apartment, and Wobbly employees lived in the other. Steve Galipeau remembers, "The bedroom was upstairs and was just a bunch of mattresses laid out like a bunkroom. The house was always cold, you couldn't get enough heat in there to save your life. You would always bring your sleeping bag when you played the Wobbly. And first thing in the morning somebody had to start the shower, because it wasn't like we could all start showering at 6:00 p.m. and the last person still have hot water. But it was our choice, and we did it for the hope of rock stardom."

Angelo Mullen of Davis Brothers also recalls that upstairs bedroom setup. "The band house had one giant room full of single beds, so we stapled sheets to the ceiling to make separate rooms. Talk about your paper thin walls when you're getting busy."

Jeff Gordon tells this story on Bali Sabo. "Bali was a really good cook, and he had a Fu Manchu moustache and hair down to his butt. We used to throw wicked parties at the band house and one night he was smoking pot and caught his hair on fire."

Steve Galipeau laughs about a celestial event at the band house. "One night we were partying at the band house, we decided to go outside, and the Northern Lights were happening like I've never seen them before or since. We were all lying out in the parking lot enjoying the show and our light man, "Shampoo" [Bob Champoux], who had a really good buzz going, ran inside and came back out with his Polaroid Instamatic with the flash cube. He started shooting pictures and someone said, 'What are you doing with the flash?' He said, 'It'll help' and I said, "Yeah, the flash will get there in about twenty years!'"

This band house story should be told anonymously. "We had a party with a bunch of girls at the staff apartment. The two guys who lived there weren't the bartenders, they were these geeky sort of guys who worked in the kitchen. Well, when the band left, of course so did all the girls. There was this connecting door between the two apartments, and we could hear the two guys talking. One said, 'You know we coulda had them girls,' and the other said, 'Yeah, well if that's all we could get I'd rather have nothing.' And the first guy said, 'Yeah, well, we got nothing!' We were listening through the door to these guys arguing and we were falling down on the floor on the other side of the door. I mean, they weren't the bartenders giving free drinks to the girls. They were always happy to have the band over to their apartment just so other people would come." Aah yes, Lenny and Squiggy making time on the band's dime.

Ken Aldrich of Tracks has this very clear memory from the Wobbly burned into his gray matter. "The one time I remember more than any other was watching Tyler Plotzke of Davis Brothers play drums while his cymbals were on fire. All I could think was, 'This barn is just aching to become ashes.' I couldn't understand how they could do that. I was scared to death they would start a fire. Now they did have guys on either side of Tyler with fire extinguishers, and it *was* a great show."

Lane Gibson explains: "We stole the idea for the fire drum solo from a group called Canary we had seen in Denver, and we thought, 'We're gonna bring this back to Vermont.' We put lighter fluid on Tyler's mallets, and used a combination of flash powder and gun powder on the cymbals. It was a wild act, and really successful, although after regular exposure to the lighter fluid and the flames, the mallet heads would eventually burn through."

Jeff Gordon, a key figure in this pyro act, continues: "One time we actually did set a girl's sweater on fire. The head of one of Tyler's flaming mallets finally burned through and flew off. It hit a wall, hit the dance floor, bounced, and set the sweater on fire. Dougie [Doug Phoenix, Davis Brothers' sound man and roadie] comes racing through the audience with the fire extinguisher, spraying all over the place, spraying the girl…somehow, no one was hurt."

Flash also describes "Another part of the show when a band would do 'Fire' by either Arthur Brown (especially) or Jimi Hendrix. We had tennis cans on either side of the stage that we loaded up. We'd fire those things off and balls of flame would go thirty feet up in the air. Of course you know the size of the Wobbly Barn, it had a huge, high ceiling but a small and pretty enclosed dance floor/stage area. Today we would probably be arrested for it. That part of the show used to scare the hell out of me, and I was running it. We always had a lot of fire extinguishers at the ready." I guess they did, because Flash practiced his pyrotechnical magic with several bands at the Wobbly Barn, and the place is still standing.

"Flash" Gordon and the Jefferson Light Show

How does a Canadian Junior A goalie, who wants to follow in his dad's footsteps and play professional hockey, end up south of the border setting off pyrotechnics that would get you arrested in most states today? And how did Jeffrey William Gordon get that nickname?

It started in a Troy, NH, woolen mill. In 1969, if a Canadian citizen came to the United States and lasted six months at a job he or she could earn a permanent visa. Jeff had finished college and wanted to come to the States, so he took a job as a loom weaver.

While in the United States, Jeff got to know some people at the Saxony Hotel in Rouses Points, NY, who were going to open a new club, The Saxony Lounge. Jeff put in his six months at the mill, said sayonara, and lit out for the Saxony.

Jeff tells the story of his first gig: "A group called the AC Apple Medicine Show was at The Saxony. I was bartending and became friends with the band, and they said, 'C'mon, do you wanna be in the road crew.' I said 'Yes,' and started earning $15 a week lugging a B-3 and other equipment. But after a while I said to myself, 'I don't really want to be a roadie, it's backbreaking work. Why don't I do something to make bands look good,' because I loved the music, and thought maybe I could add to the music. So I built this light board, it wasn't much, maybe six heavy-duty switches, almost like a keyboard, and you could plug a whole bunch of stuff in it. I had that built by an electrician, I put it together and started doing this little light thing, and immediately it took off.

"People would ask the band, 'What's that little guy doing in the corner behind the stage.' They couldn't see me working but they could see what was going on out front, and it was pretty tight. That was the start of it all."

Soon after that humble beginning drummer David Curtin left AC Apple, and Jeff hooked up with a band called the Book of Matches from Springfield, MA. "They had a record, and even though it didn't go anywhere I got into Boston and made a bunch of contacts. Then I got a call from Atlantis. They were looking for a drummer and had heard about David. He told them, 'If you want me you are going to get Jeff as well, we're a package deal.' They told David they didn't have any money and I said I would do it for free, just meals and lodging, and that's how it started with Atlantis.

"After a while I began buying equipment, then more equipment, and we were doing gigs with various bands including Aerosmith. They asked me if I wanted to do lighting for them, because they didn't have a lot of lighting equipment. Word got out that Atlantis had this little guy in the corner, playing what looked like a piano. I realized that I had to spend more to be more, so I started buying even more updated equipment."

For a time Jeff split from Atlantis and struck out on his own, doing shows through booking agencies with different bands like Dr. Hook, Black Horse, Jonathan Edwards, Edgar Winter, Foghat, Rare Earth, TNT, Steppenwolf, and others. It was "lots of one-nighters, and I was always in demand." Until Atlantis' David Curtin called. He told Jeff, "We're playing up at the Broken Ski in Killington, and we're rehearsing. What are you up to?" Long story short, Atlantis drove down to Newport, RI, where Jeff was working, loaded up their truck with Jeff's gear, and he was back on the road with Curtin, Bob Hearne, Chris Quackenbush, and Sammy "The Blade" DeSantis.

Jeff says, "We did a bunch of shows for about a year or so, a lot of them in the Boston area. By then Atlantis was fading, it just wasn't working out. David came up to me one day and said, 'This guy named Jeff Wilkes from Tracks called, they wanna bring you back to Vermont.' Well, by then I had had my fill of the big city, so I said 'I'm outa here.' Jeff drove down to Boston, picked up me and my equipment in the truck, and back we went to the farm in Hartland.

"I started doing the Tracks thing, doing the frat parties and clubs. Jeff Wilkes helped me out a lot, but in 1974 the band broke up. When Tracks broke up Davis Brothers picked me up and I was with them a long time. It was a great time with good friends and a lot of great stories. Meanwhile, Stone Cross was pounding on my door, 'Hey, we're going to Florida.' I'd heard that before, so I told them I'd think about it. I ended up talking to Lane Gibson, he was agreeable and encouraging, so off I went to Florida for a while."

Jeff "Flash" Gordon

In 2011, people who go to a rock concert expect an impressive light show. But in the late 1960s no one expected much. Remember Jeff's first light board? Six heavy-duty switches with some lights plugged in? In 1968, our Ham Sandwich light show was a foot switch and four colored lights—red, blue, green, yellow. Talk about primitive.

But "Flash" was an artist, ahead of his time even with the most basic equipment. He became a star in his own right, and the stories about him and his light show are legendary.

Jeff Wilkes exclaims, "That Flash is still alive is amazing. He had a thing for Southern Comfort, and his reputation preceded him. Wherever he went people would just keep sending over shots. When we worked together I had my sound board right next to his light board. I would look over and literally there would be ten shots of Southern Comfort lined up in front of him. During the course of a performance they would all be consumed, and at the end of the night his eyes would be crossed. I've never seen eyes crossed like his, like they were double crossed, and I was amazed he could run his equipment at all.

"And it wasn't like that equipment was sophisticated, programmable stuff. It was bare wires and duct tape and he had these car dimmer switches which he would run with his feet. It's amazing he didn't electrocute himself. The fact that he put the whole system together out of spare parts, at a cost of probably no more than $200, is incredible enough. But the truth is that the quality of the equipment almost didn't matter. Flash was a really superior light person, very creative, very skilled at synching with the music."

As for the nickname, Rick Davis stakes this claim. "One night at the Chopping Block he overloaded his flash pots, and some drunk was staggering around them when they went off. It scared the hell out of him. We were a little concerned, but aside from the scare the guy seemed okay. Then another night at the Silver Keg in Burlington, it was last call, Flash

223

overloaded the flash pots, touched them off, and blew the main circuit. They lost all the lights in the club, the power to the stage, everything. I remember the patrons coughing, sneezing, and stumbling out into the street."

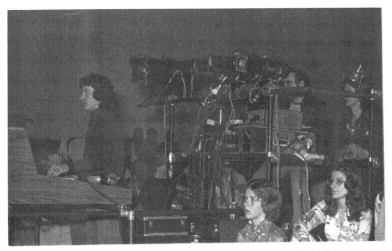

Flash (behind the railing) with Stone Cross, Scott Swain in front
on the soundboard, roadie Tim Davis to Flash's left

Rick adds, "Flash was a great guy. He was the only French Canadian we could call 'Froggy' and get away with it. Flash told Skip Truman before we played in Quebec not to ever say 'tabarnac' or 'saint tabarnac.' Skip forgot the advice but remembered the phrases, and one night at Norm Silva's Moustache Club in Montreal, trying to be cordial, Skip repeated them. We were lucky the club was dead that night or we would have been." (1)

Flash picks up Rick's narrative to tell the next two stories. "When the Jefferson Light Show was getting really hot, the Davis Brothers' music and the show fit together like a glove. Davis Brothers used to rehearse a lot, I would rehearse with them, and we were very tight. The show was never too flashy [Whoa, thirty foot pillars of flames aren't too flashy?!], and what I did depended on the type of song the band played. For a sweet, mellow song I would set the mood with the right sort of low lighting, but when things got cranked up, you could also expect visual excitement. At The Rusty Nail we'd have our smoke bombs go off from the stage, and ashes and cinders would fall down to the dance floor and onto people, but they didn't really seem to mind.

"For a time the road crew was Brad Gibson and Doug Phoenix and me. Davis Brothers used to play at a bar called Casino by the Sea in Falmouth, MA, and one night after a round of drinking the three of us decided to form this group we named the 'Mented Meenies.' We'd go down to the beach on a Sunday, the beach would be filled with families, and we would do this aquatic ballet. We'd go out into the ocean to a depth of about four feet, and the three of us would do a water ballet. Can you imagine, these three hippies doing a water ballet? But it was gorgeous, honestly, and what happened was we drew a crowd. So we did it two or three more times and drew a bigger crowd each time."

Despite his distaste for the backbreaking work, Flash did serve as a roadie, as well as the light show man, for every band with which he performed. Given that history, we are going to take an important side trip to give praise to our unsung heroes of the macadam.

Flash, Dan Avery, Greg "Bo" Bobar, Bill Bruso, Bruce Buck, Tim Davis, Peter Doucette, Chris Dunn, Perry Edson, Brad Gibson, Marc Griggs, Brad "Bear" Ingalls, Jim Minetti, Marc Mulroy, John O'Hara, Bill Osborne, Doug Phoenix, Ken Stevens, Scott Swain, Mike Thoma, Will Tracy, Lenny Warner, Jeff Wilkes, Tom Wyman, and many more whose names I do not know, did the heavy lifting for bands at all hours of the day and night and in all types of weather.

Any tribute to the road crews has to center on the legendary Hammond organ. We are talking about a beast that weighed three hundred pounds or more. Most keyboard players in the '60s and '70s insisted that the Hammond, with its accompanying Leslie, was crucial to their sound. Two people could manage a Leslie, but it took a crew to subdue the Hammond. Some bands had a carrier with handles designed specifically for a Hammond, but many just put four shoulders to the monster. (2)

Anyone who ever hauled a Hammond B-3 up the stairs at the Barre, VT, Opera House, or muscled one up the back fire escape of the YMCA in Greenfield, MA, or hefted one onto the elevated stage at The Rusty Nail in Stowe, knows that roadies are worth their weight in gold.

Perhaps the most riveting Hammond stories come from Flash's time doubling as light show wizard and roadie for Atlantis. At Stowe's Rusty Nail, most bands lifted their Hammonds up onto the stage from the dance floor, but not Atlantis. Atlantis had a truck with a thirty-four foot ramp, and they did things differently. Says Flash, "We took out part of the railing by the upstairs bar, and ran the truck ramp across the dance floor to the stage. One time we were lugging Sammy 'The Blade' DeSantis' B-3 across that ten foot drop, we were about three-fourths of the way across, and you could just feel the ramp getting ready to let go. We hustled off the ramp, it snapped, and the B-3 hit the dance floor below. I've never seen anything shatter like that."

Sammy later lost another B-3 on the back fire escape of the Opera House in Barre. The Atlantis road crew was humping the Hammond up the stairs when disaster struck. Flash recalls that "We didn't have the handle lifts they made for B-3s, so we grabbed it from the bottom, got it almost all of the way up to the top and the guy at the bottom said, 'I can't hold it!' and he let it go." The crew watched as the Hammond bumped down the stairs, taking the trailing Leslie with it. The roadie holding the Leslie jumped over the fire escape railing and hung on for dear life as the beast careened by on its way to destruction at the bottom of the staircase. Flash remembers that, "When Sam showed up to play, he asked, 'Where's the B-3?' and I go, 'C'mon, Sam, we're gonna go take a walk.'"

Flash has more stories from the Jefferson Light Show's days on the road than a postman has letters in his satchel. "One time with Atlantis we did a show with Sly and the Family Stone at one of the State Colleges in New York. At Sly's sound check Larry Graham, who had six Ampeg bass cabinets, came out on the stage and started playing some chords. *Loud* chords. They were so loud that three of the plate glass windows at the far end of the gym shattered. Needless to say we were quite impressed.

"When I was with Davis Brothers they were recording at Earth Audio Studio in North Ferrisburg, VT. Bear Ingalls, one of our roadies, was outside with a microphone trying to drop a dumpster lid while the band was trying to record a track. The band wanted the sound of the dumpster lid in their song at a very precise moment. It never worked out but the laugh factor was priceless.

"I was at The Groggery in Allston, MA, doing a show with Wiley Crawford, David Curtin, and some other guys. We were on a break, and this big guy came up and started checking out David's drums. He looked at David and said, 'You know, I can play those.' David said 'Sure' because we were in Beantown and you never know. The guy got behind the drums, made a few minor adjustments, and then asked, 'Oh, do you mind if my bass player sits in with me?' They started jamming, they jammed for about twenty minutes, and these guys were really good. I went over to my light board as usual, and did my little mood thing while they were playing. After all was said and done, the big guy came over to me, thanked me and thanked Dave for the use of his drums. Then he looked at me and asked, 'So you're the little guy who was sitting in the corner with the light board?' I said, 'Yeah,' and he told me, 'You made me really feel good, you helped me set the mood with your mood.' Then he introduced himself, and guess who it was? Buddy Miles.

"Stone Cross was playing Crandall Park in Glens Falls, NY. We were set up in this gazebo, it was probably the second set, everything was tight, the lights were tight, it was getting a little dark so it was looking pretty good. I looked to the left of where I was set up and there was this kid standing there, and he'd been standing there by himself since the show started. He was grooving to the music, having a good time. We took a break, and the kid pulled on my pants leg as I was coming down off the scaffolding. He started talking to me, but he talked like he had a speech impediment. By pointing to the stage, basically he explained to me that he was legally deaf, but he could hear the bass end. What fascinated him was that the lighting was so in sync with the bottom end, and he really got off on it. He was about fourteen or fifteen years old, and he just complimented me up and down. I felt a little humbled, because it was great to see someone else get so much enjoyment from what I did."

Flash summarizes his eleven years on the road. "With a lot of bands, I was considered a fifth or sixth member. Because of my unique style, I could adapt to any type of music, and I could create an unusual perspective and presentation of any band's music. I created the ultimate blend of their music with my lights and personalized what they did. What they performed on stage I enhanced visually. Timing was essential, it was the key to everything. When a band rehearsed I would rehearse with them, so that when we toured we were a very tight unit of sound, lighting, and music. I would produce a complete, concert-type show in a nightclub environment. Even today my visual memories of that era will never be forgotten. To all my friends, thanks for your support. To all, thanks for an unforgettable ride."

Fox Chase

"The most talented band I ever represented. There was just too much talent to live together in one house."

— Ed Malhoit, speaking of Fox Chase

The back story of Fox Chase began in two places that couldn't have been more different. In 1964, Steven Tallarico formed his first band in America's metropolis, New York City. Later that year, The Sprites assembled in the Town of Brattleboro, in southeastern Vermont. With a population of approximately 12,000, Brattleboro was a far cry from the Big Apple, although it boasted more than its fair share of quality rock bands. Fox Chase was born from the intersection of two bands in Brattleboro in the summer of 1969.

You will recall that in 1969 Steven, Don Solomon, and Frankie Ray had a band named Chain. According to Pete Bover of Nickel Misery, Steven approached him and Eddie Kistler about combining musicians from both bands to "have a five-piece band, get serious, write some tunes, and try to do something other than playing high school dances." In September players from the two bands, each represented by Ed Malhoit, joined forces and became Fox Chase.

In the 1960s and 1970s there was a widely held belief, which persists today, that Ed Malhoit was always trying to find the superstar combination, always thinking about which musicians he could mold into an act that would earn national acclaim. Says club owner Jere Eames of The Galleon, "He thought he had it with Fox Chase, and he might have." More's the pity, the group was not together long enough to test Ed's proposition.

229

What's a supergroup supposed to look like, personnel-wise? Fox Chase had incredible talent instrumentally and vocally with Eddie Kistler on keyboard and lead vocals; Steven Tallarico on drums and lead vocals; Don Solomon also playing keyboard and singing; Pete Bover on bass and vocals; and Mickey "Mouse" McElroy on lead guitar. However, this basic description does a disservice to the band's musical flexibility and multi-instrumental skill. Nick Kanakis says, "I saw them maybe three times, and they had two great lead singers and tremendous harmonies. They had two keyboard players, and then sometimes Steve would play keyboard. The fact that different band members would play different instruments on certain songs, and the fact that they didn't lose anything at all when they switched instruments, that was what really stood out in my mind."

One of the group's early shows was at The Galleon, in Littleton, NH. "The" Fox Chase (as per the poster on the next page) was the band for The Galleon's grand opening on October 25, 1969. Reflecting back on that long-ago evening, Jere Eames remembers that he and his wife, Yvonne, were "Pleased with the band." The club enjoyed a big opening night crowd and, Jere adds, "I remember Eddie Kistler, because he was such a good singer."

Jere and Yvonne had never seen either Eddie Kistler or Steven Tallarico on stage until that performance. It was their good fortune to see both these legends for the first time on the same night, in the same band, and in their own club! It also has occurred to me that the young people in the crowd that night had no idea what they were witnessing: perhaps the best band ever to form in the nexus, a band anchored by two superstars. Eddie Kistler was fated to die less than five years later, before his fame could reach a level commensurate with his talent. Steven Tallarico, playing drums that night on The Galleon's stage, was destined to become one of the world's greatest rock stars.

Advertisement for Opening Night at The Galleon, October 25, 1969

When Fox Chase formed, Steven asked his parents, Sue and Victor Tallarico, if the band could stay at the family property at Sunapee Lake. Mr. and Mrs. Tallarico graciously consented. In the early 1920s, Giovanni Tallarico had purchased a property known as Trow Hill Farm, which included a main house and more than 200 acres. The family built cabins in the mid-1930s so that Giovanni's wife, Constance, could run Trow-Rico, a music camp for some of her New York City music students. By the 1940s, Trow-Rico had become a family resort where, according to Lynda Tallarico, "Families could rent the cottages by the week, be served meals, and be treated to the most fantastic week of their lives." (1) While Kate Tyler, Eddie Kistler's widow, recalls living in the Main House with Eddie and their toddler son during the band's time at Trow-Rico, bassist Pete Bover lived in one of the cottages.

Unfortunately, the cottages had electric heat that was insufficient for the winter. When it got cold everybody in the band moved into the Main House. Pete says, "The big house was winterized, and Steven's dad understandably didn't like us moving in, but he let us do it." Lynda Tallarico told me that in the living room of the Main House, several years earlier, Steven had first played "Dream On" on the upright Steinway on which his grandmother Constance had given lessons in Manhattan.

On the property there was also a grand old three-story barn, with a huge, two-story fireplace. In the basement was a big pool table, a ping pong table, and a piano in a makeshift stage area for family gatherings and entertainment. The second floor had bedrooms for guests, two bathrooms, and a large, rectangular living area with the stone fireplace that went straight up through the roof. There were also two grand pianos and cozy seating for Sunday evening concerts. The third floor of the barn was a large attic, where the family stored all manner of treasures.

Pete Bover says that "We did our rehearsing in the barn, but it was unheated and cold as hell in the winter. It had a huge fireplace, and one time we lit up the fireplace for some warmth and the stones got too hot and ignited the music and instruments that were stored next to the fireplace. I remember running around frantically dragging our equipment out. The fire department came, and saved the barn, but there was a lot of damage." Among the items that were lost were books, music, and papers that Giovanni Tallarico had stored there.

Pete remembers that the band quickly got situated in the early fall and set about rehearsing in earnest. "We rehearsed and put together about thirty songs, so we could play out and make some money. Little by little we wrote original songs and worked to get them together, so we could record them and try to go somewhere."

The band played the Malhoit Circuit—high school dances, fraternity parties, clubs, and occasional concerts opening for big acts. Word quickly spread on the circuit that Fox Chase was an outstanding act.

Fox Chase, Fall 1969, Standing L – R: Pete Bover, Don Solomon;
Front L – R: Eddie Kistler, Mouse McElroy, Steven Tallarico

Fox Chase performed several of what Pete Bover calls "tough production numbers," including "Pinball Wizard" by The Who, and a classic that is remembered by other musicians from the nexus with exceptional clarity even after four decades—a stunning cover of The Beatles' eight minute opus off *Abbey Road*, "I Want You (She's So Heavy)."

Other songs on the play list included "Birthday" by The
Beatles, The Band's "Up On Cripple Creek," and several
Creedence Clearwater Revival tunes, including "Born on the
Bayou." Pete recalls that the Creedence numbers were "The
kind of songs Eddie knocked people's socks off with,
because he duplicated Fogarty's voice really well."

Every band experienced some not so sane moments, and Pete
Bover describes one of them during Fox Chase's time
together. "We were all living in the house in Sunapee, and
people were always coming and going. There was this nutty
guy who came around a lot and one night he came over and
said he had a speedboat out on the lake. We're all doing
nothing, getting stupid, and someone said to him, 'Hey, let's
get in the boat and take a ride.' This was about midnight, but
it was a full moon so you could see. However, it was
November in Sunapee, and the water was really cold. So
Steve and I and a couple other guys got in this boat and we
took off and went full tilt across Lake Sunapee. I just
remember being scared as hell, and now that I think about it,
if anything had happened none of us would have made it
back to shore. No more Fox Chase, no more Aerosmith,
nothing, it's all gone. There we were, a bunch of us, acting
crazy, midnight, a full moon, scooting across Sunapee, but
we made it back."

What was the engine that lifted and drove Fox Chase during
its brief flight? There is little disagreement on the answer to
that question.

According to Pete Bover, Steven Tallarico was a restive guy,
wired and ambitious. "In Fox Chase he was the guy who
pushed things along. He'd be up earlier than us, pushing us,
c'mon get up, we gotta get going. He was in on the lyric
writing and some of the riffs of the originals, he was
ambitious, and he had a lot of confidence. He said to me
once, when the band was still together, 'Pete, I've seen The

Who, The Stones, this band and that band. You know, I can do that, and I'm *gonna* do that.' That's the kind of confidence he had."

Lonna LaLonde says that "Steven was very emphatic about people doing things right, he was a perfectionist to the hilt. That's what made him what he is, that drive for perfection. And when it came to music his ears were just amazing. He would hear things that other people couldn't hear. I could never see how he got there from Point A to Point B, but he knew just how to do it."

Doug Morton mentions that "Pete told me once that Steven was a taskmaster, but Pete added that, 'Steven was right and the rest of us were wrong. We wanted to party and he wanted to work, work, work. He was pushing to do something, and we really didn't want to push that hard. He was the one who made people get up and rehearse when they wanted to sleep in and blow off practice.'" Of course, that kind of incessant, sometimes obsessive focus can be a double-edged sword.

Recalling the brief history of Fox Chase, Bobby Gagnier exclaims, "Oh, my God, that was a frightening combination—Eddie and Don and Steve. What talent!"

Doug Morton also shares this memory. "When people talk about Fox Chase, they always talk about Eddie and Steven and to some extent Don. But Pete Bover, Pete was a rock star, and Malhoit was right about that. Pete had that vibe about him all the time, always super friendly, big smile, and he was a musician's musician. He didn't flaunt it, he didn't think he was anything special, but Pete had the tone, the sound, the look, he *really* knew how to play, and he had a great ear. Plus he sang unbelievable harmony vocals. Despite his talent he was not aloof. You might think so if you saw him onstage, because he was kind of a dangerous-looking guy, a typical laid-back bass player, and a real chick magnet.

But Pete never held any grudges when Fox Chase broke up. In fact in the early stages of Aerosmith he showed Tom Hamilton some things on bass."

Tracks first met the guys in Fox Chase over the weekend of November 14-16, 1969, Dartmouth's fall "House Parties" weekend. Tracks was playing Bones Gate and Fox Chase was playing at Tri Kap across the street on Fraternity Row. Ed Malhoit, the agent for both bands, had called and told us to check each other out. He told Fox Chase to give us a listen because we were so tight and our arrangements so sophisticated. And Ed insisted that we effete, intellectual Ivy League musicians needed to study a band that had the rock star swagger down pat.

Our drummer, Ned Berndt, recollects that "While we were unloading our equipment and setting up, I saw their white van across the street so I went over and introduced myself to the drummer, Steven. He had a big smile and was very friendly. We agreed to alternate set breaks so that we could check out each other's band. I remember Steven had an oversized (marching band) 26" bass drum and played a very funky rock groove. Mainly, what sticks out in my mind was Steven's personality, happy, open and all kinda 'nice to meet you, I've heard of you guys, sure let's alternate.' No wonder he went on to be so successful with Aerosmith. He was easy to like."

The highlight of the band's brief life was a concert in Boston. According to Ed Malhoit, "I had booked them as an opening act with The Chicago Transit Authority at three different colleges, but we never got to do the second and third shows because Chicago didn't want us opening for them. I was there that night at Endicott Junior College, and as good as Chicago was, Fox Chase outdid them! The Social Director told me that she felt she was giving the big check to the wrong band, and the crowd seemed to feel the same way.

Being honest, Chicago was a better band, with the horns and their great talent and songwriting. But they were just starting out, they hadn't built their reputation yet, and they were a little different, a little ahead of the times in terms of their fusion of rock and jazz. Fox Chase was more straight ahead rock and roll, and the crowd responded enthusiastically."

Fox Chase drummer Steve Tallarico and bassist Pete Bover

In the winter of 1970 the band had saved up $600, and Steven and the guys from New York knew a studio in the city that would give the band some inexpensive studio time. Pete Bover notes that "In those days you had to go to Boston or Manhattan to record, there was no other way to do it. We booked a midnight session at this studio in the middle of Manhattan, and stayed in a cheap hotel, also in Manhattan.

'Soul Surviving Son Of A Gun' was one original, and we recorded three or four for which we did the arrangements. We struggled all night long trying to get things down, and it was really exhausting, but when we finished there was a master tape of that session, all the songs. As I look back on it, we really struggled, and it was kinda odd. Eddie and I had been in the studio with The Sprites in 1965 or 1966 in Revere, MA, and of course Steven and Don had recorded several singles. So we had done some studio work before that session, but as a player I still really didn't know anything about it, like how to get a decent bass sound. It was tiring and frustrating having to do takes over and over again in the middle of the night. We had no producer, just an engineer that the guys happened to know."

Shortly after that recording session, dissension reared its ugly head and the band broke up in March. Pete says, "I don't know exactly why it happened, but Mickey already had set up another deal to live in a house for free in New Jersey and write songs. There was a famous jingle writer named Ed Labunski, somehow Mickey got connected with him and Labunski agreed to pay our rent and fund us to write songs. When we were breaking up Steve said to me, 'Pete, you're a good bass player, and you look good, I'm gonna start a new band, you can come with me or you can do something else.' And I did something else. I went with 'Mouse' to New Jersey. I zigged when maybe I should have zagged."

It is an accepted fact that living together, especially in cramped quarters, takes its toll on rock bands. But for Fox Chase, the things that made the band so outstanding also contributed significantly to its dissolution. Don Coulombe maintains that "Steve Tallarico was a real perfectionist, that's a big part of why Fox Chase broke up. I saw them play at a high school, everybody had great voices in that band, they had a great stage show, they were truly, truly talented. But there was such an ego thing in that band." Ed Malhoit was probably right. Just too much talent assembled in one place.

Seven months, and it was over. What some people think might have been the greatest group ever to come out of the nexus, a band that might have been as famous as Aerosmith, came to a swift end. The demise of Fox Chase was lamented by musicians and fans, but their legend lives on.

In the summer of 2009, Ed Malhoit wrote, "Aerosmith did a show in August of 1994 at Stowe Resort on the mountain, and I was there. There were banners in the crowd referring to how they remembered Fox Chase. Steven did several songs with a banner draped over his back, and then had it put on the back of the tour bus as the band left the area to connect up with the helicopter ride back to Boston."

Yvonne and Jere Eames

In 1966, Jere Eames was stationed in Paris, France, as a member of the American Embassy Armed Forces Courier Service. That year French President Charles DeGaulle withdrew his country from NATO and asked all non-French NATO troops to leave. Jere was then posted to the European headquarters of the SHAPE/NATO (1) Courier Service in Brussels, Belgium.

Yvonne Stoffelen, who held a job at the American Embassy in Brussels, met Jere through mutual friends in 1967. They soon became best friends, and when Jere returned to Littleton, NH, in the fall of 1968, Yvonne accepted a position with Bell Canada in Sherbrooke, Quebec, a few hours to the north. By the fall of 1969, Yvonne had joined Jere in Littleton.

Jeremiah Eames, Jere's namesake forebear, moved up from Massachusetts to the Northumberland and Groveton, NH, area north of Littleton in 1774. Jere's father, John B. "Jack" Eames, was born in Northumberland in 1891. Jack was a businessman who came to be known as "The Dean of New England Motion Picture Exhibitors." He was in the movie business in its infancy, when D.W. Griffith directed *Birth of a Nation* in 1915. Jere's mother, Blanche Meador Eames, met Jack in Concord, NH, in the 1930s. Jack was a New Hampshire state senator, and one year while the senate was in session in Concord, the state capital, Jack had a bout of heart trouble that landed him in the hospital. His pretty young nurse, twenty-two years his junior, became his wife and the mother of his two sons.

Jack Eames spent a good deal of time in Hollywood in the late 1920s and early 1930s as the film industry picked up steam and Tinseltown vied to be America's motion picture capital. He was friends with many of the stars and star makers of the '30s, '40s and '50s, including Bob Hope, Alan Ladd, Jane Powell, and Louis B. Mayer. Jack was primarily responsible for Littleton being the site of the 1941 world premiere of *The Great Lie* starring Bette Davis, thanks to his prominence in the film industry and his friendship with Ms. Davis. She had a summer home in the Littleton area at Sugar Hill, NH, and requested that the film premiere at Jack's Premiere Theater in Littleton on April 5, not coincidentally her thirty-third birthday. A parade that day attracted a throng of ten thousand people, who lined the streets of Littleton to celebrate both Ms. Davis' birthday and the world premiere of her movie. The Premiere Theater burned down in 1949, but Jack rebuilt it two years later. It has been in continuous operation in the same spot on Main Street ever since, currently as the Jax Jr. Cinema.

Jere and his older brother, also John B., grew up in the Littleton area. The house and property where Yvonne and Jere live today on Partridge Lake, just north of Littleton, has been in the Eames family for eighty years. Jere was only eight and his brother ten when their father died in 1951 at the age of sixty. Their mother, then thirty-eight, took over her husband's business, which was unheard of for a woman in the early 1950s. Jere and John developed their entrepreneurial skills early, out of necessity, helping their mother run the family business.

During his high school years, Jere attended Riverside Military Academy in Georgia. In college at The Citadel in Charleston, SC, Jere was editor-in-chief of the yearbook. "The yearbook staff put on the big dance of the year, a spring cotillion kind of dance, it was the 'Miss Citadel Pageant' and all that." It was Jere's responsibility to hire the entertainment for that big spring event. He arranged for The Platters to give an afternoon concert, and secured Frankie Valli and The

Four Seasons for the evening's dance. Jere was also in charge of The Citadel movie theater, all of which "was a good experience for my future business."

Jere's dad was a successful entertainment entrepreneur, so it is not surprising that Jere followed in his father's footsteps. His first foray into the club business came during the summer of 1965. After graduating from The Citadel, he had some time before going into the service. "A friend named Mark Southard and I brought rock music to Littleton. The kids were going to the town fathers and saying, 'We have nothing to do.' In the town building there is an opera house, and so we rented that from the town for $15 a night and we recruited the first bands to play there. Later Ed Malhoit did the bookings.

"I especially remember a band named Heat Wave and a band named The Kravers. Heat Wave came from Berlin, NH, and they had some good-looking girlfriends! They played the first night we opened and some of the girls they brought with them were dancing out on the floor and doing such a good job that we asked them to go up on the stage and dance for $5 a night. So they would dance as Go-Go girls on either side of the stage. We never gave the place a name, but it became known as 'The Littleton A-Go-Go.' We packed that building, and it was tremendously successful. One night we had over five hundred paid admissions. But I had to go in the service so Mark took it over."

Jere was in Europe for two years, and when he returned, "There was nothing open, nothing available for kids again. It was the fall of 1968, so I started looking around for something and this building was for sale on Main Street. It was beat up, it had been a garage, the roof leaked badly and so water used to run down the walls and into the ground level. There was moss on the walls, and it had a cement floor since it had been a garage. It was a real mess, but it was in a great location."

Including a small annuity from his father, Jere and Yvonne had saved up $16,000. The building was for sale for $39,700 "or something like that. We figured we would offer what we had, and we got it for $16,000." The bank authorized an improvement loan, so Jere and Yvonne put down their entire savings and bought the building in early 1969.

The Galleon opened in late October, 1969, and Yvonne and Jere were married on Sunday, February 15, 1970. Yvonne remembers that "For our honeymoon we took off with posters for the business, up the highway, Waterville Valley, back and forth, spent the night in Plymouth, NH, there was a huge snow storm. It was a working trip for us—we ended up in Stowe, VT, giving out posters."

Besides renovating a hulk of a gas station and turning it into a great looking club, the Eameses also found quality housing for the bands that played The Galleon. Often bands would stay at Thayers Inn, a grand old place on Main Street established in 1843 and owned by the Eames family. When bands stayed at Thayers, Jere put someone he knew on duty at the hotel, just to insure that there was no foolishness, even though "none of our bands ever trashed any rooms or did anything...beyond the streaking...." One night Tom Golden (Jeremiah's bouncer) happened to be on duty and fell asleep in the lobby. He awoke in the middle of the night to find a band which shall remain nameless streaking up and down the stairs. "Tom got a kick out of it. He said they were running up and down the stairs, and running through the lobby, but he said they weren't bothering anyone.

"In addition to Thayers, my brother John owned the largest brick building on Main Street, the Tilton's Opera Block, and down in the basement there was an area that was fabulous. It had an arched brick entryway and inside it had been an old coal bin or something. Yvonne went in there and worked her magic with the decorations, and we put some bunk beds in and cleaned it all up and bands loved it down there. If Thayers was busy they would stay there, and bands would recommend it. It had a tremendous amount of atmosphere."

Talk of putting up bands leads to an important point, perhaps best summarized by Peter Lipnickas of Better Days and Company. Peter had a philosophy that functioned almost as a rating scale regarding how much he enjoyed playing at a particular club. "The fun places, the ones I liked playing the most, were places where the owners truly enjoyed having you there, where they just embraced you."

Jere's description of Yvonne's and his relationship with the bands they employed deserves a spot near the top of Peter's rating scale. Speaking of the bands who played The Galleon and later at Jeremiah's, Jere recalls, "I was glad to sit around with them and find out what they were up to. It was a two-way street. We had good bands, and we wanted those bands to come back! So it wasn't just, 'Here's your money, get out.' We wanted to build a rapport, and we especially tried to get bands back that would recognize our guests, the audience. Getting to know the bands was very important, and we enjoyed it." Yvonne adds, "We enjoyed the business and we enjoyed the bands and we enjoyed our customers. You occasionally had the nasty customer or the band that was way too loud, but that was the real minority, not even worth mentioning."

Jere continues the train of thought. "Every business we have ever been in that had to do with entertainment we'd sit around afterwards, including with the band, and postmortem the evening." Yvonne remembers many individual band members for that reason. "We'd sit around, the band guys would be exhausted, we'd give them soft drinks and left over hot dogs. Any food that was left over they would gobble that right down!"

Don Coulombe remembers that "Jere and Yvonne gave us a few dates at the club, and it meant a lot to us because we had seen so many good bands at The Galleon. Once Jere gave us a date at The Galleon, Mrs. Newell gave us dates at Newell's Casino. What a thrill that was for us, only seventeen years old at the time."

Jere and Yvonne treated their employees the same way they treated the bands; one tradition was the annual Christmas party. Jere comments on the photo below: "We always had Christmas staff parties. Almost all those people in the picture were employees. That particular year we also had members of the band, American Express, at the party. During the summers we would go out to Moore Reservoir for cookouts. And that was our social life; our business was our social life.

Christmas Staff Party at Jeremiah's, 1973, Jere seated front and center, Yvonne immediately to *his* left.

"We did pretty extensive interviews for staff positions and got a good feel for the folks we hired. We had a wonderful staff, and real longevity on our staff. We were successful and that meant that they were successful. That's a pretty simple but effective philosophy. And those people who used to work for us in the 1970s are still our friends today."

Now, see, Jere and Yvonne didn't have to do all those things, the food and lodging and the personal, social relationships. They could have just closed up each night and gone home. But that big picture philosophy of theirs is representative of both who they are, personally, and why they were such successful club owners. And that philosophy is why bands loved playing at The Galleon and Jeremiah's. It wasn't, "Hurry up, pack up your stuff, get going." The Eameses created an atmosphere in which you knew you were welcome, almost like part of a family.

Tributes to the way the Eameses ran their business, and to who they are as people, are legion. Rick Hunt, who as a teenager did the murals by the front entrance to The Galleon, says, "The Eames family has always been an advocate for young people in Littleton and for the community of Littleton itself, and I have a lot of respect for them. Back then, Jere was quite open to the kids. I remember when the place opened, it was quite the buzz and everybody attended there. I was known for doing art work, I carried around a sketch book everywhere I went, so Jere approached me and asked me to do the murals. I was flattered that he had such faith in me, and that helped to set me on the course I continue on today." Rick is an internationally known artist, earning accolades for the talent he began to develop as a teenager.

Paul Hayward, who has played in rock bands since his junior high years, likes to recall "how I met Jere. I was in the eighth grade and working on the school newspaper. We heard word that a disco was opening in Littleton and I asked for the assignment to interview the new owners for the paper. Workers were all over the place, still nailing two by fours, etc., there was dust everywhere and only weeks left to finish before opening night. Jere stopped what he was doing and gave me his complete attention as if I was Barbara Walters. I'll never forget it. I got the most interesting article of the week and he got free advertising to some 750 students."

Dale Granger waitressed at the club when it reopened as Jeremiah's. "To this day Jere is still the best boss I ever had the pleasure of working for. Why? Because he was honest, and fair, he respected you as an employee, and he had an exceptional personality. When I left Jeremiah's, any other boss would have just said, 'Well you're leaving, go.' But he always left the door open for me and anything he could do to help you, you know, if things didn't work out, he wouldn't hesitate to support you down the road."

Yvonne and Jere sold Jeremiah's in 1975, and then, says Jere, "We bought an old yellow school bus and renovated it, painted it all up, outfitted it as a motor home, and took off for a period of time. One destination was The Citadel, for my tenth college reunion. Everybody else is there in limousines and Mercedes, and I had my school bus parked on campus, feeling pretty rich indeed! We had a great trip, we were gone for six months, and then we returned to Littleton and I went to work selling commercial real estate for a local firm."

A second bus trip that began in the winter of 1978 landed the Eames family in San Diego, CA, where "We opened a Japanese restaurant called the Tengu, which translates to 'mischievous little devil.' It became the most successful Asian restaurant in San Diego county, won award after award." Things went well enough that once they got the restaurant underway they were able to step away from the day-to-day operation with full ownership, and Jere took a job at Merrill Lynch as a stockbroker. "We stayed until 1984, and made enough money that we could return to Littleton and invest both our money and our time in the town's future.

Our initial goal was to go out West for a year and then come back, but things went so well we stayed for six years."

Today, Yvonne and Jere still live in the family home on "Pahtridge" Lake—thanks, Jere, I love the accent!

Gerry Wolf toasts his friend Jere Eames. "Jere is one of the reasons that Littleton has thrived. He has put a lot of money and a lot of himself into the town. He and his family are givers. Also, he is very supportive of his friends and employees. There is only one Jere Eames. No one can measure what he has accomplished, what he has achieved, yet he is still one of the best people in the world. Jere is very personable, and really fun to be around, yet he is so self-effacing and truly humble."

Proving Gerry Wolf's point, Jere proclaims: "The true secret to my success was to marry the perfect woman to be my wife, the mother of our son, and a true working partner in all of our endeavors."

Stonewall Farm, Keene, NH, April 10, 2010, L – R: Yvonne Eames, Peter Wonson of Tracks, Jere Eames, Pete Merrigan of Gunnison Brook

The Galleon / Jeremiah's

If Gar Anderson was not my favorite club owner, Yvonne and Jere Eames were. If The Rusty Nail was not my favorite place to play, The Galleon was. In the twenty months between The Galleon's opening night on October 25, 1969, and my last rock and roll gig on June 19, 1971, Tracks played The Galleon eight times.

Those shows included New Year's Eve 1969 and 1970, and the "Grand Re-Opening" on September 5, 1970. (The Galleon had been closed for the summer in deference to the seasonal drawing power of Newell's Casino.) On one of those nights Tracks set the all-time attendance record at The Galleon with 902 paid admissions in a club with a capacity of 600. Regardless of the occasion, The Galleon was always a great gig. The crowds were eager and receptive, the owners were terrific, and the environment was special.

In early 1969, Yvonne and Jere bought a derelict, former garage on Main Street in Littleton, and set about giving the building a new life as a teen club. Despite their status as impoverished soon-to-be newlyweds, they were wise enough not to cut corners as they prepared The Galleon for opening night in October.

Jere likes to say that The Galleon "was built for sound. We went whole hog on that first sound system, which we used to crank up when the bands took a break. Dick Hammond from Hammond Electronics out of Bow, NH, did the sound system, and also did our Color Cat. It was a huge, one of a kind light and sound synthesizer with over 5,000 watts of power. It covered the whole ceiling, along with a custom made, oversized strobe light. We bought a lot of things from Roctronics, an outfit out of Cambridge, MA, run by an inventor named Dr. Richard Iacobucci. He had a shiny catalog with a mylar cover, and he sold us the psychedelic slide projectors, the shimmery curtains for behind the bandstand, the mirror ball, etc. We decided that we were going to have everything all set up on opening night.

"We had a game room set up on the second floor, so the whole second floor was another huge opportunity to make a living." Gardner Berry of Stone Cross says, "One of my clearest memories of The Galleon is the money I spent in the game room on foosball and the arcade machines."

How about the fact that the building was painted black? Jere was standing outside one day when he and Yvonne were trying to decide what color to paint the building. "I was out there, Gerry Wolf came up beside me and said, 'What are you looking at?' He was the kind of kid who was always curious, you know, 'What are you doing, what are you up to.' So I told him, 'We're trying to decide what color to paint the building' and he said right away, "Paint it black.' I said 'Black?' and he said, 'Yeah.'

"I told him I didn't think that would go over too well, because it was a brick colonial-type building. I went inside and Yvonne asked me what I had thought. I mentioned that Gerry Wolf had come along and I said, kind of offhandedly, that he suggested we paint it black. And Yvonne said, 'That's a good idea.' Well, Yvonne has always been pretty good at picking out this and that and the other and when she said it was a good idea I thought, 'Alright.' So we painted it black, and it looked fabulous."

Also fabulous were the murals Rick Hunt painted by the front door. Rick's murals were often done in fluorescent paint and shown under black lights, and they were very striking. They featured pyramids, people with three eyes, a fish with wings, a desert scene with palm trees and things melting...phantasmagorical, psychedelic stuff.

Sketch artist Rick Hunt, age 16, at The Galleon, 1969

To advertise the club Jere and Yvonne went to every single school in the North Country and put up flyers. They also stood out in front of schools as they dismissed for the day and handed out cards. Jere muses, "I don't think we could do that today."

Paul Hayward's band, Opaque Illusion, came in to test the sound and the lights on Friday, October 24. That Friday was a "soft opening"—no advertising, maybe forty or fifty people in the house, staff members and friends of the band. Paul recalls that "We appreciated Jere's kindness, giving us a chance to play. It was pretty much an afterthought, and when we finally approached him about playing, he already had a sizable lineup, and so I offered 'We're open Friday.' With all the stuff going on with the grand opening he paused to consider that and I believe he decided 'Why not have a test run.' The Color Cat and all the black lighting at the entrance was impressive, and we had a blast. We were all there the next night, too."

The Grand Opening the next night featured Fox Chase. Jere and Yvonne's advertising packed the house. Jere says that the crowd "was probably not six hundred like we averaged once we got going, but it was a very good crowd and a very good opening. It seemed packed to us because we paid the band and all our expenses and still had a few folding things left over in our pocket. Plus we had a good time!"

Rick Hunt attended opening night, and after that "every weekend when there was a band playing. I lived about three miles outside of town with my father, and I would literally walk through snowstorms to get there. The Galleon was the happening place, you went there and enjoyed the music and hung out with your friends. It was the hub of what was going on, quite unique up here in the North Country, because Jere had visited other clubs and dance places and discotheques, and brought up ideas from those—strobe lights, the mirror ball, etc."

As Gerry Wolf recollects, "The Galleon had these huge crowds. The dance floor was large, but it got so packed you could hardly breathe."

Jere adds, "We were very strict with the operation, and we took no guff from any of the patrons. My brother John, who was an attorney, would stand at the front door taking tickets or stamping hands. He always wore a coat and tie, which set a good example.

"There was no age limit—no alcohol but no age limit—so the teens and twenty-something college kids could mingle. Kids came from all over, from Berlin and Plymouth and St. Johnsbury, parents would drop them off and come get them. We did have a turnover during the night; you had the younger ones coming in around 8:00 p.m., and their parents would be back for them around 10:00 p.m., and then the older ones would come in."

Even though The Galleon was "built for sound," volume was almost never an issue, despite the club's location on Main Street. The building had been triple insulated, and unless the doors were open the club was pretty quiet on the outside. However, Jere does remember "a guy living in an apartment building next to us, 'Norm the hiker.' I was very nice to him, because he was kind of a crotchety guy but he liked to be catered to a little bit. So I'd go outside and he'd start in with 'Jere....' And I'd say, 'Norm, four hours a night, a few times a week?' That typically did the trick."

Reminiscing about the bands that played The Galleon, Jere smiles. "We had very few problems at all with the bands. We treated them well, we made sure they had clean rooms, and they showed up on time. I can't think of a single band that didn't show up on time. There was one band that was extremely loud. They just blasted away, it was deafening. That was the only band we fired. But that was the only band we had that volume problem with, and we had a lot of bands.

"We also never had a band that was a no-show. Never. We had some that rescheduled and we had to sub—Ed Malhoit would call and get a sub. You never liked that because you had been advertising, but we never had to sub with Tracks or with Opaque Illusion or Stone Cross.

"We had good bands, and when we found a band we liked, say Gunnison Brook or Tracks, we wanted those bands to come back. At the end of the night, when the band had left, then you'd pay attention to what the crowd thought. That was the biggest thing, and you learned which kids were reliable in their opinions, like Gerry Wolf. The kids would say, 'These guys are great, you gotta get them back'!"

Yvonne concurs that the bands, "Most of them, 99% of them, were all just nice guys, they really were.

"The three bands that were most popular were Aerosmith, Gunnison Brook and Tracks, and then also AC Apple. We had a lot of other bands that were extremely good, like Stone Cross and Anvil. They weren't quite as popular, but they were very talented and you'd make money. I mean, for example, Tracks was a guaranteed money maker. You played, we would be full, everybody would be happy, everybody would be dancing, and you were also a band that mingled with the guests. In fact most of the bands were very good to our clients, even the ones that were aggressively hanging onto you—the groupies!

"Of course everybody knows that Aerosmith made it really big, but back then, even though the kids loved that band, Tracks was actually more popular. I thought you guys were gonna make it big like an Aerosmith. I thought the same thing about AC Apple, and about Gunnison Brook."

Rick Hunt tells this story about one of the last times Aerosmith played The Galleon. "The club had that smallish stage tucked in the corner, and it was always dark in there. Aerosmith was playing, and it was very intimate, and I remember Steve had on a knit kind of John Lennon floppy hat. They played this Lovin' Spoonful song, 'On the Road Again.' They kicked ass with that song, it was really brilliant. I got cold chills, and I remember thinking, 'Wow, this is awesome.'"

In early 1972 business at The Galleon was still strong, but beginning to wane because a 1971 Vermont liquor law had lowered the legal drinking age to eighteen. Jere remembers that, "When the Vermont law changed, it siphoned off a good part of our business. We began to lose the eighteen to twenty-one crowd to Vermont clubs and bars. Even if we had Tracks or another top band, people would go to Vermont to listen to another band, even if it was a mediocre band, because they could also have a drink."

So, in the summer of 1972, with The Galleon closed while Newell's Casino was open and experiencing its usual booming, seasonal attendance, Jere was a very busy man. He traveled across New England and Upstate New York, checking out kitchens and club operations, and remodeled The Galleon's physical space while retooling his business plan. In August of 1972, the club reopened as Jeremiah's.

Jere notes that "The drinking age eventually did change to eighteen in New Hampshire, in 1973, but Jeremiah's was very successful from the beginning. We were open Monday through Saturday, and we had entertainment every Friday and Saturday, and sometimes during the week. The top bands at Jeremiah's were American Express, the Chris Martin Band, and others, but all the bands were 'downsized' compared to the groups that played The Galleon. Some were four- or five-piece bands, but not like the rock bands with all the big equipment.

"We employed some attractive waitresses who did some 'Go-Go' dancing, and we had a nice little stage with a corral around it and people would dance in there. We also had an open mic kind of thing, and once in a while we would have to say to an aspiring star, 'Thank you, your time is up.' The dining room area had big stained glass windows that opened up into the lounge, and after patrons got done with dinner they would stay up there. It was a coveted place to go on the weekends. You could come in and have dinner, get yourself one of the great seats in the dining room, then we'd open it up to the dance floor/stage area.

"We'd have a couple hundred people—not six hundred plus like at The Galleon—sitting down or standing at the bar or just coming to dance. The bar would be three or four deep, and we had four bartenders trying to keep up with all the customers. Upstairs we continued with the game room, and it was still very successful. We had four regulation pool tables, bumper pool, foosball, a jukebox, and fifteen to twenty electronic pinball-type games. It was a fun place and a great moneymaker up there."

Jere laughingly exclaims, "'Joy to the World'—I loved that song by Three Dog Night. It was also a big moneymaker for the club, because the words, 'Last call,' were never used by the staff. Instead, the sound system would blare out, 'Jeremiah was a bullfrog….' and hands would go up all over for last call."

The sign at the back of the club starting in 1972.

Gerry Wolf recalls that, "When The Galleon was converted into Jeremiah's, it was a great bar. Jere had bands playing there like Frostbite Falls, smaller combos, three- or four-piece smaller bands, not big rock and roll groups like before, but he still had a great following. They had great people working there, and Jeremiah's was still *the* place to go."

Dale Granger worked in the dining room at Jeremiah's for two years, beginning in 1973. She remembers the disco ball above the dance floor, and the band American Express. "They played there enough they were like the house band."

Jeremiah's had a bouncer, Tom Golden, who was also a minister. "He was the best we ever had," insists Jere. "He was sort of a short guy, and we had some pretty big bruisers coming into Jeremiah's. But Tom was just perfect because he wasn't threatening. One time he was up in the dining room area, and I got this call that Tom was in trouble and I better get up there. So I went up and here he was between two great big guys, probably both had to be 6'4". He was in the middle trying to keep them from going at each other, and they were dancing around. Tom said to me, 'Jere, good to see ya,' and he told me later I just stood there and laughed!"

Then there is the story of Jim and Janice Sherwood. Like many married couples in the Littleton area, Jim and Janice met at The Galleon while they were in high school and then continued frequenting the club after it became Jeremiah's. When the club closed down Jim grabbed every bit of memorabilia he could get his hands on, including the big frog at the back of the building, and they both saved things like stirrers and napkins. When Jeremiah's was being dismantled he took a section of the bar, and he later told Jere, "You have to see my basement, it's a shrine to Jeremiah's." He also confided in Jere that he had "borrowed" a number of items from the club, like a beer pitcher, mugs with the Jeremiah's logo on them, shot glasses, that sort of thing.

Jere and Yvonne sold Jeremiah's in 1975, under rather unexpected circumstances. Here's how the deal went down.

A young man, Michael Stevens, who was selling them novelty items—matchbooks with the club's name on them, that sort of thing—stopped by the club one day and said he had heard Jeremiah's was for sale. Jere told him he had heard wrong. A few days later, the young man was back to say his father would like to see Jere. The dad came in on a Sunday, when the club was closed, and Jere recognized that the man was an extremely good customer of Jeremiah's. He and his wife liked to come in, sit in the lounge, eat a nice meal, and have several martinis.

When Mr. Stevens walked in that Sunday afternoon, he asked Jere if he and his son could sit at the bar. The gentleman asked for a martini, and Jere gave him "two or three martinis." Then Mr. Stevens mentioned that he was interested in buying the club, and inquired as to Jere's asking price. Jere said, "I hadn't thought about it, and anyway it's not for sale." The gentleman responded, in effect, "Everything's for sale," and asked Jere to name his price.

Yvonne was on the second floor of the club, in the apartment where she and Jere lived with their young son, Jack. Jere went upstairs, and Yvonne said, "No, we're not for sale." Jere responded, "Yvonne, what's the chance of this happening?" So they came up with a price of $199,000, and Jere went back downstairs. He said to Mr. Stevens, "I talked to my wife, and surprisingly she said alright and this is the price." Then Mr. Stevens said, "I want to do some business here, can we take a look at your books." Jere went back upstairs to check with Yvonne and she said, "No, no one can see our books, they're private."

Long story short, Mr. Stevens looked over the books for about fifteen minutes, said they looked good, and wrote out a deposit check on the spot for $20,000. "And that's how we sold the club," says Jere. "I don't remember what the debt was on it, but the down payment paid off all of our debt, gave us some extra cash, and we took financing on the balance." Yvonne has never forgotten that "our mortgage payment was $1,102.17 a month, and without that payment I thought I had gone to heaven. I thought we were rich!"

Gerry's Song

"If you know Gerry Wolf you love him."

— Don Coulombe

Gerry Wolf, December 22, 1970

On December 22, 1970, Tracks played night five of a six-night gig at The Rusty Nail, a place we considered a home away from home. This was our sixth engagement at The Nail since we played the club's opening night, December 16, 1969. After finishing up at The Nail, we looked forward to celebrating Christmas with our families and friends.

We had met the young man in the photo above at The Galleon in 1969, but he was far from our thoughts that holiday season. Sadly, Gerry Wolf was far from many people's thoughts.

On that raw December day in Boston, Gerry was about as far down, about as alone, as a person can be. But Gerry is a survivor. The story of how he sank so low, and of his transformational journey to the successful life he lives today, offers inspiration to anyone willing to read on. His story is also emblematic of a belief that imbued The Sixties, that each of us could become "somebody," and that together we could make a difference in this world.

Gerry Wolf was born on May 22, 1949, in the Borough of Brooklyn. His father, Sidney, brought up there, became a shrewd, successful businessman. Gerry's mother, Marion, had escaped Hitler's Europe and was, according to Gerry, "a very unhappy woman." Marion was betrothed to Sidney in 1945 in a fashion quite out of place in mid-twentieth century America. Theirs was an arranged marriage. Marion had her first son in 1947; Gerry came along two years later.

In 1947 Gerry's grandfather, Isaac Wolf, bought a place on the outskirts of Bethlehem, NH, called Virginia's Tea Room, a sumptuous mansion and well-known establishment. Isaac converted the structure into eight different living quarters, because he had seven children. This family compound, owned by Gerry's grandparents and their children, became the Wolfs' summer residence. Isaac and his family were all in the oil business in New York, but spent the summers in Bethlehem. The arrangement was that two of the family would stay in the city every two weeks to run the business, while the other family members vacationed.

As a result, throughout his childhood Gerry lived in New York City but spent his summers in New Hampshire. He met a lot of people in Bethlehem, but went to school in his hometown of Roslyn, NY, on the north shore of Long Island. For much of his youth Gerry lived with his aunt and uncle in Manhattan, on East 96th St. between 5th and Madison Avenues, because his mother developed health problems. Gerry spent memorable, pleasant days in Rockefeller Center with his brother, but his separation from his mother was unsettling. His mother suffered from Crohn's Disease, which runs in clusters in families and appears to have both genetic and environmental components, though for a long time her doctors were unable to diagnose her condition. Gerry says, "For years as a young kid I didn't live with my mother. She was always in the hospital or in Florida. Once you were diagnosed with Crohn's back then doctors typically said you should just do nothing for two or three years. Also they misdiagnosed her several times until finally determining she had Crohn's."

As a youngster Gerry had a hard time in school. He couldn't focus, was always daydreaming, and didn't take his studies seriously. "Probably ADD," Gerry says today. When he reached high school in the early 1960s the academic problems worsened, and his parents "thought military school might straighten me out. They sent me to Valley Forge Military Academy in Pennsylvania, because they thought that if I had discipline my school work would improve." In fact his grades got worse, and Gerry struggled through what he called "a terrible year." The next year Gerry transferred to Milford Academy in New Haven, CT, and graduated in June 1968.

During high school Gerry continued to spend the summers in Bethlehem, and "Sometimes I would go up in the winter and visit, because my brother was in school at St. Johnsbury [Vermont] Academy." In 1968, right before his high school graduation, Gerry's family moved permanently to New Hampshire. Initially they lived in the family summer home in Bethlehem, which was winterized to be used year-round, but soon Gerry's father built a home in neighboring Littleton. Gerry says that "I was not up there all the time, but because I had spent all my summers in the area I knew lots of people there, and had lots of friends. I'd spent my summers going out with people, going to Newell's Casino, and soon I considered Littleton home."

In the summer of 1964 Gerry met someone who would play an influential role in his life. "I met Jere Eames when I was around fifteen. His family ran the Jax Jr. Theater on Main Street in Littleton, and they knew my family. I'd see Jere in the theater, we talked a lot, hung out, and got along very well. Jere was always there during the important times in my life. Whenever I was down or depressed, or things were going wrong, I'd sit down and talk with Jere, and he would always guide me toward something better. He gave me confidence, said you'll do fine, don't worry about things."

Another friend he met in the late 1960s was Dale Granger. Gerry had a talent for striking up a conversation with anybody, so meeting people was never an issue. Dale recalls that "He was working at the Petco gas station in Littleton, and he was behind the counter when I came in with my Volkswagon to get some gas. After pumping the gas Gerry accidentally left the gas cap off, but somehow we got the gas cap back on my car and we started talking. We ended up friends, and have been ever since."

Like high school, college was a terrific struggle for Gerry. In 1968, he matriculated at Emerson College in Boston to study speech therapy, but left after a year. Next he enrolled at the University of New Hampshire, only to drop out after a semester. He studied accounting at Bentley College in Boston for a semester in 1970, then tried Goddard College in Plainfield, VT, but again left after only a semester. At that point, "I took off college for a few years," says Gerry, "and eventually I got myself straightened out." Gerry attended six different colleges before finally earning his bachelor's degree in 1983, fifteen years after entering Emerson.

During his college years Gerry began to work as an "unpaid consultant" for Jere and Yvonne Eames at The Galleon. Jere remembers, "He was always there, and he had good ideas and was very helpful, though he was never an employee."

Being around the club all the time, Gerry knew many bands, and probably hung out with more bands than anyone else. Hanging with the bands had more than one beneficial side effect, according to Jere Eames. "I have a picture taken inside The Galleon in December of 1969. Gerry's there with his girlfriend, and she's a pretty, blonde girl, and he's got on a watch cap, something like that." Gerry was a smart young guy, and it didn't take him long to realize that hanging around the bands was one good way to get the girls.

One unsuccessful "consult" took place on Saturday night, April 3, 1971. That evening Yvonne was selling tickets at the front door, and Gerry was at the club. Yvonne recalls that, "I was very much pregnant and as I was selling tickets my water broke. I told Gerry, 'My water broke,' and he had no idea what to do. He looked at me with this puzzled expression on his face and said, 'Should I get a mop?'" Two days later Yvonne and Jere's son, Jack, was born.

The photograph on the barrel was taken after Gerry had dropped out of Bentley. Gerry remembers that "It was three days before Christmas, and I really wasn't sure where I was going or what I was going to do. During that time I was having some physical issues, I really wasn't sure what was happening with my body, and I got so down it showed up more as depression than what it really was.

"I tried to get help, I couldn't get help, I was going through really bad times, and I was going to be drafted. My family thought I was crazy, so they had me committed to a state hospital in New Hampshire for six months. I was living there with ninety other people, and they put me on these heavy psychotropic drugs like Thorazine and Stelazine. They drugged me up so badly that when I got out I went to a rehabilitation center in Roxbury called Turnabout—like a Daytop or Synanon type of rehab program. All the guys in there were very weird, addicts, pimps, nut cases. They all seemed to be heavy users, and I wasn't, but the stay there at least cleaned out all the medicinal drugs in my system."

Gerry headed back to Littleton and worked at several dead-end jobs. He wanted to try college again, but "My father said, 'No, you can't go back to college, you just keep screwing up. Why go back to school, Gerry, you're never going to do anything. You always say you're going to do it, you're a smart guy, but you never do it.'"

In 1975 Gerry's father went into the hospital for surgery to address a condition known as trigeminal neuralgia, or tic douloureux. One of the surgical options, microvascular decompression or MVD, involves making an incision behind the ear. Then, through a small hole drilled in one's skull, part of the brain is lifted to expose the trigeminal nerve. Any artery in contact with the nerve root is directed away from the nerve, and the surgeon places a pad between the nerve and the artery. If a vein is compressing the nerve, the surgeon typically will remove it. If no artery or vein appears to be compressing the nerve, the surgeon may sever part of the nerve, instead. This procedure is called a rhizotomy. MVD has a high success rate, but carries with it the risk of decreased hearing, facial weakness, facial numbness, double vision, and even a stroke or death. (1)

The surgeon inadvertently cut the nerves in the brain stem that control the respiratory system, and Gerry's father died. "That really tore the entire family apart. My mother left for Florida. Within a month of my father's death, the trauma of that event exacerbated some of my ongoing, physical problems. I went to see the doctor, which resulted in a diagnosis of Crohn's Disease. Shortly after the diagnosis I ended up in Keene, NH." Gerry wanted to go to school again, but instead spent more than a year "homeless, living out of the back of my car, with no support from my family. I had no money, I was on food stamps, and I was in and out of Social Security disability."

As luck (with a nudge from Crohn's) would have it, Gerry was eligible to participate in a state vocational rehabilitation program. He enrolled and earned a degree in Interpreting for the Deaf at New Hampshire Technical College in Claremont. "I finally got confidence that I could succeed in school. I earned some credits in Claremont that transferred to Keene State, and I got my associate's degree in safety in two years while I was working. Then I earned my B.S. in Safety Science from Keene in 1983. After I got going I aced most of my tests, and some of my professors even told me I didn't have to come to class as long as I did well on the tests. I had the safety thing down, knew it pretty well, so I was able to audit classes and keep working."

From 1982 through 1988 Gerry worked at a company in Concord, NH, called Applied Occupational Health Systems. He did well, learned the safety business from the inside out in addition to his college training, then struck out on his own.

In 1988 Gerry founded Safety Environmental Control, Inc., a business that sells personal safety products and protection equipment for the environmental industry. SECI's product line includes air sampling and air monitoring equipment; disinfectant and cleaning products for mold remediation, carpet decontamination, and air duct cleaning; protective clothing; respirators and respiratory safety products. For twenty-three years the company has done a thriving business, but two cataclysmic events in the past decade have pushed SECI to the forefront of its industry: the World Trade Center attack on September 11, 2001; and the BP Gulf oil spill in the spring of 2010.

In July 2001, after a round of standard negotiation, SECI was awarded a contract to provide respirators to the Port Authority of New York. Two months later, the company was sending far more respirators to the Port Authority than it ever anticipated. In addition to individual respirators, SECI also provided equipment after the attack to clean the air in adjacent buildings in response to what became known as "the World Trade cough." More recently, during the summer and fall of 2010, SECI provided organic respirators, Tyvek polycoat suits, and yellow latex boots ("Lots of them" says Gerry) to the Gulf region.

"The summer of 2010 was the best two months the business has ever had. SECI has prospered for twenty-three years without disasters, and I never depend on disasters to make my living. It's not what I wish for, you hope they never happen, but every time something like the Gulf spill occurs it's a boost to my business."

Today Gerry Wolf is a very successful businessman, perhaps deservedly so after what he has overcome. He has a lovely family, including four children and three grandbabies, and a second home on Martha's Vineyard. He has developed close friendships with Vineyard residents Carly and Peter Simon, and Livingston Taylor. Gerry works hard, keeps a low profile, and quietly befriends others. He wants no accolades for his philanthropy. He is loath to have his picture taken, and wants others to receive the credit for activities that would fold without him, including several recent reunions for grateful nexus musicians.

Don Coulombe says, "Gerry used to come see all the bands play, and hang around the bands. He knew them all. Later in life, all the musicians started keeping in touch with him. He was kind of like a magnet, and he started putting stuff together. Gerry is the one who is getting all the musicians back together again, sending emails and talking to each other, and it's been great."

Old friend Dale Granger admires the fact that with Gerry, "What you see is what you get. He hasn't changed a bit. Gerry is the same old Gerry we knew forty years ago, the exact same guy I met in the late '60s at the Petco station."

Gerry Wolf, 2010

Gerry recently reflected on two prominent aspects of his life. Regarding his physical condition he said, "Crohn's is no fun, but I actually look at it as a blessing. The Crohn's changed my life. Either I could become a victim or I could overcome it. I chose the latter." As far as his financial success, he told me that, yes, the material things are nice, the new cars, the house on Martha's Vineyard, and especially the financial security that allows him to help his friends. But here's the really important thing. Speaking of the money, Gerry says, "I went without for so long, if I lose it all tomorrow I wouldn't miss it." Same old Gerry....

Fox and Company

Fox and Company had its roots in The Blazing Sons, a band formed in Berlin, NH, in 1965 by Don Coulombe. The band included fifteen-year-old Don on drums; his brother Norm, then thirteen, on bass; Joel Fortier playing Hammond organ; and Louie Grondin as the guitarist. For a time, Rick Pinette replaced Joel on keyboards when Joel left for college, but after several semesters Joel returned. Rick moved on and founded a Maine band named Oak, which became very successful. The Blazing Sons played across the North Country of New Hampshire and Vermont at high school dances, town halls, and clubs like The Galleon and The Cave in Barton, VT.

In the fall of 1969, the year Don graduated from high school, Louie enrolled at the University of New Hampshire and Mike Galipeau replaced him on guitar. At the same time the band changed its name to Funkyard to capitalize on the current musical style of the same name. Shortly thereafter the band added a taxi squad member, Mike's younger brother, Steve, a guitarist who began practicing with the band and also served as a roadie.

Steve recounts a story concerning Funkyard's short-lived name. "The band bought an old school bus and had the name Funkyard written on it. Well, the name didn't go over in some places in northern Vermont and New Hampshire—people thought you were swearing at them! The band would say, 'No, no man, it's a style of music,' but the name didn't go over very well."

Early in 1970, as the funkyard style lost steam, a band broke up that the Berlin boys revered. Steve recalls, "We loved the band Fox Chase, and loved the name, so we just shortened their name and became Fox." In 1972, Joel left the band again, and the guys turned to their taxi squad. Steve says, "When Louie went off to UNH and Mike joined the band, Don was happy because he got a third voice to join him and Norm. Mike's voice was really good, and I could sing a little myself. I had been rehearsing with the band twice a week as a rhythm guitarist, and I was going on the road with them, setting up and tearing down the equipment, listening to the songs they played every night, so it was pretty easy to add me in to the lineup. Plus, we now had four vocalists in the group."

Fox played for a year or so as a two-guitar group, featuring Mike on lead and Steve on rhythm. But Steve also played bass; and Norm, the group's bassist, played keyboard as well as guitar. Soon the band's primary lineup featured Norm on piano and Steve on bass. Still, for several years Fox was like a number of other bands in the nexus (Ragweed, Anvil, Fox Chase, Gunnison Brook, Better Days) whose members switched instruments during the course of an evening.

Steve remembers that "For about two years we did the shuffle thing. At one point we did a rock and roll medley where Don came out from behind the drums, I played drums, Mike played guitar, Norm played bass and Don would just sing. But there was so much time involved in the transfers. You know, you try to keep a crowd going, and switching instruments was cute, people got a kick out of it, but it took too long. So finally it was, 'Norm, you can play guitar and keys, and I can play bass, Mike can play guitar, Don will be on the drums and we stay where we are.'"

This final note about the band's personnel. When Joel left the band he took his Hammond with him, which would lead one to think that Fox had dodged the bullet of lugging around a behemoth that bands loved to hate. Not so. Says Steve, "We actually carried a Yamaha CP-70B electric grand piano, which was about two hundred and fifty pounds for the string part and another one hundred and eighty pounds for the keyboard part." No doubt those four hundred plus pounds more than compensated for the dearly departed B-3!

There was one last name change, in 1973. Don recalls that "A lot of groups started doing the '& Company' thing, and Ed Malhoit said he thought it would be cool if we called ourselves Fox and Company. You know, you listen to the agent who's booking you because you figure if you do what he wants you to do you'll get more money." Thus the name, Fox and Company, which stuck for more than twenty years.

Fox, 1972, L – R: Mike Galipeau, Steve Galipeau,
Don Coulombe, Norm Coulombe

It wasn't hard for the band to develop an extensive repertoire because, says Don, "Everyone in the band loved what they did so our free time was always based around music. Every night we would get together after dinner and learn new songs. We worked on one original song each week, and the rest of the time we worked on the latest Top 40 hits." Four good voices gave the band the ability to choose a range of songs to cover, and there was also a unique factor in those four voices. Joy Moffat explains, "Fox and Company had the best harmonies in the world, with two sets of brothers. No one can harmonize like brothers or sisters!" Dale Granger adds that, "The Galipeaus had unusual voices, and they could do a lot of different kinds of music. Steve and Mike did a lot of Doobie Brothers, although Don did 'Long Train Running.' They also covered 'Down on the Farm' by Gunnison Brook."

In addition to Doobie Brothers songs, the band's play list included tunes by Santana, like "Black Magic Woman" and "Soul Sacrifice;" Jethro Tull songs such as "Aqualung" and "Locomotive Breath;" several Beatles' songs including "Day Tripper" and "Hey Jude;" The Stones' "Sympathy for the Devil," "Brown Sugar" and "Under My Thumb," among others; and half a dozen Crosby, Still, Nash and Young songs that showcased the group's four voices. There were also covers of America, BTO, and Aerosmith. As Eric Van Leuven recalls, "I loved Fox and Company. They were a band you could always count on, they were really, really good and they did all the songs that everybody knew."

Then there were the original songs written by Don: "Rock City USA," "Devil's Daughter," "Back on the Road," "I'll Try My Best," "Dreamers," and "Time Was My Teacher." Dale Granger says, "Fox was one of the bands whose originals the crowd really accepted." Her Waitri partner in crime, Joy, laughs as she recalls that "Dale and I used to make fun of Don because he would write a song and then go to sing it and couldn't remember the words. We always gave him a hard time about 'Rock City' for that reason…'Da da da, Rock City…C'mon, Don, you wrote the song!'"

The band recorded three albums of its music: *Fox and Company* in 1977; *Take It All*, in 1980; and *Faces in the*

Night, in 1987. "Dreamers," off the first album, was named as one of *Billboard* magazine's weekly "Top Picks" for the week of March 11, 1978. Norm remembers that "Bruce James was promoting us via 'Dreamers.' He just sent it in and got it chosen as a top pick." Steve says, "We heard about it on our local radio station one day while Mike was riding in his car. The sad part was that you couldn't find a *Billboard* magazine in Berlin to verify the story. We had to go to Littleton and get one."

Don picks up the story. "I was, and still am, friends with Alan MacIntosh, the primary song writer for Gunnison Brook. I loved the original songs they did, and I really believe that band could have made it if they had stuck it out. When Gunnison Brook disbanded in 1973 Alan and I would get together once a week and write songs. A song that Alan wrote, 'One of Those Magic Moments,' is on the first Fox and Company album. Alan always had a way with words."

Steve remembers that when Fox and Company decided "to go full time in 1975, we had a fifth member named Dana Strout. Dana was a keyboard player who had a B-3, and who was with us for about eighteen months. At the time we all worked at Converse Rubber in Berlin—Don, Mike, Dana, our sound guy Bob Champoux, me—we all made sneakers. I was eighteen or nineteen and I said, 'Guys, we don't need to keep making sneakers, we can do this full time.' We were playing Dartmouth fraternities all the time, high schools and clubs, and the money was really good. So I started in on the guys and they said, 'Okay, if Steve can get us booked.'

"Now at the time everybody had been working there for a while except me. Don had been there six years, Mike for four, but I had just been there for one year right out of high school. And the way the Converse plant worked was that everybody got vacation at the same time—the last week of July and the first week of August—and the whole plant would shut down. So one night at rehearsal everybody agreed that if I could book the whole two weeks of our vacation, fourteen days straight, we'd quit our jobs. I was like, 'Fourteen days straight, you got it!'

"I called Ed Malhoit, and I called another guy we worked with. I ended up booking six or seven nights at the Red Stallion Inn in Maine, a couple of one-nighters, and a five- or six-night gig somewhere else. The band was popular enough that it was really no problem, just gotta make a few calls.

"So the Monday following vacation we all walked into the personnel office together. The five of us paraded in there and said, 'We're giving our two weeks notice, we quit.' Personnel just freaked. All the supervisors were coming in and saying, 'What, are you guys nuts?' Then, a year after we quit, Converse closed the plant and moved out of town."

As Steve noted, Fox and Company was popular enough that it played all over northern New England. And, like every band, they had their share of memorable gigs. One of those shows was playing a van rally with Stone Cross at the Cheshire Fairgrounds outside of Keene, NH. These were huge, annual rallies to which people who owned customized vans came from all over the East Coast for three days and nights of various events, including truck pulling contests, concerts, and socializing.

The band played the van rally several years running, according to Norm. The year they shared the stage with Stone Cross, reports Steve, "There were 3600 vans in the Fairgrounds, 12,000 people, and policemen were not allowed in. You can imagine, that was kinda wild!"

Another year at the van rally Fox and Company played with Orleans, of "Dance With Me" and "Still The One" fame. Norm says, "We played several times with Orleans, at

Cheshire and at a club in Leominster, MA. We also worked with Joan Jett [and Rick Pinette's Oak] in Lancaster, NH, on the outside stage at Dubrieul's roller rink, and with Mitch Ryder and the Detroit Wheels in Boston."

The band played regularly at Dartmouth, so much that it seemed to Don "We must have played every frat party at Dartmouth from 1970 to 1980. Those are great memories, and we always had a good time. We performed many times at Bones Gate, and those shows always reminded me of *Animal House*. They had toga parties, there was beer everywhere, they were just wild, wild parties. People would climb on top of our equipment and jump into the crowd. At the end of the night the frat floor was flooded with beer, and our equipment would smell like beer for weeks."

One of the best Fox and Company stories took place in the aftermath of a Dartmouth performance. The band was staying that night in White River, in the upstairs apartment at Eleazar's, aka "Joy's Home for Wayward Musicians." Someone slipped something into Don's drink, because he was virtually comatose on arrival at Eleazar's. At the time Don wore a beard, and the mischievous proprietors of "Joy's Home," Joy Moffat and Dale Granger, decided to shave it off. Norm says, "I couldn't believe he didn't wake up during the shave, but he didn't. The next morning when he woke up his beard was gone."

Then there was the Friday night the band ended up in the wrong Manchester. Don remembers, "Ed Malhoit called us at the last minute and said, 'I got you a gig at the Round House in Manchester.' We took the job and, us being from New Hampshire, got on our bus and drove to Manchester, NH. We drove around town for about half an hour asking people if they knew where the Round House was. One guy said, 'You mean The Ground Round, they have live entertainment every week.' So we arrived at the club and had about half of our equipment set up when another group showed up and told us they were performing Friday and Saturday night at The Ground Round.

"I called Ed and he said, 'You're in the wrong town, you are supposed to be performing in Manchester, VT, at the Round House.' Well, we packed up in a hurry, drove another two hours, and got to the club at 9:00, just when we were supposed to start playing. We were ready to go by 10:00 after setting up only half of our light show and sound equipment. The place was packed, and the crowd was so drunk by the time we started playing they were ready to party all night long. That was one of the worst days and best nights all wrapped up into one."

Fox and Company followed the pattern of most rock bands when it came to transportation: start small, get bigger; start low rent, get more expensive. The Blazing Sons traveled in hearses, the signature vehicle for many bands in the mid- to late 1960s. Funkyard graduated to old school buses. Fox and Company went the bus route.

Steve claims that "Transportation troubles were our life story! About 1974 or 1975 we decided we were going to buy a really nice bus and deck it out. We bought a flatnose with the engine in the back from Nugent's Bus Company in Colebrook, NH, for about $4,000, and we probably put another $3,000 into it fixing it up." Norm continues, "We put the Fox logo on the front, we had the interior carpeted, we had a nice sound system installed to listen to, we put a partition on the back for our equipment. It looked classy, but it was always breaking down. One time right after an oil change the engine blew because the mechanic forgot to put in new oil after draining the old oil out."

Steve keeps on truckin'. "It was the worst nightmare you could ever have. For five years we broke down weekly. It didn't matter where we were, St. J. or Killington, we were broken down. Finally, one New Year's Eve we were coming home from a gig and the bus broke down near Ashland, NH. I said to the guys, 'Let's leave it by the side of the road, and I'm gonna buy a new truck on Monday. We'll just take it to the junkyard and see what they'll give us for it.' I think we got four or five hundred dollars, but we had to make payments for about six months after we got rid of it. Then we got a Chevy C-60 with an 18-foot box on the back."

Fox and Company, 1978

Beginning with The Blazing Sons in 1965, the band played together through 1994, almost thirty years. And, unlike many other bands in the nexus, Fox and Company survived the rise of disco in the mid-'70s. Steve insists that "The disco thing really didn't affect us that much. One reason was that we added some songs like the Bee Gees, and we would do enough of that so the audiences would get a taste of it. We modified our repertoire, which was just good business, but mostly we kept our old songs." The Waitri concur. Joy says, "I got them a gig down in Providence in the '80s because they adapted well to the disco era." Dale adds, "They were flexible enough to go with the flow."

More important, according to Steve, was the way the band, the brothers, got along. "We didn't have that much talent, but, damn, we had a ball. People feed off of both, if you have a band that is really talented or a band that is having a ball on stage. It seemed that it was hard for other bands to get along, but not for us. For twenty plus years we had not one argument. I was fourteen years old when I got in, and we never, never had arguments. We did do original stuff, but we also did the top covers and we always made sure we had fun. We would get on stage and there was never any tension. It wasn't like we had an argument an hour before or even a week before."

Don sums up the ride with Fox and Company. "It was the best time of my life. We had it made back then. We worked six to seven days a week performing in clubs, high schools, colleges, and concert venues. Most of us in bands played music full time and made a living at it. The bands of today are lucky if they can get a gig on Saturday night, and the money is terrible. Today people will pay more for a DJ than a full band. I wish we could all go back to the good old rock and roll days."

Newell's Casino

The Casino shimmers on the horizon of my mind, like a mystical mirage on a scorching desert.

"Wait a minute, old timer," you might complain, if you ever played Newell's Casino. "The place was a barn in the middle of nowhere!" True, but that's the least of the story.

Hilton A. Newell and his wife, Christie, had a son in 1934, Hilton's namesake, called "Buddy." The Great Depression was in full bloom and it was a tough time to raise a family, but the Newells believed they had a buffer. Hilton, a World War I veteran, building contractor, and entrepreneur, had big plans for Forest Lake in Whitefield, NH.

Christie's family had purchased much of the land around Forest Lake in the 1920s. By 1935, Hilton, his father, and father-in-law owned most of the shoreline, although it would have been generous to describe Forest Lake as isolated. The men hit upon the idea of selling 397 acres to New Hampshire for a state park. Looking to the future, they sold the land "for a song," and the promise of a passable road. With that road, they knew, would come telephone and electric service, homes, and other development at the lake. (1)

The good folk of Whitefield probably thought Hilton Newell was crazy as a loon when he announced he would build a dance pavilion on the desolate shores of Forest Lake. (2) But build he did. Buddy Newell, four years old at the time, remembers that the Casino was "a rather large building, pretty rustic, constructed out of timbers from three old barns my father had torn down. We had gasoline generators out here, two of them, so we could switch back and forth, to supply the electricity."

Newell's Casino opened as a big band dance pavilion in 1938. The occupancy limit of 1,100 rivaled Whitefield's entire population at the time. (3)

During the big band era at the Casino, which lasted until the early Sixties, the Newells' most famous guest was actress Bette Davis, who had a summer home in Sugar Hill and came to the Casino regularly. Buddy recalls that "she was so harassed in the dance hall that she asked if it would be possible for us to reserve the lower of the two balconies over the lake for her party when she came to the Casino. So we did that for her. Her party would be escorted down to the lower balcony and that would be shut off expressly for her party so they could enjoy dancing without being mobbed."

World War II was tough on the Casino, but after the war returning GIs once again filled the Casino, and roller skating was added to the entertainment. (4) On holiday weekends the Casino hosted dances that, due to the Sunday blue laws, started at midnight on Monday and ran until 4:00 a.m.

Hilton Newell's Casino was quite a place. Though it was rustic, it was unique and impressive. The dance floor was huge—one hundred feet long and seventy-five feet wide. There were no columns anywhere inside the building; the roof was supported by immense trusses. The stage, built for large musical ensembles, was more than thirty feet wide and elevated two and a half feet above the dance floor. The first level of the stage ran back ten to twelve feet, with an upper stage a foot higher and five or six feet deep. The whole building was constructed on vertical support beams that raised it about eight feet off the land at the lake shore.

Doris "Cooki" Newell, Buddy's wife, remembers that the dance hall was always dimly lit, since the only lighting was twenty colored bulbs high up on the ceiling beams. There were benches around the perimeter of the room. On the lake side of the building an oversized door opened up to a large deck that extended thirty feet out over the water. Eight to ten feet below that deck was the lower, "Bette Davis" deck.

Perhaps the most delightful aspect of the Casino was its screens. There were only six windows in the building, all on the lake side. However, on the front of the building, facing the parking lot, and on both sides, were larger openings covered with screening. They had wooden shutters that could be closed when it was cold or the dance hall wasn't being used. These openings were six feet long, four feet high, and about five feet up the wall above the benches that ringed the dance floor. When you entered the dance hall, the effect was like walking into a gigantic screened porch.

By the late Fifties and early Sixties the big band sound was losing its appeal, and for a time the Casino closed. Then one day Buddy was at his parents' house and, "This group of kids came down the road." They were The Checkmates from North Conway, NH. "They were just a bunch of kids but they wanted to try out. My dad didn't want anything to do with rock and roll. He said to me, 'Buddy, if you want to run with it, do it.'

"So I started talking to the guys and it got around to money. They said, suppose we go 50/50 and see how it goes. What did I have to lose? The first Saturday night we had maybe 200 people. They played again the following Saturday and the crowd had about tripled. Then it started getting up over 1,000. Kids were coming in, there was a need for rock and roll in this area.

"I can't remember exactly what year it was, but it was either 1964 or 1965. One of the songs The Checkmates played was that 'Surfin' Bird' song." (Cobbled together from two songs by The Rivingtons, "Surfin' Bird" was released by The Trashmen in November 1963.) Gerry Wolf, who grew up in

Bethlehem just down New Hampshire Route 116 from Whitefield, recalls that The Checkmates wore suits and had short hair reminiscent of the Kingston Trio or The Lettermen. How that would change over the next five years.

"Anyway, that's how the rock era started. Those kids wanted to come up and try it. And they were okay, they did very, very well. They had a big following here." The Casino reopened, every Saturday night from May through Labor Day, or as far into the month of September as the North Woods weather would permit.

The price of admission was $2. Don Coulombe of Fox and Company, who played the Casino in its final summer, saw bands at the Casino like Anvil, Nickel Misery, Gunnison Brook, Boston English, Aerosmith, and Tracks. Don remembers one of the signature features of those years; when you paid at the ticket window your hand was stamped with ink that only showed up under black light.

Gerry Wolf has vivid memories of the crowds packed into the Casino on Saturday nights. "The Casino was full of people who were up there for the summer and also the locals, and those two groups almost never got along or blended. Even with the screens open it used to get really hot inside on muggy summer nights next to the lake. And when the whole crowd starting dancing the building used to shake!"

With throngs of locals and summer kids in the Casino, out in the parking lot, and down by the lake, the potential for trouble was ever-present. That potential was usually headed off by Tom Gage, the chief of police for the town of Whitefield. Chief Gage would arrive and, according to Buddy, "he'd bring the officers with him he thought could handle youngsters. Back then, an older person in their fifties didn't appreciate long hair and certain attire that was common in those days, and it was better that they weren't there. Tom was good at getting the right people there at the right time so we didn't have problems with behavior, because it was nipped in the bud and everyone knew that. The parents of the kids in this area also knew that and would allow their children to come here."

Chief Gage liked to tell the story of how one Saturday night an officer chased a kid into the lake. The officer stopped at the water's edge. The kid eventually came out. (5)

Ask Sixties and Seventies band members to name the places in upper New England they most enjoyed playing, and Newell's regularly makes the top three. It wasn't elegant, that's for sure. But it was magical. When I think of Newell's I think of an American Graffiti East, the kind of place where teenagers met their old friends and made new ones, found their depth, and came of age. More than once, those teenagers met a future husband or wife.

Why did bands love to play Newell's? First, the Casino's setting. Getting there was some trip, but once you arrived the setting was its own reward with the lakeside location, the decks, and the outdoor feeling created by all the screens. Second, the stage was fantastic. Bands that were used to being soaked by beer in fraternity houses and trying to squeeze all their equipment onto postage stamp-sized stages in clubs had room to spread out.

Third, and most important, were the crowds. A thousand people—hey, that's a lot of music lovers! Looking out from the stage onto a huge dance floor packed with bodies, the feeling was amazing. Everyone having a good time, digging *your* music, the band feeding off the crowd's energy. Wow!

Of the many rock bands that played the Casino over a ten year period, Buddy Newell says that the three most popular were Aerosmith, Gunnison Brook, and Tracks. "Aerosmith was pretty popular, but you know, they weren't any more popular than Gunnison Brook or Tracks. You advertise… who's coming here the next week or the week after, and if we said Gunnison Brook or Tracks or Aerosmith the kids would say 'Good, good.'"

In 2010, Buddy mused about those three bands. "I've also thought this. Aerosmith caught on big and are still big, but if you guys in Tracks had hit the right song at the right time you could have been Aerosmith. Same for Gunnison Brook. Both bands were that good."

Regarding Aerosmith, Buddy commented that, "Steven Tyler was a great front man. He really sold them. He was a great musician, too." Perhaps as a term of endearment, Tyler used to call Christie Newell, Buddy's mother, "Mrs. Casino."

Surprisingly, not everyone thought Aerosmith was top dog. Bob Comeau of Dalton, NH, saw Aerosmith perform at Newell's. As good as they were, Comeau said, they weren't as good as Gunnison Brook. (6)

Perhaps early on even the Bad Boys from Boston felt the same way about Gunnison Brook. Nick Kanakis, who was a friend of both bands, accompanied Aerosmith on their first trip to the Casino on June 19, 1971. Joe Perry was bummed about the smallish crowd they had drawn, and Tyler gave the band a little pep talk in the dressing room. Kanakis remembers this line quite clearly: "C'mon you guys, all we gotta do is stick together and keep getting tighter and pretty soon we'll be packin' this place just like Gunnison Brook!"

The dressing room at the Casino was stage right, behind the stage. It was small and pretty bare bones, but we didn't need much in those days, certainly not bottles of Perrier or grapes flown in from the wine country of France. Pete Merrigan recalls that bands used to write notes on the walls to other bands, such as "Gunny Brook says hi Tracks" and "Aerosmith says hi Gunny Brook."

One of Buddy's oddest stories features a band that insisted on being paid in $1 bills. He doesn't recall the band's name, but when they played he had a huge stack of $1 bills ready at the end of the night.

Then there's the one about the band that never showed up. "A booking agent we used, I think Ed Malhoit, who had booked Gunnison Brook and other bands that went over big, said he had one called The Glad. They were very big, people loved them, and he advised that we book them.

"So we did. Come seven o'clock on the day they were to play no one from the band had showed up, even the roadies who were usually there by then setting up. Eight o'clock, people were starting to come in and still no Glad. Nine o'clock, time to start the show, still no Glad. We could see a potential riot coming here...people were really upset. So I went over to the house because we didn't have a phone in the Casino at that time. The house was within a stone's throw distance from the Casino, and in the big band era the lady singers would always use our house for a dressing room.

"Anyway, finally the phone rang a little after nine and it was The Glad. They were very sorry, but they weren't going to be able to make it. They had looked at a map and they were a long ways away. I asked, 'Where are you?' and the guy on the phone replied, 'We're in Springfield, Vermont' [a good two hour drive from Whitefield]. I said, 'What the hell are you doing in Springfield, Vermont?' And the guy said, 'Man, everybody's gotta be somewhere.'" "Everybody's gotta be somewhere"—a line that could only have come from the Sixties.

Times and tastes change, and the Casino fell victim to that inevitability. As Buddy tells it, "By 1974 people were into concerts. People would come in, say I had eight or nine hundred. I would have one hundred dancing, and eight hundred sitting around the edge, just sitting on the benches and the floor. They would think, 'We're paying this guy two or three dollars to come in here when we can sit right outside and not have to pay anything and still hear the music.' There was no way you could stop it. There would be boats out front on the lake that looked like the Normandy invasion! They anchored there listening to the music. And that's what killed it."

The Casino closed after the 1974 summer season. Buddy's mother, Christie, had passed away, and he held on to the building. As he put it, perhaps thinking about The Checkmates, "You never know. It finally got to where it wasn't a good decision. It was being taxed heavily, and I thought, 'What's the point of paying that tax?' So we had it demolished in 1976 or 1977. Then the tax man came by for a visit, declared that there were four building lots on the property, and the taxes went up!"

Newell's Casino, photo taken in the 1930s

285

When Buddy discusses the Casino, he speaks in reverential tones. "I was four when the Casino opened, and I remember it being built. It was like part of the family all those years. When we tore it down it was almost like a kid to us. It had been there so long it had become a part of us."

In June of 2010, Buddy and Cooki Newell gave me permission to drive their right-of-way down to the old site of the Casino. Two very nice homes stand today on that land, but neither family was there. My wife, Lee, and I got out of the car and walked around for a few minutes. When Lee retraced the thirty or forty yards from the shore to where we had parked the car, I hung back at the lake's edge. The last time I had been at the Casino was June 5, 1971. As I closed my eyes—just me, the lake, and the memories—the Casino shimmered on the horizon.

Aerosmith

Drive. Dedication. Focus. The pursuit of excellence. In our sports-crazed culture, we hear these words and think of star athletes, like Michael Jordan and his ruthless quest to win, or Peyton Manning and his legendary game preparation.

When we think of rock musicians we tend to think of the stereotype promulgated tongue-in-cheek by Dire Straits in their 1985 hit, "Money for Nothing." You know, skinny, androgynous faggots with earrings and makeup; long hairs with attitude. They climb onstage for a few hours a night, fool around and go home rich. No preparation, no "honest" sweat, no work ethic.

Don't kid yourself. The annals of every field of endeavor are littered with wrecks of the "next greatest thing," washed up on the rocks of failure because all they had was talent.

Raw talent by itself is never enough. In the world of rock and roll, if you want to look at the best example of genius-level talent combined with focus and the relentless pursuit of a goal, you need look no further than Steven Tyler.

From his earliest days on the nexus music scene, Steven was known for his drive, his focus on the goal of becoming a rock star. Still, in Aerosmith it wasn't just Steven with the steely-eyed, single-minded determination. Joe Perry had that same fire in his belly, according to those who knew him in his younger days. While Tyler held the whip, the entire band had a fierce focus.

Mario Casella of Gunnison Brook recalls, "I was visiting them in the apartment on Commonwealth Avenue, and somebody said to me, 'Go get yourself a beer, man.' So I went to the refrigerator and there was one beer in there, and one jar of mayonnaise, and like one egg, and that was *it*! While the rest of us were thinking about paying the rent, buying more gear and getting some new clothes, these guys were scraping together whatever they could to survive day to day. They were totally given to their plan, at all costs, even food didn't matter. I don't know how they did it. I know I wasn't willing to go to the edge that they were. In comparison to Aerosmith, the rest of us were all selling out, while they were willing to sacrifice just about every creature comfort in pursuit of this goal. They were sticking to their guns, and they weren't willing to compromise. Direction is everything when it comes to making it, and they knew what they were about, they were focused on that direction and a particular style."

Ned Berndt of Tracks remembers a telephone conversation he had with Steven in the fall of 1971, a conversation that illustrates Steven's almost preternatural sense of what it would take to be a rock star. "Ed Malhoit had put us in touch with each other, and Steven wanted me to come play with him. I said, 'Steven, it sounds good, but I have this loyalty streak, I've been together with these guys [Tracks] all these years, why don't you come join our band? We have a year's worth of work booked, we know where our money's coming from, we'll have plenty of time to rehearse. You can be the front man, we can do a double drum thing sometimes, you sing our songs and we'll play yours.' He said, 'Ned, you can't make it living in the woods, you gotta come to a city. I'm playing only concerts in Boston, we are gonna be rock stars.' He had a vision and he was sure he was right. Listen to the lyrics of his first song."

These days it is easy to forget, given their worldwide celebrity, that there was a time when nobody knew the name Aerosmith. The first time the band played a paying gig, November 6, 1970, at Nipmuc Regional High School in

Mendon, MA, no doubt there was more than one kid who said, "Who?" "Aerowhat?" Today of course, like so many who claim they were at Woodstock, I am certain there are 10,000 folks living in Massachusetts who will swear they were at Nipmuc that night. "Yeah, I saw Aerosmith the very first night they performed back in 1970. Ain't I happenin'!"

It's no surprise to anyone who knew Aerosmith in the band's formative years that the "Bad Boys" struggled in many ways. They talk without pretense about those struggles in *Walk This Way*, as do their peers from the nexus.

Jim Goodrum tells this story of the first time Anvil saw Aerosmith. "It was at the Savage Beast in Ascutney, VT, following a gig that Anvil had played at Windsor High School. After collecting our $600 for the high school gig we went to the club, and I remember them being extremely loud. Joe had a stack of Marshalls turned around facing the wall, and Joey had a blanket in the bass drum. We stayed until the end, 'cause they were just guys like us back then."

Aerosmith's "loud factor" permeates stories of the band's early experiences in clubs and other venues. Pete Shackett of Gunnison Brook remembers, "We used to do concerts with them around the area. More often than not, people would listen to us and then scatter when they came on because they were just incredibly loud. They sounded really good, though, from a distance." There is no disputing that volume was an ongoing point of contention, specifically Joe's volume on the guitar.

Maybe the most significant area of discord for the band early on, in addition to volume and a song selection too obscure for many of their audiences, was the issue of musicianship. Steven knew what he wanted, and as Joey Kramer and Tom Hamilton freely admit, he wasn't shy about telling them when they didn't measure up to his standards. (1)

Mario Casella thinks back to 1973, post-Gunnison Brook, when he was living on Allston Street in Boston and Aerosmith was still on Comm. Ave. "Steve came to me and asked me if I would come by the house and help out. 'We love Tom and all but there is still a lot he doesn't know.' And God love 'em, they looked at me like I was an advanced bass player, and so they asked me to come by and give Tom a lesson, give him some pointers. And I did. I would go by the house from time to time anyway, but one day I went by, we set up a bass and amp, and I showed Tom a couple of my little tricks on the bass. At that time Tom was still kind of a beginner. He definitely became a very accomplished bass player, but he had to work at it, like we all do.

"Plus, the thing about Steve, because I was invited to quite a few rehearsals and I know the way Steve works, he would tell everybody exactly what he wanted. And if it meant taking the instrument out of your hands, as he did many times with Joey Kramer, and sit down behind the drums and show him just what he wanted, then so be it. The same thing was true with all of them. Steve could see every single part he wanted and impart that to the other band members."

Don Coulombe tells of "the time in the early 1970s when we were playing Bones Gate fraternity at Dartmouth and Aerosmith was across the road playing at another frat party. The president of the frat was going to refuse to pay Steve because the band had been playing original songs all night. The guy said, 'We heard you before and you guys did lots of covers. Where are the Beatles and Stones? If you keep doing originals we won't pay you.' Steven said, 'Screw you, we're doing originals now.' That particular night there were about twenty Malhoit bands at Dartmouth, and Ed was there. When Steve and the frat guy got into that shouting match, Ed played referee, and I guess got things worked out."

Mario and Pete Merrigan also recall "a gig at Ladd's in Portsmouth" says Mario, "where people hated them because they didn't play pop. At that time they weren't doing many originals, but people still didn't recognize a lot of the songs they were doing." Pete adds, "Aerosmith had asked us to put in a good word for them at Ladd's so we did, recommending them highly. On Gunnison Brook's next date in there, we asked, 'So, how did you like Aerosmith?' The bartender gave us a really strange look and said, 'Don't *ever* send us a band like *that* again!'"

Aerosmith, 1970, L – R: Tom Hamilton, Steven Tyler,
Joey Kramer, Joe Perry, Ray Tabano

Despite Aerosmith's initial difficulties, it was also evident right from the start that this was an uncommon band. Mario says, "It was obvious to us musicians back then that they had something special. They did things musically, very edgy, very theatrical, that none of us were doing. One night I saw Ray and Joe do a double feedback thing, where they both turned around and faced their amps and got feedback. Feedback is really cool when one guitar player does it, but when they both did it the effect was just awesome. Feedback is not really controllable, mostly it just has to have that magic, and if it goes wrong you have to stop it, but if it's right you hold it there. At the time I saw them do it, it was right on. I don't remember the song they were doing, but it doesn't matter, it was just one of the things that stuck in my head. I thought that Joe and Ray were terrific together."

Carey Rush recalls that "There was nothing like them around here, they were very unique. I saw them at the Junior High in Claremont, at the March of Dimes show when they had Ray Tabano. They did 'Rattlesnake, Shake,' the Fleetwood Mac song with Peter Green, and The Yardbirds, stuff like 'Train Kept A Rollin'.' They were dark for the time, kinda more The Stones than The Beatles."

Eric Van Leuven says, "I saw them play at Kappa Sig at Dartmouth, they weren't that big yet, but they were fantastic. It was so funny because people were saying, 'Ah, they're good but they just want to be like the Rolling Stones.' But as a fellow musician, when I saw them I was impressed."

Rick Hunt offers this stunning memory. "The last time I saw them in person was at Plymouth State College and Tyler did something that was amazing. To this day I get goose bumps when I think about it. He had this old-fashioned sweater on, like a college athletic letter sweater from the '30s or '40s, and it draped down to his ankles. He was standing on the front edge of the concert stage and he was turned around so that his back was to the audience. He leaped up in the air and did a back flip in the air and landed on his feet on the floor in front of the stage. He somersaulted right off the stage and landed upright. When I think about that, I mean he could have broken his neck, the sweater could have gotten tangled up in his feet, he could have died right on the spot."

And Mario remembers "One of those magical nights" when Gunnison Brook and Aerosmith played a gig together. "It was at a Yacht Club in Sunapee, we were set up on one end of the room and they were on the other end of the room. I was a big Hendrix fan, and one of the things I got from Hendrix was the thing with the scarves. Hendrix was all about scarves, and his shirts had long, flowing sleeves, and when he moved his hand his whole arm was shimmering. The sleeves of his shirts were designed with silk streamers, and because they were silks, they moved slower than the arm, in a beautiful, graceful motion that was mesmerizing.

"Anyway, I used to put scarves through my bass strap, and they would dangle down towards the floor, and they would enhance all of my movement, spins or jumps, whatever. That night I put the scarf on my mic stand. I don't think I had done that before that night, and I remember, as we were setting up, looking across the room and seeing that Steve had a long scarf on his mic stand. I thought, 'Oh shit, I can't do that, because Steven is doing it,' and I took the scarf off the stand. The thing with the scarves on the mic stand became a trademark for Steve. He was already doing that by that Yacht Club gig, because he realized the value of amplifying his movement.

"Another trademark of Steve's was to paint his fingernails. I distinctly remember the day he came to our band house and asked Chris Dunn to show him how to do his nails. Chris was a Gunnison Brook roadie, and he was the most flamboyant member of the band. He had this thing about painting his nails in amazing detail, because he was an artist, and he painted tiny little stars, rainbows, whatever. And I remember Steve coming to the house and saying, 'Tell me how you do this,' and Chris giving him a lesson.

"Back to that night at the Yacht Club; Joe Perry drove me home that night. He had this little MG, and when I sat in it I felt like I was sitting on the floor with my legs out in front of me. It was a very weird sensation, because I'd never been in a sports car like that. Then he said, 'Hey, I've got an idea, let's go for a ride around the lake.' Well, I was convinced we were going to die that night, because he drove like a frickin' maniac, pedal to the metal, driving around Lake Sunapee with all those curves. Thank God he knew the roads like the back of his hand. It was a beautiful summer night, we both had long hair blowing back in the wind, and the best part of it was...we lived! That night surprised me, because Joe was so quiet all the time, and then he got behind the wheel and he turned into a total lunatic."

Aerosmith recorded their debut album in the fall of 1972 at Intermedia Sound Studio on Newbury Street in Boston. Soon, the band was on its way, as "Dream On" began to climb the charts. Don Coulombe tells the following story from early 1973 during Aerosmith's seemingly meteoric rise to prominence. ("Seemingly meteoric," if one is foolish enough to discount almost a decade of hard slogging in bands like Thee Strangeurs, The King Bees, the Chain, the Jam Band, and William Proud, playing high schools, clubs, and dance halls.)

"When I lived in Berlin I was booking the Notre Dame Arena, and right when Aerosmith recorded their first album I was interested in getting them to perform at the Arena. I called Ed Malhoit and said I'd like to book them. He told me they had signed a record deal, they had a record coming out, and it would be about $900 to $1,200. I said, 'Are you crazy, the last time I booked them it was four or five hundred bucks.' I told him I had to think about it and I called back about a week later, and said, 'Alright, I'm interested.' Then he said, 'Well, they just found out they're going on tour, they're opening up for Mott the Hoople, so now it will probably be about two grand to $2,200.' And I replied, 'What, are you crazy, I can't afford that.'

"I got off the phone and started talking to people and they were saying, 'Wow, this song "Dream On" is really great' and it was just climbing up the charts like crazy. Finally I said to myself, 'Okay, this song is really taking off, I can put 1100 people in the Arena, I can make a killing.' So I called back in another week and this time Ed told me, 'They just signed on with Premier Talent in New York. Premier Talent is handling them now and I don't know what it will cost you to get them.' So, just like that, in about a three-week period they went from $400 up to $900 to $1,200, then to $2,000 to $2,200, to I couldn't even afford to book them."

People used to ask Steven what "Dream On" meant. There has never been any question in my mind. The words mean exactly what they mean. Keep on pursuing your dream. Don't stop. Don't let anything stand in the way of its fulfillment. Between 1964 and 1973 Steven Tyler lived that vision, that promise to himself, and he ultimately became the rock star he saw himself destined to become.

Back in the early 1970s, across the states of New Hampshire and Vermont, you could find any number of people who would tell you that there were several bands equal or superior to Aerosmith. Those people will tell you the same thing today. Many observers credit Fox Chase, Steven's band with Eddie Kistler, Don Solomon, Pete Bover, and "Mouse" McElroy, as the best band ever to form in the nexus. Anvil, Gunnison Brook, and Tracks are also mentioned as worthy competitors.

Know what? Irrelevant. All the "would'ves, could'ves, should'ves" are irrelevant. Fox Chase flamed out in 1971. Anvil dissolved over a period of six months in 1972. Gunnison Brook disbanded in 1973. Tracks came to the end of the line in 1974. Only Aerosmith is still in the saddle.

Here's another thing. People who were around back then and like to armchair quarterback today will note that the musicians in Aerosmith were not an exceptional bunch. They will tell you without hesitation that Brad French, Kip Meeker, and Russell Pinkston were better guitar players than Joe Perry; that Mario Casella and Pete Bover were better bass players than Tom Hamilton; that David Curtin, Ned Berndt, and, yes, Steven Tyler were better drummers than Joey Kramer. Steven was the consummate front man, but Pete Merrigan and Bob Hathaway and Eddie Kistler were also outstanding singers and showmen.

Again, irrelevant. Regardless of the individual parts, the indisputable fact is that for four decades Aerosmith has been among the greatest rock acts in the world. The musical answer lies in part in an esoteric word from the world of science, synergy: the whole is greater than the sum of its parts. On the personal side, the band members had a chemistry that allowed Aerosmith to overcome the divisive, potentially destructive issues faced by every band.

Call it a team mentality, call it a family thing. Mario is emphatic that "There is no question about it, Tom, Joey, Steve and Joe especially, were truly brothers off stage. There was a cohesion, at times a love, that was plain to see." Call it what you like, the truth is that for forty years Aerosmith has ridden a wave of success that is almost unmatched. Not bad for a bunch of kids who got their start in Georges Mills, New Hampshire.

Stone Cross

Two great bands I regret never having seen, Atlantis and Stone Cross, fold easily into the same place in my mind, for the best of reasons. Both groups were loaded with fine musicians, but what helped distinguish them from other bands was that they each had a hook that made them special. Atlantis, with monster drummer David Curtin, bassist Chris Quackenbush, guitarist Bobby Hearne, vocalists Greg Dame and Rick McPherson, and Sammy DeSantis on the Hammond organ, was the only band around with a Mellotron. Stone Cross had what every other band salivated over, a Sunn Quadraphonic PA system.

From 1964 until 1969, a band from the New Hampshire coastal region, The Telstars, made a name for itself throughout New Hampshire and Vermont. Its members were Gardner (G-Man) Berry, from Kingston, NH; Bill Blaine from Hampstead, NH; Dennis Burdick; and Frank Smith. During that same period, Mike Mulroy was honing his percussion chops in the Windsor, VT, area with The Links and The Missing Links, bands that included Jeff and Rick Davis, founding members of Davis Brothers Garage Band.

When The Telstars formed, Gardner Berry was their bass player. As G-Man explains it, "I met Bill early in high school, and at the time I had a guitar. I didn't play it, but having a guitar was a prerequisite for being in a band so I learned, although I actually played bass for the first year I was in The Telstars. Bill and Frank played guitar, and Dennis was our drummer. After the first year I switched to a Vox Continental organ, and Frank became our bass player. Eventually I ended up with a Hammond B-3, which was just a wonderful instrument but a nightmare to lug around. Later on I downsized to a much more portable electric piano."

The Telstars' play list included many of the standards of the mid- to late 1960s: The Beatles, Paul Revere and the Raiders, The Young Rascals, "Louie, Louie" by the Kingsmen, and "96 Tears" by ? and the Mysterians. G-Man notes that the band played "96 Tears" four times in one night at a fraternity house at New England College in Henniker, NH. In its later years, Gardner says The Telstars "moved into Cream and Hendrix, that sort of thing, and I ended up playing more guitar. There was a lot of music in the late '60s where the keyboard took a back seat."

The Telstars first met Ed Malhoit in 1966 after he saw them play one night, probably in Laconia, NH, according to Gardner. Ed encouraged the band to enter a Battle of the Bands in Brattleboro, where they went head to head with the first band Ed ever represented, The Sprites. The Sprites were always among the favorites to win any Battle of the Bands that they entered, especially in their hometown of Brattleboro. But Ed and Gardner remember that on this occasion The Telstars beat The Sprites. G-Man laughs and says, "We drove our sorry asses into their hometown and actually won, much to the disgruntlement of all their girlfriends. At that point Ed started booking us into some gigs, and he ended up managing us for our entire careers."

The Telstars also came up big in the New Hampshire state Battle of the Bands in Manchester in 1967, when they finished second to a group from Portsmouth called the Elements of Sound.

When asked why The Telstars broke up, Gardner replied, "We were getting older and the band had run its course. In 1968 we made a record and it didn't do anything, and we took it personally and just decided the time had come."

Shortly thereafter, Stone Cross was born in the basement of a dormitory at New Hampshire College in Manchester, NH. It was March 1969, and the original lineup was the G-Man on keyboard, Charlie Rauschlau on guitar, Ron DiPerri on drums, and Bill Poulin on bass. The latter three were students at New Hampshire College, as were Bill Blaine and Mike Mulroy, who were not in the band initially. Not surprisingly, the group's first gig was at the college.

Soon after Stone Cross began playing out, Bill replaced Charlie Rauschlau as the guitarist. Ron DiPerri left the band when the 1969-1970 school year ended in May, and he recommended Mike as his replacement. The final piece of the permanent Stone Cross lineup was soon added. Bill had played briefly with bassist Phil Monastesse in 1969 in a band called Blue Cloud, and when the band decided to change bass players Phil got the call.

The name Stone Cross was suggested by Bill even before he became a member of the band. G-Man recalls that Bill got the idea from a big burial monument that stood alone in a field in Chester, NH. At some point in 1970 the band went out and did a photo shoot at that monument.

Stone Cross played weekends from 1969 through 1972. In 1972 Bill and Mike graduated from New Hampshire College, Gardner quit his day job as a drafting engineer for an electronics firm in North Andover, MA, and the band began to play full-time.

The college students in Stone Cross decided to finish their course work before turning to music full-time. In contrast, many of their contemporaries dropped out of college to pursue rock and roll's Holy Grail. Some of those rockers went back to school and completed their education later in their lives. Others chose not to finish their degrees. Please do not misconstrue these comments. I am not passing judgment. Different strokes for different folks, as a sly man once wrote in a song. I only mean to make the point that it is impossible to do music the right way as a full-time student or while working a full-time job.

Ed Malhoit says about Stone Cross, "Gardner was a great performer, he really was. And Bill Blaine was the strongest link of the band in the sense that he understood the business side of things. It was easy to work with Stone Cross. And they could all sing—the group had four terrific voices. The quadraphonic sound system highlighted their vocal talents, and we started advertising that PA because no one else had it. Then everybody else wanted one!"

Gardner Berry

Ed also maintains that "Stone Cross always had the best of sound and lights compared to other groups, especially after they got the system which put speakers in all four corners of a room. It's interesting to me that their guitar player, Bill Blaine, started a huge sound company that today does many venues up and down the East Coast."

Rick Davis remembers that "Stone Cross invested heavily in equipment, the best and most equipment including the quadraphonic PA which Davis Brothers got to play through in October of 1975 at a fund raiser in Windsor, VT."

The band's original sound engineer, Scott Swain, was succeeded by Jim Minetti. Surely both Scott and Jim enjoyed their big, shiny toy. Still, the most enthusiastic story I have ever heard about the Stone Cross PA comes from my band mate Jeff Wilkes, who was doing sound for Tracks one night when the two groups shared a show at a National Guard armory somewhere in Vermont.

"When we came in that night the armory manager looked at us like he had never seen people who appeared to be so strange, never mind that we said, 'We need three 20 amp circuits, what can you do for us?' They pulled a flat bed truck into the armory to use as the stage, and the bands were up about six feet off the floor.

"We set up one of their quadraphonic speaker towers in each corner of this armory, which was a pretty big room. Then we had the Tracks PA, so we put the entire Tracks sound system on the floor as monitors. I built this thing out of pipes and clamps right in the middle of the room to raise me up in the air, sort of like a scaffold, to run the sound. Their system was four-channel but it had a joy stick, and you could put anything through that joy stick and then send it all around the room, or even over the top of the room from one corner to the other. I remember Ned [Berndt] doing a drum solo and I put him into that joy stick and he was just flying around the room. It was freaking out the audience, and I was in hog heaven. As an audio person that was the most fun I ever had. It was astounding, because I could send the sound right over my head, and I was smack in the middle of the room."

Early on, when the band was just starting out, Stone Cross opened for Sly and the Family Stone at the New Hampshire state armory in Manchester. The sound company for the concert was Hanley Sound of Boston, fresh from doing the sound at Woodstock. G-Man recalls that "It was when Sly was right at his peak. We were the opening act and it was kind of a challenge for us because a lot of the cover stuff we did was Sly material. That was the first big show that we did in the band, and the first time we had used monitors. We thought we had died and gone to aural heaven because they had a monitor system bigger than our whole PA system at the time. There were 7,000 people in the crowd, it was our first major gig, and we played as well as we ever had to that point because of the energy in the room.

"We finished our set and they said to us, 'Okay, you've got to get off the stage because we have to get it ready for the featured act.' So we struck the stage in about forty-five seconds, and then the promoter came up to us and said, 'Hey, can you play a little longer, Sly's not here yet.' He showed up eventually and played an absolutely unbelievable show."

Through its coveted sound system, Stone Cross pumped out songs by the Allman Brothers, J. Geils, Gary Wright, Dave Mason, and a Beatles Medley. The group covered several Joe Cocker songs, and Three Dog Night classics like "One," "Try a Little Tenderness," "Celebrate," and "Eli's Comin'." G-Man notes that "We always had a great following and had a great time. We were a cover band, but not a Top 40 cover band. Our play list was pretty much album music, but it was popular. We always focused on the big British bands—

Queen, Led Zeppelin, Jethro Tull, that was our forte. We did "Bohemian Rhapsody" as the opener of a Queen medley, and we also did a very popular medley of songs by Spooky Tooth, one whole side of *The Mirror* album."

Notice the common thread that runs through the Stone Cross play list: the *sine qua non* of outstanding vocals!

L – R: Phil Monastesse, Bill Blaine, Gardner Berry, Mike Mulroy

Stone Cross was one of several bands from the nexus that studied with Dante Pavone in Boston. G-Man remembers that "We used to go down there, all four of us, on a Monday night. I am going to say, without hesitation, that Dante really changed my life. He is the reason that I still have a voice at

303

sixty years of age and still can go out and do it seven nights a week and maintain some resilience. I rarely lose my voice, and it's really because of the way Dante taught me to sing. I sing with three bands, sometimes twenty-five or thirty nights in a row. The point is I can work all week and my voice is stronger than it has ever been."

In addition to the Sly concert, another favorite Stone Cross memory is the van rally at the Cheshire Fairgrounds in Swanzey, NH, a night that is also remembered vividly by Fox and Company. That year the two bands played to over 12,000 people at the Fairgrounds, and, as Gardner recalls, it was "just one of those nights when everything clicked."

Pete Shackett has a pair of memories about Stone Cross. "I'd go see them play when we were both at Dartmouth. I'd run over to whatever fraternity house they were playing and listen to a few songs on our break. I remember being totally impressed with the surround sound PA.

"The one time I partied with them on a personal level was in Lake George at Mother's. They had left an amp behind at a gig we were next at. I strapped it on my motorcycle and rode it over to Lake George. They were all super friendly and great guys to party with and talk to. I had a great time, caught the show that night, stayed over with them, then headed back the next day. They also came to see Gunnison Brook at our final gig at Ladd's in Portsmouth in April of 1973. On the live tape you can hear our lead singer, Pete Merrigan, saying 'And there's Stone Cross. Thanks for coming' or something to that effect."

Stone Cross continued playing out until 1983, and was just as successful and popular at the end of its run as it had been at the beginning back in 1969. G-Man recalls that the group had a great following, and others enthusiastically concur.

Norm Coulombe of Fox and Company remembers "how great the surround sound was, and what a popular band Stone Cross was back then."

Tom Day, the owner of Eleazar's in White River Junction, recalls that "Stone Cross, Tracks, Davis Brothers, and Better Days were bands I could make a living off of. They were very talented."

L – R: Phil Monastesse, Mike Mulroy, Gardner Berry, Bill Blaine

Rick Davis says, "Stone Cross really impressed with their vocals, their four-part harmonies. To me they were the best vocal band, hands down."

Here's how Steve Galipeau, also of Fox and Company, sums up Stone Cross: "One word—vocals! We got to know them reasonably well, and they were really fun to listen to. They were just excellent, an incredibly talented band."

Joy's Home for
Wayward Musicians

...aka Eleazar's, in White River Junction, contrasted notably with some of the other venues that bands in the nexus played. Newell's Casino, The Galleon (before it became Jeremiah's), and The Barn, all technically non-alcoholic, entertained younger crowds. Clubs like the Wobbly Barn in Killington and The Rusty Nail in Stowe catered to the well-heeled ski crowd. But like the Chopping Block in Proctorsville, Eleazar's was much closer in atmosphere to the quintessential road house.

Says Gardner Berry of Stone Cross, "It was just what you would expect a 'road house' to be...a hard drinking crowd, everyone hooting and hollering and having a great time." Jeff "Flash" Gordon of the Jefferson Light Show echoes the G-Man's sentiments. "Eleazar's and the Chopping Block were the road houses of the era. You could expect a brawl almost any night, and then a call to the cops."

Eleazar's opened in November 1972, and while former patrons remember its owners as Tom Day and Vern Hatt, in fact the men who first owned the club were Tom and two Dartmouth students, Rick Carvolth and Allen Atkins. In 1972 Tom was in a family catering business in New York City that his grandfather had started, and he wanted to "get the hell out of the city." Rick was a neighbor in New York, and Tom had been looking at restaurant possibilities in Vermont, so the three joined forces at Eleazar's. When Rick and Allen graduated from Dartmouth in June of 1973, Roger Davis came on as Tom's new partner. After a couple years Roger left the business and Vern came on board.

Before it became Eleazar's, the building had been an Italian restaurant named Ponzi's. Ponzi's was a favored destination of Dartmouth College students if their families visited on weekends. I mean, you wouldn't want to take your mom to the fraternity basement for a beer on Saturday night, right?

One advantage Eleazar's had in regard to hiring bands and drawing crowds was that it was easy to get to, located as it was at the crossroads of Interstates 89 and 91. As Don Coulombe notes, and other musicians affirm, "Eleazar's seemed to be in the middle of where everybody came from— Burlington, Brattleboro, Manchester, Littleton, or Berlin. It didn't seem like it was more than a couple of hours away so you didn't ever mind doing the gig."

Eleazar's was built against a hillside. You entered the club on the lower level, where the bar and kitchen were located, along with tables and chairs for customers and the foosball table that was constantly in use. Up a staircase to the second story, you found yourself at the back of a relatively small dance floor. Across the dance floor at the front of the club was a good-sized stage. Behind the staircase were tables for patrons, and to the left of the stage up two steps was an area known as "the deck," which also had tables.

More than one musician expressed surprise that the stage at Eleazar's was so big, when the club itself was fairly small. The answer, says Tom Day, lies in the fact that original partner Allen Atkins played in a band named Galactica at Dartmouth. "When we built the place, Allen insisted that we needed a big stage, because he'd been in bands." Allen remembers vividly the conversation about the stage. "Tom envisioned this tiny stage, like for a jazz combo. I'd been playing clubs all over New England in Galactica, and I thought we should have a better stage than average. Tom said that a big stage would take up table space, and that we weren't going to make any money because there wouldn't be anywhere for people to sit and drink. I told Tom that if we didn't find a way to make the bands happy no one was gonna show up anyway. I can't emphasize enough, however, that Eleazar's wouldn't have succeeded without Tom Day. We had a lot of fun, but he was also a really good businessman, and he knew the details."

As for the foosball table, Don Coulombe remembers the tournaments in the afternoons before gigs at Eleazar's. Tom recalls the "owner-band" contests pitting himself and Vern Hatt against Rick Davis and one of his cohorts from Davis Brothers. All part of the fun.

In a former life, before it was Ponzi's, the building had been a grain and feed store, with an apartment upstairs in the back, which Rick and Alan shared during their senior year at Dartmouth. The apartment had a kitchen, separate rooms where the waitresses later lived with some degree of privacy, and a large room with bunks where visiting bands stayed.

Despite Eleazar's rough crowds, bands kept coming back. Gardner Berry says, "I loved it there, we had such a good time. We played Eleazar's when it first opened. It had a wild crowd, everyone dancing their asses off, and you were supposed to end at midnight, but you couldn't end at midnight. You'd just keep playing and playing and you didn't care. You don't see that sort of thing anymore, that kind of enthusiasm."

Rick Davis claims, "Eleazar's was like a wild west frontier town bar. In its heyday we played there Thursdays through Sundays. The Sunday show was an afternoon 'matinee.' It was a wild-ass place, people would get falling down drunk, but the waitresses were cool, everybody was cool."

In its prime, Eleazar's offered a Wednesday happy hour, with bands Thursday through Sunday. On occasion a Sunday matinee would be open as a "one-nighter." Don Coulombe recalls that "Ed Malhoit would call us sometimes on Saturdays, we'd be up at the Pickle Barrel in Killington, for example, and he'd say, 'Listen, Eleazar's needs a band on Sunday, do you want the gig?' Sometimes you'd pick up an extra $400-$500 bucks there so we'd do it. Play there Sunday and then go home after that. You'd make enough money to make it worth your while."

The patrons also loved the place. Annie Dolan, who saw most of the bands in the nexus at several venues, including The Barn, the Wobbly Barn and the Chopping Block, says Eleazar's was, "Insane, I don't know how they stayed open, that place was totally insane. How that place ever even survived I don't know. The cops hated going there. It was a crazy place but the music...there were so many good bands that played there. It was all about the music, we came for the great music."

Dale Granger came to work at Eleazar's in 1975, followed within two or three weeks by Joy Moffat. The two young ladies quickly became known as "The Waitri." They worked the upstairs level of Eleazar's exclusively, since the bar was downstairs, thus Tom and Vern saw no need for waitress service on the lower level.

Joy was told "they had never been able to keep a waitress for any length of time prior to our arrival. Eleazar's was such a rough club, there were fights almost every night. The rumor is that one of our predecessors had lost a tooth. The club had a glass front door that seemed to get broken every week, there was a mirror over the bar, it was like an old-time saloon. There were constant fights and harassment.

"But Dale and I came in and we just handled it. We were both in the middle of many fights, but neither of us was ever seriously injured. I did put one guy in the emergency room. He hit me first. They grabbed our asses, we grabbed back!"

Dale remembers that "When I first started working at Eleazar's, I had this huge black eye from a car accident. I was driving in a blizzard, my car spun out and I hit the guard rail on the I-91 bridge over the White River. The black eye worked to my advantage at Eleazar's, being the kind of bar it was, because the guys were like, 'Wow, where'd you get that black eye?' For a while it covered the whole side of my face, and I started telling them all sorts of stories. Once I went down to the kitchen for an order and Vern said, 'What are you telling them up there?' Having the black eye kind of endeared me to the customers."

"Waitri?" Says Dale, "There was never a singular for Waitri, because the two of us were always together. One day, one of us, I can't remember who, came up from behind Tom Day and asked him a question. He turned and looked at whichever one of us it was and said, 'What do you two want now.' And the one of us said, 'Tom there's only one of us,' and he said, 'Naw, you're always together.'"

The Waitri in their Fox tee shirts, 1975, Dale on the left, Joy on the right

Joy remembers "A ton of bands that used to play the club. The top three were Better Days and Company, Davis Brothers Garage, and Stone Cross. Better Days, they were almost like our house band, and it seemed to me the combination was always 'full moon, Better Days, fight!'"

Joy also says that, "Dale's section was in the back of the club facing the stage, and mine was 'the deck' which was up a couple of steps and had a railing on the side of the stage. For some unknown reason ninety percent of the fights broke out on the deck."

There are so many wild stories that are part of Eleazar's lore, stories that just can't be true. Except that so many different people vouch for their authenticity.

Allen laughs, remembering that, "When we first started Eleazar's, there was a Vermont motorcycle gang called the Vermont Mindbenders. They heard about the club, cheap drinks and good music, and they said, 'Wow, this is great.' So a group of them would come in, but they were bringing guns and knives with them. Right away we instituted a policy of checking weapons at the door. Tom was in charge of that, taking a weapon off somebody. He would politely say, 'You're welcome to come in, but there's no weapons in here. You can leave them here at the front, and I'll give them back to you when you leave. That policy worked well, but we always hired one or two off-duty policemen as well."

The most infamous tale is the melee of '75. Tom recalls, "Some cops had been called to the club the week before. I wasn't there, but the guy that Vern called the cops on told the cops to get lost, that he'd kill them or something, so the cops went away. The following week some guys were making trouble in front of the bar, and the cops got out of their car and because they'd been called chicken the whole week they just overreacted. It was close to closing time, and the next thing I knew Route 5 was wall to wall police, from Hanover, Norwich, Lebanon, 'Staties' from both New Hampshire and Vermont, there were probably ten or fifteen cop cars there. The local cops are running around with shotguns at high port, and I'm going, 'Don't shoot anybody, will ya!' Well, they didn't shoot anybody, but the following day the headline in the *Valley News* was 'Melee at Eleazar's' or some damn thing.

"A week or two later the town selectmen called me and Vern for a special meeting, because we were bad, because we'd had a melee. I brought my license with me, and I was gonna throw it on their desk. They were going through all this bullshit, and this guy named Paul Whitney, who owned the Holiday Inn in White River, gets up to speak. And he says, 'Look, if you close Eleazar's, all the freaks are gonna be in my bar. With Eleazar's open you know where they are.' He was just telling the truth. It was a wahoo group at Eleazar's. As a result, they didn't ask for our license." However, as part of the town's punishment for the melee the club had to close at midnight on Saturday nights rather than the usual town-wide closing time of 1:00 a.m. for bars.

Remember the Ray Stevens tune, "The Streak?" One night in the middle of winter Roger Davis decided to streak the bar wearing a ski mask to hide his identity. He launched his run from the upstairs apartment, went streaking through the bar, and continued out the front door on his way back to the apartment by way of the outside stairs. One problem. Roger neglected to close the apartment door after him, so his German Shepherd Rex ran right through the bar behind him. An observant soul behind the bar noticed Rex running after the streaker, and put two and two together. That individual, who shall remain nameless, went up to the apartment from the bar and locked the outside door, leaving Roger naked in the cold. Rex liked the weather just fine.

Dale recalls that "A lot of the customers at Eleazar's would go over and hang out at the Dartmouth frats and listen to bands. There was one band we had, The Beams, from Boston, and we tried to promote them by plastering Hanover with posters, you know, 'Come down to Eleazar's and see The Beams.' Well, unfortunately, the Dartmouth crowd did come, and it was a mess. We had our regulars at Eleazar's, guys named Hog Man and others, and we knew how to handle them and take care of them the same way we did the guys in the bands. After that night we told the owners that we would never want to have Dartmouth students again. Frat row comes to Eleazar's, not a good scene. We're looking at these Ivy League guys and thinking, 'This is the cream of the intellectual crop in America?' Oh, my God!"

Then there is the story about the food fight, which also happened when The Beams were playing. Dale swears The Beams started it. "There was stuff all over the place, food, soap suds, everything. We were climbing out the windows onto the back roof and water hosing each other and at one point half of us locked the other half out of the building. I don't know whose shoulders I was on, but I was trying to climb in the window on the front of the bar, in this red nightgown. The cops drove by, slowed, and then just sped up and kept going, because the cops really didn't like coming to Eleazar's, and when they did they came in pairs. Joy just locked herself in her room and said, 'Just clean it up in the morning.' And we did clean it up, for Joy."

Tom Day was a big guy, about 6'4" and two hundred fifty pounds. Tom and Vern never hired a bouncer because, well, Tom was a big guy. One night some kid somehow broke a nice watch Tom was wearing, and Tom picked the kid up and shoved his head through the sheetrock wall into the kitchen of the upstairs apartment. The hole in the wall actually came in handy for The Waitri. They covered it with a cloth, kitchen towel calendar, and "If we were late for work we could just move the calendar and look out to see if anyone was sitting in our section."

Dale muses about her Waitri pal. "After the two of us were at Eleazar's for a few weeks Joy just sort of nested in and we cleaned up the apartment, because basically it was just walls and some mattresses on the floor. Somehow we managed to scavenge sheets and blankets and stuff and made the band room nice, and our rooms were nice, and we cleaned up the kitchen. Joy was the one who cooked; I didn't have any skills in that area, so I became the clean up person.

"We lived together with the bands that stayed up there at the apartment with its bunk room arrangement. Joy and I each had our own rooms with locks on the doors." The apartment at Eleazar's was not big, but both Joy and Dale maintain "There was always room for one more." In addition to the bands playing at Eleazar's, all the bands on the Malhoit Circuit knew they could stay at the Eleazar's apartment and be pampered at Joy's Home For Wayward Musicians.

Joy recalls proudly that "The band guys would often request to stay with us, like if they were sick or if they had three or four days off, because they could stay in a home-like atmosphere and get cooked for." Plus, while playing at Eleazar's, as Don Coulombe notes, "It was nice that you had a bedroom right there in the club, since you could then drink all night and pass out in a bunk only six feet away."

According to Dale, Eleazar's "was a place that guys liked to come to. In fact, bands would end up socializing there, since White River was a crossroads for bands that would be heading north up toward Burlington or Canada, or going down to Boston. Tom and Vern probably didn't appreciate the fact that it was supposed to be only for bands that were playing there that week; but other bands would drop in and they'd get to meet each other and spend some time together. It was hard for bands to meet each other, even though they played the same circuit, since they were always playing. Bands would arrive at Eleazar's early for their gigs so they could rehearse and also hang out."

After the melee of '75 and the ensuing meeting with the town selectmen, Tom says that "I'd had enough of bar life, so I just gave the bar to Vern." Vern did a lot of work inside the bar and renamed it Hatts Off. Vern stayed on for about two more years, and then the club, under new ownership, became known as The Ritz Cafe. The Carey Rush band played the last show at The Ritz, in 1983.

Don Coulombe offers this epitaph. Eleazar's "was one of my favorite places, probably because so many bands played there. We used to run into a bunch of bands there and just as you'd be coming in to set up another band would be breaking down. We got to know Better Days there, and the guys from Tracks. It's almost surprising they got the caliber of bands to play there that they did, since it was such a small place, and really kind of a dive. But they just had cool people who went there, and it was fun to stay there and play there."

Musicians not only remember the club itself, they also remember Joy's Home for Wayward Musicians. In the summer of 2010, while experiencing a temporary health setback in her Utah home, Joy Moffat got a call from the East Coast. It was from Paul Lee Owens, the bass player of a band named Spoonfeather that played Eleazar's in the mid- and late 1970s. Joy smiles when she recounts the bass player's message. "Cupcake, you gotta take care of yourself! You're responsible for a generation of rock musicians in New England."

Better Days and Company

Steve Hirsch was hanging out in the University of Vermont student union in Burlington one spring day in 1971 when a pal said to him, "Hey, I know a band that needs a guitar player." Steve checked it out, joined up, and Better Days and Company began a five-year run as one of the most popular bands in the nexus.

The band Steve joined was Daze of Time. Its lineup was Alan Hammang on keyboard, Peter Lipnickas on bass, Bruce James on drums, Dave Pittman on rhythm guitar, and Tim Hughes on lead guitar. The group had success as the five-piece Fabulous Daze of Time starting in 1965, but in the spring of 1971 things began to come apart. Tim had gotten married and was ready to get off the road, and Bruce was preparing to leave. Steve says that "I started talking with them and we said, 'Let's put a new band together.' That's when the name of the band changed to Better Days."

In addition to finding a new guitar player in Steve, Better Days also went in search of a drummer. The band's first drummer was one of Steve's college roommates, Marty Goldstein. When Marty headed back to college at the end of the summer of '71, a Canadian named Bruce "Bucky" Berger took over on the skins. Bucky left the band in January 1972 because he couldn't get a work permit to stay in the United States.

In early 1972, Bobby Gagnier parted ways with Anvil. Better Days and Anvil had played some shows together, and the guys in the band knew Bobby G. was a talented drummer, so they welcomed him aboard. For the next eighteen months Better Days operated as a four-piece band. Regarding that time period, Steve remarks that "As a four-piece band, we did dreadfully in terms of income. We were starving, but boy did we have fun. We were jamming a lot, and I think that was musically maybe the most fun that I ever had. We weren't even trying to be a commercial band, we were just doing what we wanted."

Those four-piece days continued until Pete Shackett arrived on the scene in late June 1973. Pete recalls that "Gunnison Brook had broken up in April of 1973, and I went to work for my brother Dave laying hardwood floors. After working for a couple of months and jonesin' to play drums again, I put a call in to Malhoit asking if there were any bands in the area looking for a drummer. Ed told me that Better Days and Company were looking. So I met them at the Chopping Block in Proctorsville, sat in with them that night, and things seemed to go well. They invited me to play drums and I was back in the business.

"Better Days and Company was already an established band when I joined them. They had been around for a couple of years and were doing very well, and I wondered why they wanted a drummer because Bob was so good. With Bob on drums, Steve on guitar, Peter on bass, and Alan on keyboards they sounded tight and polished."

Bobby explains that "My going out front was a group decision, spurred on by a suggestion from Malhoit, to reach a broader audience by having someone out in the front position. I'd had the experience of sharing drums and fronting with Bob Hathaway in The Other Man's Grass and Anvil, and we felt that if we were able to find the right drummer it would work out. Pete was such a fine drummer, and adding him also offered the possibility of my going back on the kit for a set each night. Best decision we made!"

Pete continues, "When I joined, Bobby went out front for lead vocal, timbales, congas, and percussion. I played drums most of the time but developed a set on lead and rhythm guitar so Bob could still play some drums each gig. That concept worked out well for us, and my guitar set eventually became a nightly part of the act. Steve was a huge help in getting my electric playing off the ground. He taught me a lot of licks and technique. Steve's a hell of a good guitarist, and I'm glad he's still playing out all these years later. And Alan, he was from Valdosta, GA, and he turned me on to the Allman Brothers with the double guitar leads. We all got along pretty well for a diverse group of individuals."

Front, in the chair: Bobby Gagnier, L – R: Pete Shackett,
Steve Hirsch, Peter Lipnickas, Alan Hammang

About his guitar playing, Pete adds, "We also had one of the neatest openings to a forty-five minute continuous set of Led Zeppelin. I opened 'Stairway to Heaven' on acoustic guitar while sitting on the drums. Eventually Steve came in on electric, and I put down the acoustic and picked up the drum part where it started in the song. It sounded really good."

Steve Hirsch says that "Playing with two different drummers was a really interesting part of every evening, and a great draw of the band. We never went with two drummers at the same time, but we did use a lot of percussion. For example, we did a lot of Santana stuff with Pete on drums and Bobby G. on timbales and congas. Bob played drums on most of the American and Southern rock, and Pete played drums on the British stuff. We did a lot of Allman Brothers, 'Rambling Man' and others, 'Sweet Home Alabama' by Lynard Skynard, that sort of thing."

In addition to the Zeppelin set, Santana, and a lot of Southern rock, the band covered The Beatles, "Casey Jones" by the Grateful Dead, "Takin' Care of Business" by Bachman-Turner Overdrive, and songs off Aerosmith's first album. Better Days also covered Russell Pinkston's, "Mexican Bird," and two Rare Earth numbers. Steve recalls that "'I Just Want to Celebrate' and 'Hey, Big Brother' were our signature tunes. Peter had an absolutely fantastic rock and roll voice, maybe one of the best, a growly, nasty voice with incredibly good pitch, and he used to sing both of those."

The band played all over New England, and frequently in Upstate New York, with a good following wherever it went. The boys were regulars at Dartmouth fraternities; after Tracks broke up in 1974, Better Days slipped into the role of "house band" at Bones Gate, known for its wild parties and Sunday afternoon blowouts on big College weekends. The Bones Gate connection was how Better Days came to cover "Mexican Bird." Peter Lipnickas recalls that "We played there so often after Tracks that the guys there who had really liked Tracks wanted us to learn a Tracks song, and so we did 'Mexican Bird.' And we loved playing it. Instead of one person doing the lead singing we would share the lead. Bobby would do a verse, Alan would do a verse, and I would do a verse. It was awesome—we loved that song."

Ladd's in Portsmouth, NH, was a favorite destination, with Bill Esslinger, the doorman affectionately known as "Shitslinger," and Mike Smith, who Steve says was "a great club manager and treated us well. Ladd's was probably my favorite place to play—we always had the whole crowd in the palm of our hand." For Pete Shackett, playing at Ladd's "was always a little strange to me because of my established past with Gunnison Brook. Ladd's was both the very first place and the very last place that Gunnison Brook played together. Better Days did really well there, however, and Ladd's was a regular employer." So regular, in fact, that Peter L. remembers that "It got to the point at Ladd's that when we would play there people would line up to come and see us. When people were standing in line outside and you were walking in it gave you a feeling that was just indescribable. People were lined up waiting for somebody to leave so they could go in and hear you!"

As noted in the previous chapter, Eleazar's was also a regular stop. To Waitri Dale Granger and Joy Moffat, Better Days and Company was there so frequently that it almost seemed like the house band.

While it's almost inconceivable, at no time in its five-year history did the band live together. As Steve Hirsch puts it, "We were literally all over the state of Vermont. Alan was in Lyndonville, Peter L. was in Poultney, I was in Burlington, and Bobby and Pete S. were in Killington. For a while after Tracks broke up I lived at the Tracks house in Hartland, and we did use the Tracks practice room in the barn a couple of times. But for the most part we didn't practice except at gigs. Then again we were playing all the time, six nights a week." Pete Shackett concurs: "We would meet to practice in the afternoons at the clubs where we were playing weeklong gigs. Many arrangements and parts to songs were worked out after hours at whatever band place we were staying."

Every band has its tall tales to tell, and Steve relates a trio of Better Days' gems. "One event that does stand out is when Better Days got caught at ground zero of the flood of June 28-30, 1973. It was the first week that Pete Shackett was slated to perform with us, and we were working at The Mill in South Londonderry, VT. We awoke to one of the employees banging on the door at 6:00 a.m. in the morning to warn us that we better move our vehicles out of the lot. Quickly! A little stream that trickled by the lot in a twenty-foot-deep gully (The West River, a tributary of the Connecticut) was a roaring torrent about to crest the top.

"We burst out of the back door of the club to rescue the truck and our cars within minutes, and just in time to see a VW tip over the crumbling bank and go bobbing off down the river! After driving all the vehicles up a steep hill on the other side of the main road, we sprinted back and formed a 'bucket brigade' to put all the equipment up on tables at the highest point of the club. There was not enough time to move the gear, as water was licking under the front door by that point and the police were ordering everyone out of the building. We ended up trapped in town for three days due to every major route being flooded or washed out. Not my idea of fun, but quite memorable."

The second memory involves both Better Days and Atlantis. "Atlantis rented their band house from the owner of the Chopping Block. It was a creaky, three-story firetrap that sat about fifty feet from the club. One night after finishing five sets at the Chopping Block, a few of us went over to party with the folks from Atlantis.

"I spent the first hour or so jamming with their keyboard player, Sam DeSantis. A bit later I was talking with Ed Malhoit and Dave Curtin's drop-dead gorgeous girlfriend in a second story room. I happened to catch something out of the corner of my eye and looked over at the window just in time to see a screaming body fall past it. This was incongruously followed by roars of laughter from outside. Dave and the Atlantis roadies had dragged every last mattress out of the house and made a huge pile of them in the parking lot. He took the dare and made the twenty-foot drop first. Once the shock wore off, we all took turns jumping out of the third floor window. People shouldn't be allowed to have that much fun!"

Steve tells this final, scary story about the time that Alan Hammang got stabbed at the Hampton Manor in New York. "It was during the gas crisis and we were packing up. Alan had the truck backed up to the door, and as he walked around to get something out of the front of the truck he found some guy siphoning gas out of the tank. Alan was a big, tough guy, and he dived on the guy and grabbed him. But the guy had a knife in his hand, and he turned around and stabbed Alan. Alan was so amped up that he didn't even realize he had been stabbed. He was out there wailing away on this guy, and one of the bouncers came out. The guy got loose from Alan and jumped in his truck, but the bouncer ran over with a baseball bat in his hand and smashed the guy's window, and was chasing him hanging on to the door handle trying to pull him out of the truck.

"This whole thing happened in about thirty seconds, and I'm sitting there with my jaw hanging open. By the time Alan came back to where I was I looked and said, 'You're bleeding.' He had this really heavy jacket on which probably prevented a serious injury, and we ended up driving to the ER in Rutland and spending the night at the hospital."

Better Days and Company played out for more than three years with its five-piece lineup, and all told the band was together longer than five years. At its peak the group commanded top dollar, anywhere from $700 to $1200 a night. At one point in its run Bobby G. recalls a month the group played twenty-eight out of thirty days. Not a bad living, back then. Money aside, Peter Lipnickas says the main thing for him was, "Other than the birth of my daughter, being in that band was without a doubt the best time of my life." Bobby G. agrees: "We had a very fine run, one of the best times of my playing career."

L – R: Pete Shackett, Steve Hirsch, Bobby Gagnier,
Peter Lipnickas, Alan Hammang

So, why did the band break up? The precipitating event, according to Steve Hirsch, was that Pete Shackett wanted to move to Florida and play a duo act with former Birth and Gunnison Brook band mate Pete Merrigan. "Pete actually wanted to leave in 1975 but I talked him out of it. Then one day the next year he sat down with us and said, 'I'm moving to Florida in July' and that was it. By that point Alan had just gotten married and was ready to ditch the band life, and everybody was kinda getting on everybody else's nerves. So we decided, 'Let's bag it.'" Peter L. adds, "We were getting tired and running down, and it was getting to be work instead of fun."

Pete Shackett echoes the feeling. "Near the end it was getting harder to find gigs, and one of the big reasons was that many of the clubs we used to depend on were turning to disco. That miserable rage lasted into the '80s and ruined many bands. They were also turning to smaller groups like single acts for their happy hours, plus duos and trios that didn't cost them as much money. After a while it just seemed like it was time to pack it in. We weren't really going anywhere, gigs were getting tougher to find and many of them really sucked. From my perspective, I was getting tired of rock and roll and all the loudness, and I was longing to play acoustic. So I gave my notice, but oddly enough I don't remember the discussion being contentious. I think everyone was ready to call it quits."

In July of 1976 Better Days and Company turned out the lights for the last time with one final gig at Eleazar's. Shackett headed to Florida. Peter L. and Steve helped found the Burlington-based band Plum Crazy, with Sammy Spear on guitar, Scott Mathieu on drums, and Bob Butterfield on harp (yes, that's his real last name). Bobby G. joined a group from Plattsburgh, NY, called Hawkeye, a great funk / R&B / soul group whose previous drummer was John Wilcox. Known as Willie Wilcox, he went on to work for many years with Todd Rundgren, playing drums on the rock classic, "Bang the Drum All Day." Alan gave up life on the road for marital bliss.

Here's the thing about band breakups, and about Better Days' "no fault" breakup, their parting of the ways by mutual agreement. Better Days was the exception to the rule, because band breakups were often acrimonious, and always distressing to at least some of the members. What had begun months or years earlier with high hopes and soaring optimism, with a belief that *this band* was gonna make a lot of money and be the next rock sensation, would all come screeching to a halt. The clash of egos, the defections, the disenchantment, the tensions of living and creating art together...when it all came crashing down, everyone involved had to wrestle with and fend off bruised feelings and negative emotions.

Still, time eventually heals most wounds. In the summer of 2010 Doug Morton was ruminating on band breakups, and he summed it up quite neatly. "The intensity of being together, making music together, the emotions...people begin to play roles that they don't even know they are playing, and that they are not prepared to play. You go through the gauntlet together. Why do bands break up? A lot of different reasons. But in spite of it all you know you're still brothers. Time passes and with its passage the good memories come back, even for the people who were at odds when the band broke up."

Aha!

In July 2009, Steve Calvert and I discussed the research survey I would send to musicians for this book. Steve suggested the following question. "Describe the single, best 'aha' moment you had on stage, when you looked out over the audience or the dance floor and saw all these people loving the moment and the music and it hit you, 'Hey, the 'mates and I are responsible for this incredible scene and all this joy.'"

Wise man, that Calvert. At a significant level, that's what this book is all about—how music brings people together; the inspiration derived from music; and the profound, spiritual experience at those moments when the musician is completely one with his or her music.

So glad I asked. Here are several survey responses, plus my own "aha" moment.

Pete Bover, The Sprites and Nickel Misery

The simplest and best one was our very first Sprites' gig at a little town hall in Winchester, NH. There were about twenty-five or thirty gorgeous teenie bopper girls out there, and they were all looking at us google-eyed. They were smiling, some people were dancing, and I said, "Oh man, this is what I wanna do!" It was clear as a bell, just a wonderful feeling. It was absolutely overwhelming, that first gig. What a moment.

(Author's note: Pete was fourteen years old when The Sprites played their first gig. Barely a teenager, albeit a very talented one, he was living what an artist friend of mine refers to as "The dream of every American male.")

* * * * *

John Maxfield, Gunnison Brook

When I did my first gig with Gunnison Brook, rejoining two members of Birth in their new band, we ended the night with the second side of the album *Abbey Road*. The audience exploded as if we were at Shea Stadium. It might have been for the wrong reason, doing someone else's music, but it was still a trip being responsible for several hundred people's group fantasy.

* * * * *

Dan Sibley, Gunnison Brook

One such moment was when we were playing at Plymouth State College, opening for Miles Davis. Miles elected to go on first, I imagine so his band could "get out of Dodge" early. We were all sitting on the gymnasium floor, transfixed, listening to this incredible music. Keyboardist Keith Jarrett and percussionist Airto were both in his band at that time. After they were done, we opened with the Stones' "Honky Tonk Women" and everyone jumped up shrieking happily and started dancing. We really felt appreciated.

* * * * *

Jimi Slate, The Sprites and Nickel Misery

I was drumming for AC Apple, living in Plattsburgh, and the Amboy Dukes farewell tour was going on. Halfway through their Plattsburgh concert, 10,000 people in the room, the drummer got sick. Ted Nugent asked if there was a drummer in the audience who could finish up the concert.

I was sitting in the back, and I said to myself, "There must be at least a hundred drummers in this place right now." Well, nobody went up, and that was my job anyway, so I thought

"I'll bet I can do it." So I walked all the way down to the front and walked up on stage, went back stage, and the drummer was lying down on a couch and he looked really sick. I told him I might have to rearrange his drums and cymbals, etc., and he said, "Do what you gotta do."

I went out on stage, rearranged the drum set and I told Ted Nugent, "When the song is over give me one final sweep of the guitar down, so I know that's the end." And I played half the concert with Ted Nugent. It was just straightforward, hard-driving rock, and I love playing that sort of rock. I pulled it off, didn't screw anything up. Wow!

* * * * *

"Leadah", Tracks

For me that "aha" moment was a concert Tracks played with the James Gang on January 15, 1971, in Webster Hall at Dartmouth College. Webster Hall seated about 850 people, and we opened both 7:00 p.m. and 9:00 p.m. shows for Joe Walsh and the boys. I recall that the room was mostly filled for the first show, and packed for the second.

We were pretty amped, and played well enough in our first set that we earned an encore. The James Gang, however, was so painfully loud that halfway through their 7:00 p.m. set the room was virtually deserted. No encore there.

Our 9:00 p.m. set was even better, maybe the best we ever played while I was in the band, and we received a standing "O" when we did our encore. The James Gang also played an encore for that packed second show (obviously they had figured out they needed to turn down) but without the standing ovation.

As we left the stage after our second set, I was headed down the back stairs to the dressing room. Joe Walsh was coming up for their set, and as we passed in the stairwell he said, in his classic stoner voice, "Nice set, man."

* * * * *

Don Coulombe, Fox and Company

We had many of those moments. Probably the best one was when we opened for the Guess Who from Canada, at an outdoor event in Glens Falls, NY. Every summer they would have a "Concert in the Park" series. This particular concert was the biggest event to date in that town. When we got on stage all we could see was thousands and thousands of people, having the time of their lives. The next morning the front page of the newspaper read, "Fox and the Guess Who crammed Crandall Park with twenty-five thousand people." Biggest turnout in the summer parks series, what a rush.

* * * * *

Bobby Gagnier, Anvil

We had a bunch of those moments, but probably when we opened up for Mountain with Felix Pappalardi on bass and Leslie West on guitar. There were 5,000 people in Patrick Gymnasium at the University of Vermont, and a lot of them had come to see us. It was such a peak for Anvil, when you have so many people in a crowd that size who are there to see you. It was kinda like we could validate that Mountain is a band to go see because we, Anvil, are opening up for them.

Another cool thing about that night was we got to meet and hang out with one of the classiest people ever, Felix Pappalardi. Anyone who wears snakeskin boots is alright with me! I had some homemade cookies my mom had sent me, and

I offered them to Felix, 'cause I thought, "When was the last time he had homemade cookies." Felix liked our band a lot.

Leslie was not in a good mood, and I think one of the reasons was that a lot of these big bands would come to a little town and think they could just bring their "B game" and everybody would be blown away. But when they saw Brad French and what we did for the opening set, they realized it was a challenge, and they were gonna have to step up.

* * * * *

Gardner Berry, Stone Cross

We used to play up in Lake George a lot at Mother's. We would play at Mother's Tuesday through Sunday and the local radio station from Glens Falls would come up and they got us to do "Concert in the Park" on the Monday nights that we were off. We did that from about 1973 to 1977. At times it got rained out, but it was always a fun show.

In 1977 it happened that Monday fell on the 4th of July, and so they had the concert at a bigger park called Crandall Park, and it was one of those nights when everything worked. The weather was perfect, there were upwards of 10,000 people there, there were fireworks at the end, it was just…amazing. It's an amazing feeling playing for that many people. Stone Cross was the only band, and all those 10,000 people were there just to see us; it was really fabulous.

* * * * *

Lane Gibson, Davis Brothers Garage Band

We were playing at the Casino Vail in Vail, Colorado, in 1971 when Stephen Stills came in with a whole bunch of people. We got wind he was sitting up in the back there, so we played "Suite: Judy Blue Eyes" for him. There's a section towards the end of that song where the three-part chorus goes, "doo doo doo, doo doo, deet doot, doo doo doo doo." The lead vocal line over the chorus is in Spanish, which Stills sang on the original. Anyway, not knowing Spanish I was completely winging all of those Spanish words. I had no idea what they meant, I was trying to phonetically pronounce what I'd heard from the way Stills sang it.

So after we did the song he clapped over his head. Shortly after that he comes up to me on stage, and he's got what looks like a piece of paper in his hand. Turned out it was the inside of a Marlboro box. He had pulled out the inside of the box because he needed something to write on. What he did was write down the Spanish words to that section of the song and he handed it to me and he said, "Here, you need these."

Then he picked up a guitar and jammed with us on a couple of tunes: "Livin' in the USA" by Steve Miller Band; "Crossroads" by Cream, which he wanted to play, he was just really into the tune; and "Funk #49" by the James Gang.

Stephen Stills with Davis Brothers Garage

* * * * *

Wanna know what happened to that handwritten note from Stephen Stills, a piece of memorabilia any musician would treasure? Okay. Lane is originally from Metuchen, New Jersey. During the years when Davis Brothers was playing out West, they used to come back to the East Coast in the summer for a two- or three-week vacation. Lane would stay with his parents in New Jersey and would try to get to the shore as often as he could because he loved to go surfing.

One day he was at the shore, and he had his wallet in the pocket of his surf jams. In the wallet, which he forgot to take out of his pocket when he went out on his board, was the note written on the inside of the Marlboro box. Alas, Stephen Stills' handwritten note went to sleep wid da fishes off da Joisey shore.

"Huh? What?"

So, your plane is idling at the departure gate. The pilot has just come on the intercom to apologize for what he says will be a "slight" delay. Yeah, and you know those flying pigs will get from Boston to Chicago before you.

You look out the window, scope out the dudes working the luggage carts on the adjacent jet and the guy driving the fuel truck. The lady with the fluorescent wands you wish was guiding you onto the tarmac for your flight through the friendly skies is snapping gum, arms limp at her sides. Doesn't matter if it's June or January, all the folks on the ground are wearing those cute ear muffs. Maybe the first time you saw them you wondered why. Not any more.

The human ears are wondrous anatomical equipment. But like a toe we never think about until it is stubbed, we take our hearing for granted until it starts going south.

In May 2003 my wife, Lee, and I attended a Doobie Brothers concert at the Roanoke (Virginia) Civic Center. It was a great concert, and it was L-O-U-D! The Doobies deployed three drum sets that evening. Sometimes one drummer was primarily a percussionist; sometimes all three drummers were hammering away on their full kits simultaneously. Imagine the amps used by the other players to keep up with that percussive explosion.

As the concert wound down, Lee and I left a little early to beat the traffic. As we exited the building into a parking lot filled with sleeping horsepower, it sounded like I was standing on the median of a freeway with cars zipping by in both directions. Except that the nearest freeway was a couple hundred yards away.

Then Lee turned to me and said, "What's that sound?"

"What sound?"

"There's this whooshing noise in my ears."

"You mean like traffic on a freeway?"

"Yeah, or some kind of white noise."

I smiled ruefully. "That's the sound I used to hear every morning after a Tracks gig."

Sketch by Rick Hunt

I wish I didn't have so much company when it comes to hearing loss, though I am not at all surprised. Virtually every former band member I talk with suffers from it.

Gardner Berry: "I'm pretty hard of hearing, I have some substantial hearing loss on the high end. I don't go to movie theaters any more because it's really hard to distinguish the dialogue. So I do Netflix and use the English subtitles."

Pete Bover: "I know I have hearing loss. I don't quantify it but I know I have it. I played through four fifteen-inch JBLs when I was sixteen and seventeen years old. That's a lot of noise coming at me, and I remember a funny feeling in my ears when I was in the wrong position on the stage, and waking up in the morning with the white noise in my ears."

Brad French: "I have hearing loss on the high end from standing in front of stacks of Marshalls all those years. People tell me I talk too loud, a sign of hearing loss."

Peter Logan: "I definitely have hearing loss. I remember that about an hour into playing, my ears would stop hurting. At the time I didn't recognize that as a bad sign."

Don Coulombe: "I have hearing loss in my right ear. My monitor was huge and the fact that I was a drummer meant I needed that damn thing as loud as the band just so I could hear myself. My wife keeps telling me that she is going to get me a Miracle-Ear one of these days."

And finally, this story told by Pete Merrigan about the late, great Harry Dailey, bassist for both Jimmy Buffett's Coral Reefer Band and Shackett and Merrigan's Mad Beach Band. "Harry and his wife were watching television one night in the late 1980s. A show was being broadcast about Terence Trent D'Arby, at that time one of the hottest performers around. The commentator said that D'Arby was certain to be the 'James Brown of the Nineties.' Harry didn't hear exactly what was said, and with a puzzled look on his face asked his wife, 'Why would anyone want to be James Brown in a nightie?'" Shades of Emily Latella.

Then there is tinnitus, which is usually described as a ringing noise in one or both ears or in the head. The most common cause of tinnitus is noise-induced hearing loss. Yours truly shares this condition with many former rockers, perhaps because the way Tracks set up on stage placed me more or less directly in front of Russell Pinkston's guitar speakers. Man, those tinkling, high-pitched bells are annoying!

Musicians are not the only ones who suffer from the ravages of excessive decibels. For example, Gar Anderson, who as owner of The Rusty Nail was constantly exposed to bands' searing volume, asks tongue-in-cheek: "So is this what caused my tinnitus?" And #1 Gunnison Brook fan Joy Moffat has a condition called Bellman's Curve hearing loss as a result of her years sitting right at the front of the stage when her heroes were playing. Joy says, "Certain frequencies kick out, certain sounds mask other sounds. For example, if I'm in the kitchen with the water running I can't hear the phone ringing in the next room."

In addition to hearing issues resulting from years of standing in front of screaming guitars, crashing cymbals, and crackling snare drums, there is other damage as well, including polyps and other throat issues. In 1969, while Tracks was playing a summer-long gig on Cape Cod, I made several trips to an ENT specialist in Fall River, MA, for help with a developing polyp problem. Part of my cure was beginning voice lessons with Dante Pavone and learning correct singing mechanics. In August 2006, Steven Tyler had laser surgery in Boston to seal a blood vessel on his right vocal cord which had popped as a result of more than forty years of extraordinary vocal acrobatics.

Drug and alcohol abuse and their attendant consequences were, and continue to be, a reality. One rocker tells these stories on himself and a band mate. "We both contracted hepatitis from shooting up with the same needles, and I ended up in the hospital. One time we tripped on very strong LSD. It was Thanksgiving and we went to my parents' house for dinner. The food was crawling on our plates!"

And there's this story of a "good" trip. A guitarist was observed by a member of a different band attempting to tune up before a rehearsal one night at Dartmouth's Webster Hall. "He would hit a note and he would giggle, and he'd kinda, he was tracking something in the air that appeared to be bouncing off his guitar. Then he'd hit another note, watch it flutter off into the ozone, and giggle again. He never did get tuned up because he couldn't figure out how to. But wherever he was, off by himself, he was definitely having a good time." Now that's gotta have some flashback potential.

Second only to hearing issues are repetitive use injuries. Within the past three years, Bobby Gagnier has had surgery on both hands. In early 2008, he had a bone replaced on the back of his right hand. In February 2010, "I had arthrosis surgery, because of an arthritic condition that finally gets to the point that it's deteriorating the bone. It's called basal joint arthritis, and it's a repetitive use injury. Basically I had my left thumb restructured."

Gunnison Brook guitarist Dan Sibley has also needed several hand surgeries due to repetitive, motion-induced damage.

Gardner Berry says, "I had an issue with my hip. What happened was that for thirty years I stood up to play keyboards, keeping one foot on the sustain pedal. All of my weight was on my left leg, and it gave me a condition that my chiropractor called a reverse hip. She worked on that and it got to a point where it's comfortable for me now. These days I sit down when I play."

Oh, and there was one more condition that wasn't talked about very much. Every so often some of us, myself included, would come down with a bad case of anal-cranial reversion, usually after admiring ourselves in a mirror or reading our press clippings. Fortunately, the condition was reversible upon being treated with sufficient and unblinking peer pressure.

Perhaps the most amusing story on this whole subject of rock-and-roll-induced injuries comes from Dave Cross. After Ragweed's short-lived 1970-1971 foray into the Pacific Northwest, Dave, a born and bred New Yorker, decided to stay on the West Coast. For more than thirty years he has played drums with rock bands in the Tacoma, WA, area. Since 1992, he's drummed for the Rockodiles, a three-piece band specializing in '50s and '60s rock: Beach Boys, Ventures, Elvis, Stones, Chuck Berry, and classic tunes like "Summertime Blues" and "Wipe Out." One night in 2010 at a Rockodiles practice in Dave's basement, the fifty-something bass player complained, not for the first time, about chronic pain in his left index finger. Dave asked him if he thought it might be a repetitive use injury. The reply: "Nah, I've been playing too long for that."

Where Do We Go from Here

By the mid-'70s the wheel was inevitably, inexorably turning; the live music scene in upper New England was changing. According to club owners Jere Eames and Gar Anderson, and to many musicians, the sense of community, the sense of family of the late '60s and early '70s, was fading. Personal, friendly relationships between band and club were becoming "strictly business." Unfortunately, strictly business wasn't always good for business.

Worse, the connection between band and audience was shorting out. Disco had arrived, and with it an emphasis on DJs and fashion and de rigueur dance steps and flashing lights on the dance floor. People didn't come to clubs anymore to listen to the music. They came to see and be seen. As one rocker trenchantly put it, the club patrons declared that *they* were the reason to come out on a Friday or Saturday night.

Buddy Newell closed down Newell's Casino in 1974. Gar sold The Rusty Nail a second and final time; he had sold it the first time in 1972, then took it back when the new owners from Florida drove his brainchild to the brink of ruin. Jere and Yvonne sold Jeremiah's in 1975. A golden era was coming to an end.

Brad French delivers this epitaph: "In the mid- to late '70s, I played in some really, really good show bands. You know, matching tuxes, we made really good money, we played five or six nights a week, and I did that for a few years. But towards the end I knew the end had come for me because it just wasn't fun anymore. It was just a job, and at a lot of the places where we performed you were thought of as just a jukebox, just a marionette."

Many of the rockers who inhabit this tale had reached or were approaching thirty. Thirty, the magic age, beyond which—so we had been told a decade earlier—one was never to be trusted. Some began to regard playing rock music as an expression of sowing their youthful oats, and started planning to move on, to join the establishment.

For many in the upper New England rock scene it seemed time to turn to different pursuits. For example, John Maxfield enrolled in med school to become Dr. John. Pete "Nuke 'Em" Shackett took up nuclear medicine and authored a definitive book on the subject. Peter Logan went to law school and today practices law in San Francisco. Peter Christenson, Stanford Ph.D., is a Communications professor at Lewis & Clark College in Portland, OR. Russell Pinkston went back to Dartmouth, majored in music, and earned his Ph.D. at Columbia. Since 1983 he has been a professor at the University of Texas-Austin, and director of their electronic music lab.

There are, of course, exceptions to the "cut your hair and get a job" mentality my mother preached at me every time we talked on the phone. Some of our mates from back in the day are "lifers." They continued to play out right along, which they do today as, ahem, middle-aged gentlemen. Pete Merrigan, Gardner Berry, Bobby Gagnier, Rick Davis, Norm Coulombe, the gents in Aerosmith. Again, these are but a few examples.

Some bands played on into the '80s—Stone Cross, Fox and Company, Davis Brothers Garage. More frequently, in the middle '70s, there was a sense of passing the torch to younger musicians and new bands—Dave Abair, Paul Hayward, Bob Leitgeb, Doug Morton, Carey Rush, Lazy Livin', Spoonfeather, The Fraank Band, 8084, and others.

* * * * *

Fast forward to April 2010, when Gerry Wolf, Pete Merrigan, and Jere and Yvonne Eames threw a party at Stonewall Farm in Keene, NH. "Flashback" played host to upwards of 150 people. More than two dozen musicians from the Sixties and Seventies made fine, fine music for six hours, and there were many reunions among old friends that night. For me, the most significant of those reunions involved members of Gunnison Brook.

Alan MacIntosh had been in Las Vegas for many years, and the other band members had lost touch with him. Alan had not attended a 2008 Gunnison Brook reunion, didn't even know about it. But in 2009 the Gunnison Brook boys reconnected. Alan and his wife, Martha, flew out from Vegas for the party in Keene, and on Saturday, April 10, 2010, he was onstage with his former band mates for the first time in thirty-seven years. In the run-up to the party, he composed a tribute to his old band titled "Back in the Day." Alan tells the story:

"A July 2009 letter in the mail from Peter Wonson set off a chain of 'events of the heart.' It was a revelation to learn that the old members of Gunny Brook has been searching for me, had failed, and had gone ahead with an official Gunnison Brook Reunion performance without me.

"Having been the lead culprit in breaking up the group in 1973, there was plenty of hurt to go around. But these fellows had the hearts of mature men, and had been willing to set their hurts aside. I was heartened to know that now I had been handed a second chance to appreciate the five other musicians in Gunnison Brook.

"So, my emails went out, one after the other. Then I waited. I was prepared for indifference, but I received warm and generous replies. Now, this is something to live up to, I thought. Well, if they want me for the next Gunnison Brook Reunion, I'd better get busy.

"Not only did my appreciation for the guys revive, my urge to write also revived. All of a sudden, I wanted to write a new song, this time about the old Gunnison Brook, with each member present. And I knew right away it would be onstage, in performance, at Ladd's in Portsmouth. It would evoke Peter and Mario up front doing their thing, and the bridge would involve Joy, our #1 fan.

Mario Casella and Pete Merrigan of Gunnison Brook, at Stonewall Farm

"Writing 'Back in the Day' was fun, but singing it was nearly impossible. Too emotional. You can't sing when you choke up, because it stops the flow of air through your vocal cords." But, somehow, Alan managed, that evening in

343

Keene. In the lower level of Stonewall Farm's main building, where the event was held, a Korg electric piano had been set up in an anteroom outside the green room. At the end of the night, after most people had left, Alan sat at that keyboard and played his song for an intimate group. Martha was there, as was #1 Gunnison Brook fan, Joy Moffat. Joy had told Bobby Gagnier about the song, and he had come downstairs to listen. I was also privileged to be present at that private concert. A couple of times while Alan was playing and singing I glanced over at Joy, and saw a tear in her eye. For me it was the most magical moment of a magical evening.

Two months later, in June 2010, Tracks and The Night Watchmen played two reunion shows in New Hampshire and Vermont, the first time Tracks had convened onstage in over thirty-five years. The first gig was for the 40th Reunion of Dartmouth's Class of 1970 (Russ Pinkston, Jeff Wilkes, and Peter Logan's class). The second night, Thursday, June 17, the bands played in White River Junction, at the American Legion Post. That night, old Tracks fans from the '60s and '70s drove from places like Boston, Manchester, the coast of New Hampshire, Burlington, and the town of Derby in far northern Vermont to be part of the reunion. One of those fans was Donald Mahler, an editor with the *Valley News* in White River. The week after the performances, he published a piece about the June 17 show. It read, in part:

"I went to a family gathering the other night. It was an extended family, even though none of us were actually related. While nobody knew everybody, everybody knew somebody. I promise you, if we all held hands the circle would never be broken. That's what music does: it brings people together. Longhairs, gray hairs, strangers, old friends, old flames, old hippies and former rowdies all brought together for the same reason: the music.

"About two hundred fugitives from the Land of Oz showed up at the White River Legion Thursday night to be part of the return to the local stage of veteran bands The Night Watchmen and Tracks. Forty years just flew off the calendar on the sweet voice of Skip Truman, bringing back the old memories with the old harmonies. Russell Pinkston's guitar still had the crackle of lightning that time could not diminish; Ken Aldrich's keyboards were soaring and Ned Berndt kept the whole thing in beat banging away on the drums.

"One old friend put it best: 'This is just paradise.' You could see it in the smiles and the hugs, in the feet tapping and arms swinging. Sometimes the downbeat coming from the stage was accompanied by a heavy sound of a dozen or so boots hitting the dance floor at exactly the same time as the drumsticks. The guys may have been up on stage, but we were all part of the band.

"The building was full of old musicians, bands that made up the Upper Valley music scene back in the day. 'I remember following these guys all around the Dartmouth fraternities,' recalled one old drummer. 'They still sound great.'

"Music was so important then, our voice to the world. Little has changed. The old songs still produce a rush of feeling and memory, and live music just intensifies the emotion for all of us old geezers.

"As one of the band members said as they were leaving the stage at the end of the night, 'Our sets get shorter and our breaks get longer and we just keep getting older.' The biggest challenge the band had all night was finding a coherent way to end some of its songs. And that's a problem...why? End them? Don't stop the music now. We are all living the game of musical chairs one day at a time these days. The last thing we want to hear is the silence. So play on, old friends. Don't ever stop the music." (1)

* * * * *

And so we have our memories—recent ones, which we continue to create; and the old ones, frayed around the edges like that baseball card you have from the Fifties. If you hadn't played with it on the sidewalk or put it in the spokes of your bicycle as a kid it might be worth a lot of money to some collector. But to you it is priceless, because when you hold the card in your hand it conjures up indelible memories.

A recurring theme of everyone I interviewed for this book is how fortunate we were to have been a part of that magical time known as "The Sixties." It was an era that will never be replicated, those years when music was inextricably woven into the fabric of our lives.

Once music has cast its spell over you, it remains forever an essential part of who you are, of how you exist. It touches your soul, and your life is never the same.

The Last One Night Stand

August 16, 2038. **The expansive** wood deck skimmed the ground in the back yard that led down to the ever gorgeous waters of Sunapee Lake.

They had flown in the day before to Manchester's airport, except for the one who still lived on the shores of the lake. They traveled light, like the old days, each carrying a single bag, since this was a one-night stand. The youngster of the bunch had just turned eighty-five. The oldest was ten days short of ninety.

They brought no equipment with them. The host's sixty-two-year-old kid had arranged all that through a local music store. It didn't matter that they didn't have their own instruments, even the beloved '59 Les Paul. The sound they made wouldn't matter, because what they would hear when they closed their eyes, what they always heard, was how it used to sound.

Several grandkids who had their own bands lived within an hour's drive. They were the road crew that day, and also handled the sound checks.

When it was time, the old men eased out onto the deck. For twenty-five years they had returned for the one-night stand, and if it rained the roadies set up in the basement. But vintage 2038 was the kind of day they always wished for, and somehow usually got. A hint of a breeze off the lake, warm sun, patchy clouds. It felt right, and on days like this they felt particularly alive, even young again.

Back in 2013 there had been fifteen or twenty of them, and truly they made a joyful noise. Now there were five. So many of them, most of them, were gone. Each year since '31 one of them had cracked a dark joke about actuarial tables.

What had once been a sixty-minute set, with interchangeable players to keep the energy level on high, had gradually shrunk to last year's two songs. This year they again settled for two songs, the tempo slowed noticeably to accommodate the arthritis and ancient muscles, the tunes dropped two keys in deference to pipes all but rusted through.

For the past decade they hadn't bothered to rehearse. It was enough to get through the one-night stand, to exit the other end of the tunnel, maybe breathing a bit heavily, maybe cramping a little, hearts racing, but having finished the gig for another year.

They played, lost once again in the joy of what they had shared for so long, and in the joy of the music. But each was lost as well in his own world, buoyed by the hazy memories of when they were young and planned to live forever. After restarting the opening song, barely into the first verse, when the singer had a coughing jag and stumbled over the lyrics, they caught their breath and pushed on.

When it was over, the second and third generation applause faded and the afternoon air fell silent. One final, muffled beat came from the drummer's floor tom. The old man lay against the tom, head resting on the rim, eyes wide, contentment etched on his face. Then, with a hint of a smile from long ago, the youngster said, "Coda."

Acknowledgements

I continue to be astonished by the support of and energy from hundreds of people, without whom this book would not exist. I can most accurately characterize the indefatigable efforts of my many co-authors by using the following example. Without exception, every interview we held for the book ran too long, yet ended too soon.

I worry that I have overlooked some individuals, because thanks are owed to so many. My apologies for any such inadvertent omissions.

First things first. My thanks to Pete Merrigan, the catalyst, without whom I never would have begun this project. One afternoon in June of 2009 I sent an email to Pete— unannounced after a four decade hiatus, on a whim, a vague voice from the distant past. The next day there was a very generous reply and a copy of a forward Pete had sent to eight other ancient folks, inviting them to get in touch with me. They did, one thing led to another, and in short order I had committed myself to this book. Over the course of the past two years Pete has been a friend, a source of contacts and information, a sounding board, a reader and critic, and also the author of two splendid chapters in this tale.

Great thanks to Steve Calvert, whom I have known for forty-seven years, since we were Pea Green freshmen in the fall of 1964. Dr. (English Ph.D.) Calvert was a founding member of both The Night Watchmen and Tracks, and he has been a true friend for the past two years. Early on Steve offered to serve as my editor. He knew what he was getting himself into, the enormous commitment of time and energy. He signed up anyway. I am indebted to him for that; for being a mentor who was always available; for "The Café Bizarre;" and for our ongoing conversation about music and life.

To Yvonne and Jere Eames, whom I have known for forty-two years, for their friendship and their unflagging support, in so many different ways, of this book.

To Rick Hunt, an extraordinary artist, who generously offered to create the sketches that grace this book.

To Dartmouth musical colleagues Russell Pinkston, Ned Berndt, Jeff Wilkes, Peter Logan, Dave Cross, John Maxfield, Alan MacIntosh, David Soren, Gene Mackles, Eric Ebbeson, Peter Christensen, Oliver Hess, Andy Raymond, Jim Shafer, Tom Parker, Nels Armstrong, Eric Van Leuven, Allen Atkins, Rick Saltman, Bob Lundquist, Dave Fuchs, and Kirby Nickels.

To musicians Ken Aldrich, Skip Truman, Bob Neale, Pete Shackett, Mario Casella, Dan Sibley, Bobby Gagnier, Brad French, Peter Yanofsky, Jim Goodrum, Rick Davis, Lane Gibson, Angelo Mullen, Don Coulombe, Norm Coulombe, Steve Galipeau, Steve Hirsch, Peter Lipnickas, Pete Bover, Jimi Slate, Gardner Berry, Bill Blaine, Mike Mulroy, Pamela Brandt, Doug Morton, Brian Bull, Paul Hayward, Carey Rush, Bob Leitgeb, Cher Mitchell Aubin, Sandy Alexander, Dana Flewelling, Roger Bartlett, and James Mahoney.

To Ed Malhoit, Joy Moffat, Dale Granger, Gerry Wolf, Gar Anderson, Ken Strong, Vinnie Buonanno, Buddy and Cooki Newell, Tom and Beth Day, Rick and Noreen Carvolth, and Scott Harrison.

To Lynda Tallarico, Victor Tallarico, Jeff "Flash" Gordon, Mitch Wonson, Carol Mulroy Morton, Kate Tyler, Karen DeBiasse, Bob Reich, Jon Newcomb, Annie Dolan, Lonna

Lalonde, Nick Kanakis, Susan Helie, Mary Casella, Melinda Merrigan, Gerry Bell, Ford Daley, and Dan Salomon.

To Britanny Lavin, Laura Pici, and all the talented people at Infinity Publishing.

To Steve Morse from *The Boston Globe*, Donald Mahler of the *Valley News*, Jeff Woodburn of *WhiteMtNews.com*, Mike Boila of Gear Publishing Company, Jerry Carbone of the Brattleboro Public Library, Kathleen Hurley, Laura Osborne and Laura Jean Whitcomb of *Kearsarge Magazine*, Robert Blechle of *The Caledonian Record*, Ron Garceau at *SooNipi Magazine*, Gordon Ploker of Photo USA, George Mitchell, Dave Prentice, and Boyd Johnson.

To my Roanoke friends: Ralph Berrier (who has written a terrific book about family and bluegrass music, *If Trouble Don't Kill Me*); Kim Kristensen; Annette Chamberlin, who eagerly read a number of chapters; and especially Gates DeHart, who proofread the full manuscript.

To all the musicians from the nexus. In the past eighteen months I have collected a lot of music from "back in the day." Know what? It holds up really well, because it is really good. I salute you, your phenomenal talent, and your great music. Without you, there would be no book.

Finally, to my wife, Lee, who encouraged and supported me from the beginning of this project. I lost track of the times she had to endure my jumping out of bed after we had settled in for the night, my voice trailing behind me as I headed down the hall to my office…"I just need to write down one quick thing."

* * * * *

One of my favorite songs is "Almost Cut My Hair," by Crosby, Stills, Nash and Young. This last word is both a thank you, to everyone from "The Sixties" who made the magic happen; and a reminder, to all of us from that era who are still standing. Listen to David Crosby's song, and remember what our music stood for.

PW

Endnotes

Nodah

1. Abenaki language: Wobigentekw = White River; Kwanitekw = Connecticut River; Sobakw = Atlantic Ocean; Kinnikinnick = a mixture of sumac or red willow bark, native tobacco, spicebush, and bearberry; Nodah = Hear me; Ketsinioueskou = Great Spirit; Ndakinna = homeland

2. The oldest known musical instrument found to date, a vulture bone flute discovered in a cave in Germany, is 35,000 years old.

"Momma, Are They Body Snatchers?"

1. On July 29, 2009, out of the blue, Ken Aldrich wrote me a creative email that inspired this chapter, is the basis of the chapter's first and second paragraphs, and is one of many contributions Ken made to the book.

2. "Scapegoat" lyrics reprinted with permission of Dr. Russell Pinkston.

Tin Soldiers

1. Richard Nixon's middle initial was M. for Milhous. Archie Bunker referred to Nixon as "Richard E. Nixon." I'll leave the F. to your imagination.

2. Printed with permission of Mr. Robert Reich.

Wayne Wadhams

1. That first 45 was "The Pocket Book Song" by Leroy Van Dyke—not exactly an all-time classic. Pamela Brandt, who played in the Moppets, Ariel, and Deadly Nightshade, remembers her first 45 purchase—the 1956 double-sided hit by the King of Rock and Roll, "Hound Dog" and "Don't Be Cruel." Now that was a purchase for the ages.

2. A video of The D-Men performing their song, "I Just Don't Care," on Hullabaloo in 1965 can be seen at:
http://www.youtube.com/watch?v=4rY50GBqstM

3. "Ding Dong! The Witch Is Dead" can be heard at:
http://www.youtube.com/watch?v=tFvDFTiHQfU

Back Stories and the Road to...Good Intentions

1. The American Civil Liberties Union was founded in 1920. Historical license is a lovely tool in a pasquinade.

Whitcomb's Music Center

1. The term straight meant something different forty years ago to a musician. Reference the classic song "Dear Mr. Fantasy" by Traffic.

The Barn

1. K.M. Hurley, "Walk that Way," *Kearsarge Magazine*, Summer, 2010, 48-49.

2. Hurley, 49.

Rodney Diamond and the Studs

1. Reprinted with permission of Pete Merrigan.

Then The Muse Tapped Me on the Shoulder

1. David Bradley, *Robert Frost: A Tribute to the Source*, (New York, NY: Holt, Rinehart and Winston, 1979).

An Italian Opera Singer

1. As related to John Maxfield of Gunnison Brook.

2. Steve Morse, "Voice Coach for the Rockers," *The Boston Globe*, July 9, 1993.

3. Morse, "Voice Coach for the Rockers."

4. Morse, "Voice Coach for the Rockers."

Hard Times on the Road

1. Lyrics to the second verse of "Turn the Page," Written by Bob Seger, Copyright 1973 Gear Publishing Company (ASCAP), reprinted with permission.

"Hey Leadah..."

1. In 1981 an errant elbow in a pickup basketball game put a visible S curve in the center of my face. I was given general anesthesia before the doctor repaired what he called "the Rice Krispies" inside my nose where solid bone and cartilage should have been.

2. After a twenty-two year hiatus, Ned is back to playing in a rock, funk and R&B band in Miami that goes by the name C. O. Jones.

Gar Anderson

1. Monson Academy became Wilbraham & Monson Academy in 1971.

The Rusty Nail

1. In the eighteen months between Friday, December 19, 1969, opening night at The Rusty Nail, and June 19, 1971, the night I played my last gig with Tracks, the band played seven separate times at The Nail, for a total of thirty-nine days.

2. My first wife, Maggie, and I slept in three different locations at The Nail. The most charming was the final one, a spacious bedroom with a king-sized bed at the back of the building. The room's ceiling had not been finished when we stayed there, and it was covered with plastic sheeting. Through the plastic we frequently saw tiny field mice scurrying about overhead.

3. One resident of The Nail who had no trouble negotiating the spiral staircase was Metzi, Gar's beloved dog. Metzi used to launch late night commando raids up the staircase to the stage, snatch Ned Berndt's drumsticks, and gnaw on them at her leisure under cover of the dark. Ned typically discovered her handiwork the next time he sat down to play.

Davis Brothers Garage Band

1. According to the Kansas Department of Transportation, the east-west distance across the state of Kansas is 411 miles.

"Flash" Gordon and the Jefferson Light Show

1. Tabarnac and saint tabarnac are considered "sacres," or profanities, in Quebec French.

"Flash" Gordon and the Jefferson Light Show (continued)

2. According to Hammond, the original B-3 and C-3 models each weighed over 400 pounds.

Fox Chase

1. Stephen Davis, *Walk This Way: the Autobiography of Aerosmith* (New York, NY: itbooks/HarperCollins Publishers, Inc., 2003), 20.

Yvonne and Jere Eames

1. SHAPE = Supreme Headquarters Allied Powers Europe
   NATO = North Atlantic Treaty Organization

Gerry's Song

1. MayoClinic.com, *"Trigeminal neuralgia: Treatment and drugs"*, (http://www.mayoclinic.com/health/trigeminal-neuralgia/DS00446/DSECTION=treatments-and-drugs)

Newell's Casino

1. Jeff Woodburn, "Newell's Casino: a place of adolescent memories," *WhiteMtNews.com*, August 13, 2010. (http:/www.whitemtnews.com/?s=Newells+Casino)

2. *WhiteMtNews.com*, August 13, 2010.
3. *WhiteMt.News.com*, August 13, 2010.
4. *WhiteMt.News.com*, August 13, 2010.
5. *WhiteMt.News.com*, August 13, 2010.
6. *WhiteMt.News.com*, August 13, 2010.

Aerosmith

1. Stephen Davis, *Walk This Way: the Autobiography of Aerosmith* (New York, NY: itbooks/HarperCollins Publishers, Inc., 2003), 104-105.

Where Do We Go from Here

1. Donald Mahler, "At Rockers' Reunion, the Whole Family Was There," *Valley News*, June 24, 2010.

Photo Credits

(I regret that for the vast majority of photos in the book the actual photographer is unknown.)

Cover Photo

Tracks in concert at the Bema, Dartmouth College, Hanover, NH, April 19, 1970, Wonson collection

Wayne Wadhams

Page 19, courtesy Jeff Wilkes

Sixties Dartmouth Bands

Page 25, courtesy David Soren

Page 31, Wonson collection

The Café Bizarre

Page 35, courtesy Peter Logan

The Acorn and the Tree

Page 38, courtesy Gardner Berry

Page 45, courtesy Carey Rush

Back Stories and the Road…to Good Intentions

Page 49, courtesy Pete Shackett

The Sprites / Nickel Misery

Pages 52 and 58, both courtesy Pete Bover

The Barn

Page 70, courtesy Mike Mulroy and Carol Morton Mulroy

Page 75, Wonson collection

Ed Was an Empire

Pages 80 and 84, both courtesy Ed Malhoit

Page 82, courtesy Dale Granger

Anvil

Pages 90 and 92, both courtesy Peter Yanofsky

Can't Get Theah from Heah

Page 106, Wonson collection

Ragweed

Pages 115 and 117, both courtesy Dave Cross

Gunnison Brook

Page 122, courtesy Pete Shackett

Home Is Where the Band House Is

Page 135, courtesy Jeff Wilkes

Page 141, courtesy Mary Casella

Then The Muse Tapped Me on the Shoulder

Page 150, Wonson collection

"Hey, Leadah…"

Page 172 and 176, both Wonson collection

Page 180

Top, courtesy Eric Van Leuven. Bottom, courtesy Peter Yanofsky.

Page 181

Top, courtesy Jeff Wilkes. Bottom, Wonson collection.

Gar Anderson

Page 189, Wonson collection

The Rusty Nail

Page 192, courtesy Gar Anderson

Page 196, courtesy Susan Helie

Davis Brothers Garage Band

Pages 205 and 207, both courtesy Rick Davis

The Wobbly Barn

Pages 212 and 214, both Wonson collection

"Flash" Gordon and the Jefferson Light Show

Page 222, courtesy Jeff Gordon

Page 224, courtesy Bill Blaine

Fox Chase

Page 231, courtesy Jere Eames

Page 233, courtesy Doug Morton

Page 237, courtesy Pete Bover

Yvonne and Jere Eames

Page 245, courtesy Jere Eames

Page 248, Wonson collection

The Galleon / Jeremiah's

Pages 251 and 256, both courtesy Jere Eames

Gerry's Song

Pages 259 and 267, both courtesy Gerry Wolf

Fox and Company

Pages 270 and 276, both courtesy Don Coulombe

Newell's Casino

Page 285, courtesy Jeff Woodburn and Whitefield Historical Society

Aerosmith

Page 291, courtesy Jere Eames and Ed Malhoit

Stone Cross

Pages 300, 303 and 305, all courtesy Gardner Berry

Joy's Home for Wayward Musicians

Pages 308 and 311, both courtesy Dale Granger

Better Days

Page 319, courtesy Pete Shackett

Page 324, courtesy Dale Granger

Aha!

Page 332, courtesy Rick Davis

Where Do We Go from Here

Page 343, courtesy Gerry Wolf

Back Flap

Courtesy Gerry Wolf

Players Index

(More than one person suggested it would be helpful to have a "where are they now" index. My apologies for the fact that the whereabouts of several people are unknown. Please remember our many friends who have passed away.)

Gar Anderson of The Rusty Nail still lives in Stowe, VT, with his wife, Moira, and daughters Metzi and Robyn.

Allen Atkins traveled the country after Eleazar's with a band named Mantis, and is now a professor of Finance at Northern Arizona University in Flagstaff, AZ.

Rick Carvolth of Eleazar's is an Emergency Physician, CEO of Team Health West, and lives in Santa Rosa, CA.

John Conrad of the Barn is deceased.

Tom Day of Eleazar's lives with his wife Beth in White River Junction, VT, and is retired after thirty years in the swimming pool construction business.

Yvonne and Jere Eames of The Galleon and Jeremiah's are semi-retired and living in Littleton, NH, where they continue to be tireless promoters of the town of Littleton and New Hampshire's North Country.

Jack Giguere of the Wobbly Barn is deceased.

Jeff "Flash" Gordon is retired from IBM and lives in Essex Junction, VT, with his wife and eight-year old son.

Dale Granger-Eckert is married, living in Newburyport, MA, a runner and Alzheimer's advocate.

Vern Hatt of Eleazar's lives in Eastham, MA, on Cape Cod, and owns Appropriate Home Designs.

Rick Hunt lives in Littleton, NH, is a professional visual artist, and is half of Laughing Couple Interactive Storytelling with his wife, Carolyn.

Ed Malhoit still lives in Claremont, NH, and works for Toyota Sales.

Joy Moffat works for Best Friends Animal Society in Kanab, UT, where she spends her free time sewing and playing music.

Buddy and Cooki Newell of Newell's Casino live in Whitefield, NH, and are retired.

Dante Pavone is deceased.

Wayne Wadhams is deceased.

Don and Lady Eve Whitcomb are deceased.

Gerry Wolf lives in Dublin, NH, and owns SECI, an environmental products company.

Aerosmith:

Tom Hamilton, Joey Kramer, Joe Perry, Steven Tyler, and Brad Whitford are still playing out.

Ray Tabano trained as a chef at the French Culinary Institute. He owns and operates 5 Star Gourmet Catering in Yonkers, NY.

Anvil:

Brad French lives in Colchester, VT, where he owns and operates Brad French's Guitar Restoration Lab.

Bobby Gagnier is living in Springfield, VT, and still playing as much as possible.

Jim Goodrum lives in Sunapee, NH, is a financial planner, has been married for thirty-seven years, has three children, and an eight handicap.

Bob Hathaway is deceased.

Peter Yanofsky is living in Burlington, VT, enjoying retirement.

Better Days:

Bobby Gagnier, see Anvil.

Alan Hammang was last known to be living in the Atlanta, GA, area.

Steve Hirsch lives in Burlington, VT, where he writes chip verification software for IBM and plays with his band "High Mileage" whenever folks will tolerate them.

Peter Lipnickas lives in Allenstown, NH, and works in the data processing field for a major direct mail company. His current musical interest is in home recording.

Pete Shackett lives in the Tampa Bay, FL, area, is a songwriter and the producer of *Grouper Republic*, a practicing Nuclear Medicine Technologist, and has authored a book on Nuclear Medicine Technology.

Davis Brothers Garage Band:

Jeff Davis lives in Claremont, NH, and is co-owner of the Davis Frame Company, a timber frame business. He still plays out with brother Rick.

Rick Davis lives in Ascutney, VT, and is owner/operator of The Rick Davis Music Co. Services include: One Man Band; Rick Davis Band; Davis Bros. Band (Rick & Jeff); 24 track Digital Recording Studio; DJ/Karaoke; Used Musical Equipment; Audio, Video, Photo Archivist.

Tyler Plotzke is deceased.

Lane Gibson owns and operates a recording studio in Charlotte, VT, Lane Gibson Recording and Mastering.

Skip Truman lives in Enfield, NH. He works for Subaru in Business Development and Customer Relations Management. He is playing with his funk/soul band Soul Line, and also playing Chicago Blues with harp player Johnny Bishop.

Brad Gibson lives in Manahawkin, NJ, and has his own painting and finishing company. He plays drums regularly in The Brass Tacks, a sixteen piece big band that plays '40s swing music.

Craig Miller was last known to be living in Los Angeles, CA, promoting rock shows.

Burt Sisco is a professor at Education at Rowan University in Glassboro, NJ.

Nobby Reed lives in Swanton, VT, currently gigging with The Nobby

Reed Project, playing original music in the blues vein. He has released nine CDs since 1997 through Pump Audio (now Getty Images).

Bob Miles lives in Aurora, CO, and runs a family business.

Frank Barnes lives in Bennington, VT, where he is an English teacher and assistant principal at Mount Anthony Union High School. Frank still plays out with 8084. He and Andre Maquera (8084 guitarist) own West Street Digital recording studio in Fairfield, VT.

Angelo Mullen resides in Manchester, NH, is an enabler of computer solutions and actively performs with bands in the greater Boston area.

Bill Dworske is an account manager for a cable company in Colorado Springs, CO.

Fox Chase:

Pete Bover lives in Vernon, VT, and works at J.J. Discount in Spofford, NH. Pete says: "I hung up my bass at age forty-five after too many years in the bar wars!"

Eddie Kistler is deceased.

Mickey "Mouse" McElroy was last known to be living in New Jersey.

Don Solomon, whereabouts unknown.

Steven Tyler, see Aerosmith.

Fox and Company:

Don Coulombe lives in East Freetown, MA, owns a travel company in Lincoln, RI, and has a comedian/singer/impersonator show called the Don Who Show.

Norm Coulombe lives in Berlin, NH, and still plays out full-time.

Mike Galipeau lives in Gorham, NH, still plays out with Norm Coulombe, and is a level one wastewater treatment plant operator.

Steve Galipeau is living in Lancaster NH, still playing solo, and is owner of Commercial Divers Plus.

Dana Strout lives in Berlin, NH, and works for the U.S. Postal Service.

Joel Fortier was last known to be living in Berlin, NH, and working with troubled youth.

Gunnison Brook:

Mario Casella lives in Asbury Park, NJ, with his wife, Mary, has three boys in their twenties, and is playing music in an all-original band called The Blackberry Blues Band and a cover band called The Intentions. Mario is approaching retirement as a union painter.

Bill Kendall is deceased.

John Maxfield is an emergency physician living variably in New Hampshire and Ohio and probably working until he drops, still playing piano but only to torture his neighbors.

Alan MacIntosh is a professional guardian and fiduciary and lives with his wife, Martha, in Las Vegas, NV.

Pete Merrigan is still playing music professionally, splitting his time between NH and Florida with his wife, Melinda, and their cats.

Pete Shackett, see Better Days.

Dan Sibley is retired and living in Piedmont, CA, and is currently playing with his band The Incurables every Friday night. (Plus any additional jam he can pick up!)

Ragweed:

Peter Christenson lives in Portland, OR, and is a professor of Communications at Lewis & Clark College.

Dave Cross drums for the classic rock band, The Rockodiles, teaches private drum lessons, does substitute teaching and marvels at how time flies in Tacoma, WA.

Oliver Hess lives in Ojai, CA, where he is a lawyer practicing in the employ of the State of California.

John Maxfield, see Gunnison Brook.

Andy Raymond lives in Los Angeles, CA, and has had a long career in retail business.

Sprites / Nickel Misery:

Pete Bover, see Fox Chase.

Chuck Holden was last known to be living in northern Vermont.

Bear Johnson is deceased.

Eddie Kistler, see Fox Chase.

Jimi Slate lives in Elizabeth City, NC, with his wife of thirty-eight years, and has five children. He still plays out almost every week in clubs on the Outer Banks of North Carolina, plus retirement homes and churches.

Gene Struthers was last known to be living in Clearlake Park, CA.

Dave Trombley is deceased.

Stone Cross:

Gardner Berry lives in Manchester, NH, and still plays music full-time with Mama Kicks (classic rock) and Four Sticks (Led Zeppelin tribute). G-Man plays solo, duo and freelance, also has had one ebook published.

www.mamakicks.com   www.four-sticks.com

Bill Blaine lives in Gilford, NH, where he designs and builds concert sound and lighting systems for New England venues.

Phil Monastesse lives in Warner, NH, and works for the Derry Schools as a custodian. Playing rocking blues and originals with the Rod Welles Band, out of the seacoast area.

Mike Mulroy lives in Mitchell, MD, and works as a Facility Manager for a Regional School in Maryland, for the Archdiocese of Washington.

Tracks:

Ken Aldrich and his wife, Jane, live in Lebanon, NH, where he is a semi-retired computer technician working for local school districts. He still records his own music and works with local musicians.

Ned Berndt lives in Miami, FL, where he is a luxury real estate broker. He continues to perform with his band C.O. Jones. Smile if you speak Spanish.

Steve Calvert is "retired" in Bristol, RI, as a full-time writer of novels, screenplays, and stage plays; he practices a lot, and plays out (keys, guitar; sings a little) when invited.

Wiley Crawford, whereabouts unknown.

Eddie Kistler, see Fox Chase.

Peter Logan is a lawyer and plays drums in San Francisco, CA.

Bob Neale lives in Seattle, WA, and is currently playing bass on cruise ship gigs around the world on Holland America.

Russell Pinkston lives in Austin, TX, where he is a Professor of Music Composition and Director of Electronic Music Studios at the University of Texas at Austin.

Dominick "Pooch" Puccio is deceased.

Skip Truman, see Davis Brothers Garage Band.

Jeff Wilkes lives in Washington, D.C., where he advocates for environmental education and works with the music program at his local public elementary school.

Index

Abair, Dave, 341

Abenaki, 4-5

AC Apple, 220-221, 254, 328

ACLU, 49

Acoustics, The, 70, 72-73, 231

Aerodrome, The, 77, 94

Aerosmith, 46, 82-83, 136, 139-141, 160, 221, 234, 236, 239, 254, 271, 281-284, 287-296, 320, 341

Aiken, Dwight, 142-143, 216

Airto, 328

Albums:

Abbey Road, 124-125, 233, 328

After Bathing at Baxter's, 199

Beggar's Banquet, 155

Faces in the Night, 271

Fox and Company, 271

Grouper Republic, 49

Jesus Christ Superstar, 197-198

Meet the Beatles, 35

Rough and Ready, 91

Sgt. Pepper's Lonely Hearts Club Band, 56

Sounds of Silence, 183

Take It All, 271

The Mirror, 303

Aldrich, Ken, xi, 29-32, 42, 60, 63, 72, 107, 150, 152, 155, 168-178, 196, 206, 218, 345

Algonquian Confederation, 47

Allman Brothers, 89, 93, 206, 302, 319-320

Allman, Duane, 93

Allman, Gregg, 93

Amboy Dukes, The, 328

America, 271

American Express, 245, 255, 257

American Stone, 140

Amos 'n' Andy Show, 45

Anansi, 175

Anderson, Al, 58

Anderson, Gar, 148, 182-201, 203, 249, 337, 340

Anderson, Metzi, 189

Anderson, Moira, 188-189

Anderson, Robyn, 189

Anvil, xi, 38, 64, 69, 83, 86-97, 137, 154, 254, 269, 281, 289, 295, 317-318, 330-331

Apple Pie Motherhood Band, 108

Appleton, Jon, 178

Applied Occupational Health Systems, 265

Arey, Steve, 97

Ariel, 21, 44, 77, 136, 169, 196, 199

Argent, 206

Armstrong, Nelson, 23-24

Arnold, Bruce "Humpty," 200-201

Askew, Don, 14

Atkins, Allen, 306-308, 312

Atlantis, 83-84, 221-222, 226-227, 297, 322-323

Aubin, Cher Mitchell, 65, 81

Avery, Dan, 225

Azoff, Irving, 100

Bach, Johannes Sebastian, 151

Bacharach, Burt, 56

Bachman-Turner Overdrive, 320

Back Room, The, 146

Baden, Joel, 151

Baggy Knees, The, 185-186, 210

Baker Library, 21

Band, The, 112, 124, 169, 234

Baraw, Chuck, 195

Baraw, Stu, 193

Barn, The, 67-76, 204, 306, 309

Barnes, Frank, 210

Barre Opera House, The, 226

Barrows, Bill, 202

Basie, Count, 61

Battle of the Bands, 51, 54-56, 174, 298

Baxter, Frank, 72

Baxter, Jeff "Skunk," 164, 169

Beach Boys, The, 339

Beams, The, 313-314

Beatles, The, 15-16, 27-28, 30, 35, 50, 52-53, 57, 87, 124, 128, 144, 197, 206, 233, 271, 290, 292, 298, 302, 320

Beaver Brown Band, The, 196-197

Beck, Jeff, 88, 90-91, 93, 169

Bee Gees, The, 277

Beethoven, Ludwig van, 34, 41

Belden, Bill, 87, 89

Bell, Archie and The Drells, 24

Bell, Gerry, 28

Bellisimo, George, 72

Bellman's Curve, 337

Benefit Street, 195

Berger, Bruce "Bucky," 317

Berklee College of Music, The, 20, 86, 88

Berndt, Ned, 10, 18-19, 150, 168, 172, 175-178, 206, 236, 288, 296, 301, 345

Berry, Chuck, 22, 339

Berry, Gardner, xi, 38, 81, 206, 213, 215-216, 250, 297-305, 331, 336, 338-339, 341

"Bert and I," 104

Better Days and Company, xi, 44, 47, 155, 163-164, 177, 179, 244, 269, 311, 316-325

"Betty Lou" (Joy Moffat), 147-148

Big Bopper, The, 44

Bigfoot, 48

Billboard magazine, 15, 210, 272

Birth, 98, 111, 119, 120, 324, 328

Black Horse, 221

Blaine, Bill, 297-301, 303, 305

Bland, Bobby "Blue," 57

Blazing Sons, The, 231, 268, 275, 277

Blind Faith, 112

"Blitz," 113, 115

Blue Cloud, 231, 299

Blues Project, The, 24

Blue Tooth, The, 93

Bobar, Greg "Bo," 225

Boncaddo, John, 170

Book of Matches, The, 221

Booth, Margot, 151

Bosch, Heironymous, 17

Boston English, 281

Boston Skyline Music, 20

Boulevard de Paris, 95

Bover, Pete, 50-53, 56-57, 59, 64,
81, 230, 232-235, 237-238, 296,
327, 336

Bowen, Anne, 77, 137

BP Gulf oil spill, 265-266

Brahms, Johannes, 41

Brando, Marlon, 57

Brandt, Pamela, 21, 44, 77, 137,
169, 199

Broken Ski, The, 83, 221

Brooklyn Bridge, The, 77

Brooklyn Philharmonic, 35, 39

Brown, Arthur, 30, 219

Brown, James, 337

Brubeck, Chris, 197

Brubeck, Dave, 34, 197

Bruce-Douglas, Ian, 165

Bruso, Bill, 224

Bryant, Bob, 104

Buck, Bruce, 225

Buffalo Springfield, 112

Buffett, Jimmy, 336

Bull, 196

Bull, Brian, 170

Bummerville, 66

Bunyan, Paul, 163

Buonanno, Vinnie, 182-183, 186-
187, 199-200

Burdick, Dennis, 297

Butterfield, Bob, 325

Byrds, The, 15, 72, 215

Café Bizarre, The, 27, 33-37

Calvert, Steve, 6, 17-18, 26-27, 33-
37, 168, 181, 327

Canary, 219

Canned Heat, 176

Capitol Records, 215

Carne, Judy, 140

Carnegie Hall, 41, 125

Carton, Johnny, 72

Carvolth, Rick, 306

Casella, Mario, xi, 43, 120-123,
126, 128-129, 140-141, 143,
148, 160, 287-288, 290-294,
296, 343

Casino by the Sea, 225

Casino Vail, The, 203, 331

Catello's, 66

Cave, The, 268

CBS, 33-34, 169

Chain, 59, 70, 229, 294

Chain Reaction, 67

Chambers Brothers, 24, 176

Champoux, Bob, 218, 272

Chandler, Rodney, 74

Charlie Daniels Band, The, 215

Checkmates, The, 280-281, 285

Cheshire Fair Grounds, The, 273,
304

Chickering, John, 175

Chris Martin Band, The, 255

Christenson, Peter, 27-28, 111-119, 136, 154, 341

Chicago, 113, 236-237

Chopping Block, The, 120, 145-146, 164, 205-206, 223, 306, 318, 322

Cipriano, Gene, 185

Clapton, Eric, 36, 91

Clayton, Merry, 176

Clinton, Bill, 12

Club Soda, 65

Cocker, Joe, 112, 124, 302

Cohen Hall, 23

Cole, Nat "King," 45

Coleman, Cy (Seymour Kaufman), 40-41

Collins, Lee, 68

Comeau, Bob, 283

Coming Thing, The, 21-22

Com Tu Club, The, 68

Connolly, Frank, 82

Conrad, John, 67-68, 75

Conrad Manor, 67-68, 70-72

Coral Reefer Band, 336

Corinthians, The, 23-24

Cosell, Howard, 136

Costner, Kevin, 11

Coulombe, Don, ix, 54, 57, 63, 107-108, 213-214, 238, 244-245, 259, 266, 268-277, 281, 290, 294-295, 307-309, 315-316, 330, 336

Coulombe, Norm, xi, 268-276, 305, 341

Country Joe and the Fish, 30

Cozy Cabin, The, 183

Crabtree, Mike, 23

Crandall Park, 228, 330-331

Crawford, Wiley, 175, 227

Cream, 17, 27, 57, 93, 169, 207, 298, 332

Creedence Clearwater Revival, 234

Crescent Beach Motor Inn, 113 162

Crests, The, 77

Crohn's Disease, 261, 264-267

Crosby, Stills, Nash and Young, 12, 172, 177, 206, 271

Cross, Dave, 21-23, 27-28, 107, 111-115, 118-119, 135, 154, 162-163, 339

Crowd, The, 22-23

Cunningham, Richie, 9

Curtin, David, 83-84, 221-222, 227, 296-297, 322

Curtis, John, 215

Daddy Warbux, 165, 196

Dailey, Harry, 336-337

Daley, Ford, 5, 43

Daltry, Roger, 53

Dame, Greg, 83-84, 297

Dartmouth College, 4-5, 12, 14-23, 25-26, 28-31, 33, 43, 47, 94, 98-100, 102-103, 111, 116, 121, 125, 127, 157, 174-175, 178, 236, 272, 274, 290, 292, 304, 306-308, 313, 320, 329, 338, 341, 344-345

Dartmouth Film Society, 16, 18

Dartmouth Fraternities:

Alpha Theta, 28

Bones Gates, 236, 274, 290, 320

Kappa Sig, 292

Phi Tau, 43

Sigma Nu, 29

Tri Kap, 236

Davis, Arthur, 202

Davis, Bette, 241, 279-280

Davis Brothers Garage Band, 54, 67-68, 141, 155, 179, 202-211, 213, 216-219, 222, 224-225, 297, 301, 305, 311, 331-333, 341

Davis, Rick, 67-68, 72, 81, 141, 202-211, 213, 215-216, 223-224, 297, 301, 305, 308-309, 341

Davis, Jeff, 67, 71, 201-205, 296

Davis, Miles, 328

Davis, Roger, 306, 313

Davis, Tim, 224-225

Day, Tom, 305-308, 310, 312-315

Daze of Time, 317

Deadbeats, The, 73

Deadly Nightshade, The, 44, 77, 199

Dean, James, 57, 145

Dean, Lonny, 194

"The Death of the Hired Man," 132

Deep Purple, 128

DeGaulle, Charles, 240

Dhaulagiri, 25

D-Men, The, 14

de Besche, Austin, 19

DeSantis, Sammy, 82-83, 225-226, 296, 321

Diamond, Lee, 170-171

DiPerri, Ron, 299

Dire Straits, 287

Dirty John's, 207-208

Dodge, Marshall, 104

Dolan, Annie (Cole), 69, 71, 206, 309

Doobie Brothers, The, 164, 206, 271, 334

Doors, The, 57

Dorr, Donnie, 73

Doucette, Peter, 225

Dream Engine, 5, 27-28, 108, 111-112, 154

Dr. Hook, 221

Dubrieul's roller rink, 274

"The Duke" (Mario Casella), 143-144

Duncan Phyfe, 231

Dunn, Chris, 225, 293

Dworske, Bill, 205

Dylan, Bob, 168

Eagles, The, 215

Eames, Blanche Meador, 240

Eames, Jack, 263

Eames, John B. "Jack," 240-242

Eames, John, Jr., 241, 243, 252

Eames, Jere, 229-230, 240-258, 340, 342

Eames, Yvonne, 230, 240-254, 257-258, 340, 342

Earth Audio Studio, 227

Earthworm, Nigel, II, 165

Ebbeson, Eric, 23-25

Edgar Winter's White Trash, 95, 221

Edson, Perry, 225

Edwards, Jonathan, 108, 195, 221

Egg and Machine Shop, The, 94-95

Einstein, Albert, 102

Eisenhower, Dwight, 11

Eleazar's, ix, 127, 274, 305, 306-316, 321, 324

Elements of Sound, The, 298

Ellington, Duke, 42, 61

EMA (Ed Malhoit Agency), 64, 79

Embryos, The, 26

Emerson, Lake & Palmer, 206, 210

Emmanuel, Rahm, 159

Engler, Rick, 14

Epstein, Brian, 15, 50-51

Ericson, Leif, 47-48

Erik the Red, 48

Ertegun, Ahmet, 177

Esslinger, Bill, 321

"Eugene" (John Maxfield), 143

Evans, Ken, 14

Everett, Boyd, 25

Facebook, 155

Fakawi tribe, 47-48

Falzarrano, Doug, 72

Famous Charisma Records, 211

Farina, Mimi and Richard, 24

Fat Band, The, 195-196

Fat City, 136

Ferrante, Arthur, 41

Ferrara, Doug, 14

Fifth Estate, The, 14-16, 18

Filthy McNasty's, 208

Fleetwood Mac, 292

Floyd, Eddie, 24

Flynn Theater, 94

Fogarty, John, 234

Foghat, 221

Fortier, Joel, 268-269

Fountain (Pinkston), Margaret, 38

Four Dimensions, The, 87

Four Tops, The, 17

Fox, 269-270

Fox and Company, ix, xi, 54, 107, 210, 213-214, 268-277, 281, 304-305, 330, 341

Fox Chase, 175, 229-239, 252, 268-269, 295

Fraank Band, The, 341

Franklin, Aretha, 57, 156

Fred, 116

French, Charles, 44

French, Brad, 38, 44, 86-92, 96-97, 137, 154, 296, 331, 336, 340

Frost, Robert, 132, 149

Frostbite Falls, 256

Funkyard, 268, 275

Gabriel, Peter, 211

Gage, Tom, 281-282

Gagnier, Bobby, xi, 72, 87, 90, 92-95, 97, 317-321, 324-325, 330-331, 338, 341, 344

Galactica, 307

Galadriel, 115-116

Gale Farm, The, 184-185, 189-191

Galipeau, Mike, 268-272, 276

Galipeau, Steve, 213, 217-218, 268-277, 305

Galleon, The, 229-231, 243-246, 249-257, 259, 262-263, 268, 306

Gaucheault, Dave "Mad Dog," 216

Genesis, 210

Gibbs, Philip, 13

Gibson, Brad, 210, 225

Gibson, Lane, 54, 68, 202-208, 211, 213, 216, 219, 222, 331-333

Giddings, Steve, 23-25

Gifford, Brent, 216

Giguere, Jack, 212-213

Gilliatt, Dave, 27, 108

Gitt, Bob, 20

Glad, The, 83, 284

Godfrey, Arthur, 42

Goldberg, Rube, 33

Golden, Tom, 243, 257

Goldstein, Marty, 317

Goodrum, Jim, 64, 69, 72, 87-88, 90, 92-97, 137, 289

Gordon, Jeff "Flash," 206, 209, 215, 217, 220-228, 306

Grace, Ron, 130

Graham, Larry, 227

Granger, Dale, 247, 256, 262, 266, 271, 274, 277, 309-311, 313-315, 321

Granliden Hotel, 40

Grant, Hayden, 72

Grass Roots, The, 53

Grateful Dead, The, 320

Green, James, 13

Green Key, 98-99

Green, Peter, 292

Greenfield, MA, YMCA, 226

Griffith, D.W., 240

Griggs, Marc, 225

Groggery, The, 226

Grondin, Louie, 268-269

Guess Who, The, 330

Gump, Forrest, 141

Gunnison Brook, ix, xi, 43, 47, 63, 68, 83, 108-109, 120-131, 134, 139-141, 145-148, 152, 154, 156-157, 160, 214, 248, 253-254, 269, 271, 272, 281-284, 287, 289-291, 293, 295, 304, 318, 321, 324, 328, 337-338, 342-344

Gunnison Manor, 121-122, 130, 133-134, 136, 139-141, 152, 174

Gunnison Manor House Party, 139-141

Haley, Bill, 44

Hall, Eldon, 22, 29-30

Hamilton, Tom, 73, 204, 236, 289-291, 296

Hamm, Richard, 76

Hammang, Alan, 317-319, 321, 323-325

Hammond, Dick, 249

Hammond Electronics, 249

Hampton, Lionel, 68

Hampton Manor, The, 4, 27, 31-32, 87, 94, 210, 323

Ham Sandwich, The, 28-32, 42, 72, 168, 175, 223

Hanley Sound, 302

Hanover High School, 5, 25, 26, 29, 69, 177

Happy Days, 11-12

Harley, Anthony "Fa Fa," 23

Harris, Emmylou, 215

Harris, Vic, 187, 199-200

Hartt School, The, 87

Hassles, The, 37

Hathaway, Bob, 87, 89-93, 97, 180, 296, 318

Hatt, Vern, 306, 308, 310, 312, 313-314

Hatts Off, 315

Havens, Richie, 95-96

Hayward, Paul, 179, 246, 251, 341

Hawkeye, 325

Hearne, Bob, 83-84, 221, 297

Heat Wave, 242

Hendrix, Jimi, 24, 27, 30, 37, 57, 91, 93, 169, 174, 199, 219, 293, 298

Henniker High School, 127

"Herc" (Dan Sibley), 143

Hess, Oliver, 97, 111, 115-119

High Altitude, 64

Hipwell, Brian, 78

Hirsch, Steve, 164, 177, 317-325

Hitler, Adolph, 260

Hobbits, The, 73

Hokum, 175

Holden, Chuck, 50

Holliday, Billie, 156

Homer, 34

Hooke, Helen, 77, 199

Hooker, John Lee, 168

Hope, Bob, 241

Hopkins Center, The, 5, 16, 18, 26

Hughes, Tim, 317

Hullaballo, 15

Hunt, Rick, 140, 246, 250-252, 254 292

Hurley, K.M., 76

Iacobucci, Richard, 250

IBM, 85

Improper Bostonian, 165

Ingalls, Brad "Bear," 225, 227

Inkspots, The, 61

Inside the Hits, 20

Intermedia Sound Studio, 82-83, 294

Invaders, The, 72, 87

Isaacson, Peter/Clay Canfield, 199

Jackson, J.J., 171

Jackson State College, 13

Jack's Drum Shop, 24

Jagger, Mick, 70, 129, 156, 176

Jam Band, The, 73, 204, 294

James, Bruce, 272, 276, 317

James Gang, The, 329, 332

Jarrett, Keith, 328

Jax Jr. Cinema, 241, 262

Jefferson Airplane, 27, 178, 199

Jefferson Light Show, The, 209-210, 215, 220, 224, 227, 306

J. Geils Band, 95, 215

Jeremiah's, 243-247, 249, 255-258 306, 340

Jerome Mystic (Bob Davis), 88

Jerome Mystic Movement, The, 88

Jethro Tull, 271, 303

Jett, Joan, 274

Joel, Billy, 37, 215

Joey Dee and the Starlighters, 6

John, Elton, 207

Johnson, Jerry "Bear," 50, 52, 64

Johnson, Lyndon Baines, 27

Johnson, Rich, 23

Jones, Calvin, 22

Jones, James Earl, 11

Jordan, Glenn, 121, 152

Jordan, Michael, 287

Joys Home for Wayward Musicians (Eleazar's), 274, 306, 315-316

Jubilee Records, 16

Juilliard School, The, 38-41

Kanakis, Nick, 69-70, 72, 75, 230, 283

Kangas, Frances, 65-66

Kangas, Jeff, 65

Kangas, Paavo, 65-66

Kaplan, Al, 26

Kearsarge Magazine, 76

Keg, The, 203

Kemeny, John, 98, 100, 102-103

Kendall, Bill, 121

Kennedy, Bobby, 11, 167

Kent, Clark, 145

Kent State, 12-13, 99-100

Keystone Kops, 207

King, B.B., 61

King Bees, The, 294

King, Martin Luther, Jr., 11, 167

King, Rock, 185

Kingston Trio, The, 281

Kinks, The, 53

Kinsella, Ray, 11

Kissinger, Henry, 98

Kistler, Eddie, 50, 52-54, 56-59, 68, 175-177, 206, 229-230, 232-235, 238, 296

Kitchen Kats, 42

Kraft Music Hall, 43

Kramer, Joey, 288-290, 294-295

Krause, Allison, 13

Kravers, The, 241

Laber, Grant, 124

Labes, Jeff, 108

Labunski, Ed, 238

Ladd, Alan, 241

Ladd's, 123-124, 291, 304, 321, 343

Laing, Corky, 96

LaLonde, Lonna, 70-71, 235

Lane, Lois, 145

Latella, Emily, 337

Lazy Livin', 179, 341

Lebanon High School, 70

Led Zeppelin, 93, 174, 303, 319-320

Left Banke, The, 36

Leh, George, 198-199

Leitgeb, Bob, 341

Lennon, John, 15, 156, 254

Lesnevich, Georgia, 198

Lesnevich, Gus, 198

Lettermen, The, 281

Levitt, William, 86

Leverone Field House, 100-102

Lewis, Jerry Lee, 44

Life magazine, 12, 197

Lime Cirrus, The, 26, 33, 170-171, 196

Lindbergh, Charles, 37

Links, The, 73, 202, 297

Lipnickas, Peter, 244, 317-321, 324-325

Liszt, Franz, 36

Little Feat, 206, 215

Littleton A-Go-Go, 242

Locanto, Ralph, 170-171

Loeb, William, 102-103

Logan, Peter, 26-27, 33-37, 168, 336, 341, 344

Lovin' Spoonful, The, 15, 17, 27, 33, 254

Lucas, Phil, 23

Lundquist, Bob, 21-22

Lynard Skynard, 320

Lyons, "Queenie," 87

MacIntosh, Alan, 121-124, 126-127, 130-131, 143, 152-154, 156, 158, 170, 272, 342-344

MacIntosh, Martha, 342, 344

MacIntosh, Steve, 29

Mackles, Gene, 16-17, 20, 24-25

Mad Beach Band, The, 336

Maddron, Tom, 27

Maestro, Johnny, 77

Magnolia Trio, The, 43

Mahler, Donald, 344-345

Malhoit, Ed, 51-52, 59, 61, 64-65, 77-85, 94, 175, 179, 229, 235-239, 242, 253, 270, 273, 284, 288, 290, 298, 300-301, 309, 318, 323

Malhoit Circuit, The, 94, 205, 233, 314

Mamas and The Papas, The, 25

Manchester Union-Leader, 102-103

Mandala, 17

Mann, Terence, 11

Manning, Peyton, 287

Maranville, A.J., 72

March of Dimes concert, 83, 292

Martin, Dean, 68

Mason, Dave, 302

Mathieu, Scott, 325

Matteson, Doug, 200

Maxfield, John, 27, 73, 98, 100, 108-109, 111-112, 114-115, 119-123, 127-128, 143, 154, 328, 341

Mayall, John, 93

Mayer, Louis B., 241

Mays, Willie, 37

McCartney, Paul, 156

McElroy, Mickey "Mouse," 230, 233, 238, 295

McGuire, John, 73

McPherson, Rick, 83, 297

McQueen, Scott, 29

Meeker, Kip, 97, 196, 296

"Mented Meenies," The, 225

Merrigan, Pete, xi, 68, 73, 76, 98-103, 111, 119-125, 128-131 133, 136, 139-141, 142-146, 148, 152, 156, 158, 160, 283, 291, 296, 324, 336, 341-343

Miles, Bob, 204-206

Miles, Buddy, 59, 228

Mill, The, 322

Miller, Chris, 5

Miller, Craig, 203

Miller, Jeffrey, 13

Miller, John, 186

Miller, Vern, 197

Minetti, Jim, 225, 301

Missing Links, The, 43, 202, 297

Mitch Ryder and the Detroit Wheels, 274

Moffat, Joy, ix, 127, 130, 147-148, 206, 215-216, 271, 274, 277, 309-311, 314-316, 321, 337, 343-344

Mogenson, Topper, 183, 186

Mohegan Sun, 46

Monastesse, Phil, 299, 303, 305

Monday Night Football, 136

Monopoly, 17

Moppets, The, 21

Morgan, Terry, 74

Morgenroth, Dan, 29-31, 72, 137, 175, 180

Morrison, Van, 108, 112

Morton, Carol Mulroy, 43, 46, 61, 71-73

Morton, Doug, 52-53, 64, 235, 326, 341

Mother's, 109, 304, 331

Mothers of Invention, The, 77

"Motorhead Red" (Pete Shackett), 49, 109, 143, 145, 148

Mott the Hoople, 294

Mottola, Tommy, 177

Mountain, 95-96, 330

Moustache Club, The, 224

Movies:

A Hard Day's Night, 128

Animal House, 5, 99, 274

Birth of a Nation, 240

Eddie and the Cruisers, 197

Field of Dreams, 11

Great Lie, The, 241

Rosemary's Baby, 157

Snow White, 16

Wizard of Oz, The, 15

Mr. Lucky's, 204

Mullen, Angelo, 155, 210, 217

Mulroy, Joe, 43

Mulroy, Marc, 225

Mulroy, Mike, 43, 46, 72-73, 202, 297, 299, 303, 305

Murray the K, 17

Music Box, The, 72

Mussolini, Benito, 156

NAR, 188, 190

NATO, 240

Naumburg Competition, 38

Naylor, Hare, 29

Nazz, 112

NBC, 44

Neale, Bob, 19, 44, 174-177, 206

Neilson, Steen, 193-194

Nelson, Harriet, 11

Newell, Buddy, 278-286, 340

Newell, Christie, 245, 278, 283, 285

Newell, Doris "Cooki," 279, 286

Newell, Hilton, 278-280

Newell's Casino, 57, 107, 245, 249, 255, 261, 278-286, 306, 340

"New Hampshire," 149

New Hampshire Hall, 22

New Heavenly Blue, 196-198

Newport Folk Festival, 24

Newman, Randy, 215

Nickel Misery, 50, 54, 57-59, 64, 229, 231, 281, 327-328

Night Crawlers, The, 29

Night Watchmen, The, 6, 26-27, 33, 35, 168, 344-345

Nipmuc Regional H.S., 288-289

Nixon, Richard, 11-12, 48, 98-99, 103

Northeast Kingdom, The, 104-105

Northern Lights Music, 66

Notre Dame Arena, 54, 294

Nugent, Ted, 328-329

Nye, Dave, 175

Oak, 268, 274

O'Hara, John, 90, 94, 225

Old Orchard Beach Casino, 58

Olin, Rich, 23

Olsen, Jimmy, 145

Opaque Illusion, 251, 253

Orleans, 273

Orson Welles Film School, 20

Osborne, Bill, 225

Osborne, Keith, 115-116

Other Man's Grass, The, 64, 69, 72, 87-89, 91, 318

"Over in the Meadow," 42

Owens, Paul Lee, 316

Oz and Ends, 173

Page, Jimmy, 88

Pappalardi, Felix, 96, 330-331

Paquette, Ron, 200

Parker Brothers, 17

Parker, Jimmy, 73

Parker, Tom, 23-24

Patrick Gym (UVM), 56, 93, 330

Paul Butterfield Blues Band, 24, 28, 112, 120, 124

Paul Revere and the Raiders, 53, 298

Pavone, Dante, 124-125, 156-160, 175, 303-304, 337

Pentagon, The, 48

Peppermint Lounge, 6

Perrotto, Patty, 80

Perry, Joe, 73, 136, 140, 204, 283, 287, 289, 291-294, 296

Petrucci and Atwell, 169

Phillips, Michelle, 25

Phineaus, Mitch, 200

Phoenix, Doug, 210, 219, 225

Pickett, Wilson, 24

Pickle Barrel, The, 213, 309

Pilobolus Dance Company, 5

Pinette, Rick, 268, 274

Pinkston, Betsy, 39

Pinkston, James, 39

Pinkston, Malcolm, 44

Pinkston, Margaret, 39

Pinkston, Russell, ix, xi, 7, 13, 19, 26-27, 33-37, 39-40, 45, 149-152, 162, 168-179, 206, 320, 337, 341, 344-345

Pitney, Gene, 15

Plant, Robert, 53

Platters, The, 241

Playboy magazine, 68

Plotzke, Tyler, 204-208, 218-219

Plum Crazy, 325

Plymouth State College, 292, 328

Polo Grounds, 37

Ponzi's, 307-308

Port Authority of New York, 265

Poulin, Bill, 299

Pousette-Dart Band, The, 215

Pousette-Dart, Jon, 215

Powell, Jane, 241

Praetorius, Michael, 15

Premier Talent, 295

Presley, Elvis, 36, 44, 91, 339

Procol Harum, 128

Projection Room Lounge, The, 187

Puccini, Giacomo, 34

Puccio, Dom "Pooch," 30-31, 168, 175, 178, 181

Purple Hat, The, 164, 171, 173

Pypo Club, The, 117-118

Quackenbush, Chris, 83-84, 221, 297

Quechee Gorge, 1, 4

Queen, 303

? and the Mysterians, 298

Ragweed, 108, 111-121, 135, 154 162, 269

Raitt, Bonnie, 108, 215

Rare Earth, 221, 320

Rauschlau, Charlie, 299

Rawls, Lou, 61

Ray, Frankie, 229

Raymond, Andy, 27, 98, 111-115, 119-120, 154

Razz, 155

Redding, Otis, 24

Red Stallion Inn, 273

Reed, Nobby, 210

Reich, Bob, 12

Reichardt, Lou, 26

Remains, The, 197

Rhinehart, Joanie, 200

Ritz Café, The, 315

Rivers, Johnny, 91

Rivingtons, The, 280

Roberts, Ray, 194

Roctronics, 249

Rodney Diamond and the Studs, 124, 142-148

"Rodney Diamond" (Pete Merrigan), 130, 142, 144-146, 148

Rogers, Beverly, 136

Rolling Stone magazine, 132

Rolling Stones, The, 27-28, 35, 53, 73, 124-126, 129, 155, 168-169, 176, 206, 235, 271, 290, 292, 328, 339

Romero, George, 155

Ross, Bernie, 74

Round House, The, 128, 146, 274-275

Rowan & Martin's Laugh-In, 140

Ruder, Steve, 203

Rundgren, Todd, 325

Rush, Carey, 45, 54, 60, 62, 66, 72, 91, 292, 315, 341

Rush, Tom, 176

Russell, Don, 23

Rusty Nail, The, 125, 145, 148, 182, 185-188, 190-201, 203, 205, 214, 249, 259, 306, 337, 340

Ruth, Babe, 136

Sabo, Bali, 216-218

Salomon, Dan, 66

Sam Ash Music, 66, 173

Saltman, Rick, 5, 27

Santana, 89, 93, 96, 168, 271, 320

Savage Beast, The, 204, 288

Save Vermont Barns Project, 138

Saxony Lounge, The, 220

Scheuer, Sandra, 13

Schroeder, William, 13

Schubert, Franz, 41

Scott, Dave "Pudge," 73

Seatrain, 124

SECI, 265-266

Seger, Bob, 161, 165

Seidman, Dave, 24-25

Serkin, Rudolph, 18

Sesame Street, 77

Seton, Chuck, 178

Seymour, Thad, 12

Shackett, Bertha, 49

Shackett, Bill, 44

Shackett, Pete, 44, 47-49, 63, 73, 98, 109, 111, 119, 120-122, 134, 143, 148, 157-159, 163, 170, 289, 304, 318-322, 324-325, 336, 341

Shackett, Wilfard, 49

Shadows of Knight, The, 29

Shafer, Jim, 23

Sha Na Na, 142

Shea Stadium, 328

Shed, The, 185, 193-194, 201

Showcase East, 212

Sherwood, Janice, 257

Sherwood, Jim, 257

Shull, Kathy (Kasaras), 79-80

Shute, Bill, 14

Sibley, Dan, 121-122, 124, 128, 143, 214, 328, 338

Simon and Garfunkel, 183

Simon, Carly, 266

Simon, Peter, 266

Sinatra, Frank, 34, 68

Silver Keg, The, 151, 155, 205, 223

Sisco, Burt, 203

Sister Kate's, 185

Slate, Jimi, 50-52, 54, 56-59, 64, 97, 328-329

Slick, Grace, 156

Sly and the Family Stone, 168, 171, 173, 206, 227, 302, 304

Sly Dog, 179

Smith, Frank, 297

Smith, Mike, 321

Snyder, Sherry, 113

Solange, 27, 33-34, 36-37

Solomon, Don, 175, 229-230, 233, 235, 238, 295

Songs:

16 Candles, 77, 144

96 Tears, 298

A Man from Afghanistan, 93

Ain't No Mountain High Enough, 171

Ain't Superstitious, 90

All Over the World, 130

All Along the Watchtower, 155, 168-169, 174, 179, 201

Almost Cut My Hair, 352

Aqualung, 271

As My Guitar Gently Weeps, 57

Baby Let's Wait, 53

Back in the Day, 342-344

Back on the Road, 271

Bang the Drum All Day, 325

Beautiful, 112

Black Magic Woman, 271

Blue Moon, 144

Blue Suede Shoes, 144

Bohemian Rhapsody, 303

Born in Chicago, 28

Born on the Bayou, 234

Brown Sugar, 125, 271

Can't Get Enough of It, 171

Can't Wait to Get Back Home, 126

Caroline, 30

Casey Jones, 320

Celebrate, 302

Chest Fever, 112, 114

Close Quarters, 112, 136

Color My World, 113

Come On Up, 53

Crossroads, 36, 332

Daddy Was a Jockey, 168, 178

Dance With Me, 273

Day Tripper, 271

Dead Flowers, 125

Devil's Daughter, 271

Ding Dong! The Witch Is Dead, 15-17

Dock of the Bay, 24

Domino, 112

Don't Tell Me Tomorrow, 126

Down On The Farm, 126, 271

Dream On, 136, 140, 232, 294-295

Dreamers, 271-272

Duke of Earl, 143

Eight Miles High, 72

Eli's Comin', 168, 302

Everyday Dreamer, 179

Exodus, 41

Expressway to Your Heart, 30

Feelin' Alright, 174

Find the Cost of Freedom, 12

Fire, 30, 174, 219

Funk #49, 332

Get a Job, 144

Get Together, 101

Gimme Shelter, 176

Gimme Some Lovin', 36, 171

G-L-O-R-I-A, 29, 73

Good Lovin', 53, 73

Good Times, Bad Times, 88

Goofin' Song, The, 17-18

Guiding Hand, 126

Heigh Ho!, 16

Hey, Big Brother, 320

Hey Jude, 271

Hey Mister, 153

Higher, 173

Hitchcock Railway, 112

Hoedown, 210

Hold On, I'm Comin', 24

Honky Tonk Women, 125, 129, 207, 328

Hound Dog, 36

Humble Pie, 126

I'm A Man, 57

I Can Tell, 37

I Don't Want to Miss a Thing, 46

I Just Want to Celebrate, 320

I'll Try My Best, 271

In the Ghetto, 91

Isengard, 170, 177

I Want to Hold Your Hand, 36

I Want You (She's So Heavy), 233

Jackson-Kent Blues, 13

Jingo, 93

Joy to the World, 256

Jumpin' Jack Flash, 125, 129-130

Keep on the Sunny Side, 77

Knock On Wood, 24

Lady Madonna, 30

Late Late Show, 126, 153

Lazy Living, 126

Lethargy, 149-150, 177

Let It Bleed, 125

Light My Fire, 30, 57

Live With Me, 125

Livin' in the USA, 332

Locomotive Breath, 271

Lonesome Me and My Dog, 126

Long Tall Texan, 23

Long Term Wrong Turn Blues, 126, 153

Long Train Running, 271

Lookin' for the Money, 210-211

Louie, Louie, 29, 73, 298

Love In Vain, 125

Love Is a Beautiful Thing, 34, 53

Love the One You're With, 174

Magic Carpet Ride, 167

Marmalady, 126, 153

Marnie, 151, 179, 207

Medicated Goo, 155, 168, 178

Mexican Bird, 151-152, 179, 320

Midnight Cowboy, 41

Midnight Hour, 24-25, 28, 73

Money for Nothing, 287

Monkey Man, 125

Mustang Sally, 24

My Girl, 24, 30

Nasty Situation, 210

Ninety Nine Percent, 126, 130-131, 153

Nowhere Man, 87

Now What, 178

Ohio, 12-13

Old Cat Lady, 126, 152-153

Old Dear Friend, 121, 126

One, 302

Only At Your Convenience, 126, 153

On the Dark Side, 197

On the Road Again, 254

Pawnbroker, 151, 179, 207

Peaches en Regalia, 124

Pinball Wizard, 233

Poor Side of Town, 91

Rattlesnake, Shake, 292

Reap What You Sow, 126-127

Rock City USA, 271

Roundabout, 170

Ruby Tuesday, 125

Satisfaction, 73

Scapegoat, 7-8, 179

Sea of Love, 23

Shotgun, 30

Situation, 91

Somebody to Love, 199

Song of Job, 124

Soul Sacrifice, 93, 271

Soul Surviving Son Of A Gun, 238

Stairway to Heaven, 319

Steppingstone, 126, 153

Still The One, 273

Street Fighting Man, 155, 168, 168, 178-179

Suite: Judy Blue Eyes, 168, 196, 332

Summertime, 56-57

Summertime Blues, 339

Surfin' Bird, 280

Sweet Lorraine, 30

Sweet Home Alabama, 320

Sympathy for the Devil, 125-126, 129, 271

Takin' Care of Business, 320

Teen Angel, 144

Terpsichore, 15

The Night They Drove Old Dixie Down, 112

The Streak, 313

The Worst that Could Happen, 77

Tighten Up, 24

Time of the Season, 54, 57

Time to Kill, 124

Time Was My Teacher, 271

Tonight, 41

Took A Vacation, 126

Train Kept A'Rollin', 292

Try a Little Tenderness, 28, 302

Turn the Page, 161

Under My Thumb, 271

Up On Cripple Creek, 234

Voodoo Child, 93

Walking the Dog, 51

Wailin', 126

Well All Right, 112

White Rabbit, 199

Whole Lotta Love, 174

Wipe Out, 163, 339

Wooden Ships, 172

You Can't Always Get What You Want, 125

You Keep Me Hangin' On, 30, 57

Soren, David, 18, 22-25

Soren, Noelle, 25

Soul Survivors, The, 30

Southard, Mark, 242

Southern Comfort, 223

Spaulding Auditorium, 18, 24

Spear, Sammy, 325

Spencer Davis Group, The, 27, 57, 169, 171

Sphinx, 24-25

Spice, 140

"Spike" (Alan MacIntosh), 143, 147

Spooky Tooth, 303

Spoonfeather, 316, 341

Sports Illustrated, 67

Springsteen, Bruce, 6

Sprite Promotions, 78

Sprites, The, 50-54, 56, 68, 78, 174, 229, 238, 298, 327-328

St. Mary's Gym, 78, 81

Standish, Tom, 212

Steely Dan, 164, 206

Steppenwolf, 167, 221

Steve Miller Band, The, 13, 169, 206, 332

Stevens, George, 212

Stevens High School, 65, 128

Stevens, Ken, 225

Stevens, Michael, 257-258

Stevens, Ray, 313

Stills, Stephen, 12, 174, 331-333

Stingrays, The, 29, 63

Stoffelen (Eames), Yvonne, 240

Stone Pony, The, 197

Stonewall Farm, 248, 342-344

Stone Cross, xi, 43, 46, 73, 81, 130, 157, 206, 210, 213, 222, 224, 228, 250, 253-254, 273, 297-306, 311, 331, 341

Stop, Look, and Listen, 140

"Stopping by Woods on a Snowy Evening," 149

Stoweflake Motel, 195

Strong, Ken, 185-186, 193-194, 201

Strout, Dana, 272

Struthers, Gene, 57

Studio B, 20

Sugar Shack, The, 212

Summer of Love, The, 11

Sumner, Brad, 170-171

Suntreader Studios, 178

Superman, 145

Swain, Scott, 224-225, 301

Swallow, 196-198

Sydnor, Ocie, 23

Tabano, Ray, 291-292

Tallarico, Constance, 40-41, 231-232

Tallarico, Frank, 40-41

Tallarico, Giovanni, 40-41, 231-232

Tallarico, Lynda, 40-42, 46, 231-232

Tallarico, Michael, 40-41

Tallarico, Pasquale, 40-41

Tallarico (Tyler), Steven, 40-42, 46, 59, 67-72, 82, 136, 140-141, 160, 175, 229-239, 254, 283, 287-296, 337

Tallarico, Susan, 41-42, 231

Tallarico, Victor, 40-41, 46, 231-232

Talley House, The William, 9, 162

Taylor, James, 156, 215

Taylor, Livingston, 266

Ted Herbert's Music Mart, 66

Teicher, Louis, 41

Telstars, The, 81, 297-298

Tet Offensive, 167

Thayers Inn, 243

Thee Strangeurs, 67-70, 72, 294

Thoma, Mike, 225

Thomas, Rufus, 51

Thompson, Chris, 73, 202

Thompson, Nate, 73, 202

Three Dog Night, 256, 302

Tilton's Opera Block, 242

TNT, 221

Tolkien, J.R.R., 116

Topliff Hall, 16-17, 31

Toussaint, Allen, 120

Townshend, Pete, 73

Tracy, Will, 90, 93-94, 225

Tracks, ix, xi, 7, 9, 13, 18-19, 44, 55, 77, 82, 107, 110, 125, 134-135, 149, 151-152, 154-157, 162, 164-165, 167-179, 181, 185, 191, 195-196, 201, 206, 218, 222, 231, 236, 249, 253-254, 259, 281-284, 288, 295, 301, 305, 316, 320- 321, 32, 335, 337, 344-345

Tracks:
Hartland Farm, 135, 137, 151, 174, 176-177, 321

Traffic, 112, 168-169

Trashmen, The, 280

Trent D'Arby, Terence, 336

Trigeminal neuralgia, 264

Trombley, Dave, 50, 52, 57

Trophies, The, 51

Trow Hill Farm, 231

Trow-Rico, 231

Troy, John, 215

Truman, Ralph, 42-43

Truman, Skip, 29-31, 42, 72, 168, 171-173, 175-177, 206-207, 224, 345

Truro, Ronnie, 216

Tyler, Kate, 232

Ultimate Spinach, 164-165

Uncle Sam, 196

Uncle Tom's Cabinet, 23-24

Valley News, 312, 344

Valli, Frankie and the Four Seasons, 241-242

Van, Billy B., 67

Vanilla Fudge, 30, 57

Van Leuven, Eric, 125, 127, 170, 271, 292

Ventures, The, 339

Vermont Mindbenders, The, 312

Vermont Transit Line, 162

Virgil and the Poets, 73

Virginia's Team Room, 260

Wadhams, Wayne, 5, 14-20, 169, 177, 179

Wadsworth, Olive, 42

Wain Music, 64, 79

"Waitri, The," ix, 271, 277, 310-311, 314, 321

Walker, Junior, 30, 36

Wallace, George, 12

Walsh, Joe, 329-330

Walters, Barbara, 247

Warner, Len, 90, 94, 96, 225

Warwick, Dionne, 56

Watchband, The, 202

Watergate, 11

Webster Hall, 14, 21-22, 26, 28, 176, 328, 337

Wertz, Vic, 37

West, Leslie, 96, 330-331

Wet Magic, 86

Wheelock, Eleazar, 4

Whitcomb, Aaron, 66

Whitcomb, Don, 60-66

Whitcomb, Lady Eve, 60-62, 65-66

Whitcomb's Music Center, 9, 60-66, 79

Whitney, Paul, 312

Who, The, 27, 233, 235

Wilcox, John "Willie," 325

Wilkes, Jeff, 26-27, 33-37, 135, 137, 167-168, 172-173, 175, 177, 199, 209, 211, 223, 225, 301-302, 344

Wikipedia, 48

Wildweeds, The, 58

William Proud, 294

Windsor High School, 202, 289

Wintermeister, 188

Winwood, Steve, 36, 57

Wobbly Barn, The, 142, 145-147, 205, 210, 212-219, 306, 309

Wolf, Gerry, 248, 250, 252-253, 256, 259-267, 280-281, 342

Wolf, Isaac, 260

Wolf, Marion, 260-261, 263-264

Wolf, Sidney, 260-261, 263-264

Wonder, Stevie, 206

Wonson, Lee, 286, 334-335

Wonson, Mitch, 104-105, 181

Woodstock, 173, 185, 203,
    289, 302

World Trade Center, 265-266

Wright, Gary, 302

Wrought, 174

E.U. Wurlitzer Music and
    Sound, 66, 83

Wyman, Tom, 225

Yanofsky, Peter, 72, 87-97, 137

Yardbirds, The, 93, 292

Yasgur, Max, 173

Yes, 170

Young, Jesse Colin, 101-102

Young, Neil, 12

Youngbloods, The, 101-102, 111-
    112, 123-124, 130

Young Rascals, The, 27, 30, 34, 36,
    53-54, 298

Zappa, Frank, 77, 124

Zaks, Jerry, 5

Zip Codes, The, 51

Zombies, The, 54, 57, 67

4 South College Street, 134, 173

1954 World Series, 37

1968 Democratic Convention, 167

8084, 341